CLOUGHIE

CLOUGHIE

WALKING ON WATER

MY LIFE
BRIAN CLOUGH

with John Sadler

headline

First published in 2002
by HEADLINE BOOK PUBLISHING

10 9 8 7 6

A CIP catalogue record for this title is
available from the British Library

ISBN 0 7472 6567 4

Typeset in Ehrhardt by
Letterpart Limited, Reigate, Surrey

Text design by
Ben Cracknell Studios

Printed and bound in Great Britain by
Mackays of Chatham plc, Chatham, Kent

HEADLINE BOOK PUBLISHING
A division of Hodder Headline
338 Euston Road
LONDON NW1 3BH

www.headline.co.uk
www.hodderheadline.com

**To absent friends – those we've
lost and miss so much**

CONTENTS

ACKNOWLEDGEMENTS

My thanks to John and Jo. To John Sadler for his patience, skill and unfailing good humour and his wife Jo for all her hard work. And for putting up with him!

STILL STANDING

The snowdrops were gorgeous again this year, tiny, white and pure, ages old but always new and fresh and reassuring with their welcome message that another winter is on its way out and another spring only just around the corner. Then there were the crocuses, and the daffs – my but it's good to be alive!

I saw them all this year and hope to see them for a few years to come although I know there are a lot of people out there with the impression that I've been pushing them up along with the daisies since before the millennium. I thought it was about time I let people know that Old Big 'ead is still alive and kicking. In the words of that rousing Elton John song 'I'm Still Standing' – not as steadily as I used to because the old knees are not clever but I'm certainly not falling over, contrary to what you might have heard.

Aye, they used to say I could walk on water when I was in my pomp as a manager and I like to think there were days when I could walk the River Trent from one bank to the other! Those were the days – winning matches, breaking records, winning the championship and lifting that lovely big European Cup, not just the one season but retaining it the season after. That's why

I relish the sights and sounds of another approaching spring-time. Time to reflect on the magic of it all and to remind myself that I made a little contribution here and there to improve the lives of others, if only for a moment or two.

I wish the career hadn't ended the way it did. Oh, how I wish that! Not every hour or every day but never a week goes by without me regretting that final season, 1992–93. It was the very first season of the exciting new English Premiership and I took Nottingham Forest to the bottom and relegation. Walk on water? I know most people out there will be saying that instead of walking on it I should have taken more of it with my drinks. They are absolutely right.

I ended my first book in 1994 by saying I would tackle my drinking habit the way I have tackled all obstacles and chal-lenges in my life – head on and with determination to take control and overcome it. Well, I have tried, and I'm still trying.

I don't watch as much football as I used to because the hype and hysteria that surround every televised match in order to make it sound like a World Cup final drive me potty, but I do admire genuine quality – Alex Ferguson's achievements with Manchester United, for instance, and Arsene Wenger at Arsenal even though he should be ashamed of their disciplinary record. Some forty red cards in his first five years or so at Highbury? For heaven's sake, doesn't he know how to impose decent standards of behaviour on a team? If he did, their talent would show through even more.

I admire the way Gerard Houllier transformed Liverpool and won a treble. I was relieved to see him out and about again after his heart problem and I hope he takes good care of himself. I like the look of David O'Leary and the way he went about creating a talented team at Leeds. He's inclined to moan a bit about absentees but to reach the semi-finals of the Champions League the season he had two players spending much of their time in court trying to make sure they weren't sent to jail – hey, that was some achievement in itself. I still can't believe Leeds sacked him – their reported reasons sounded more like excuses to me.

I have no difficulty in acknowledging the ability of other managers – even Sven-Goran Eriksson although I would have preferred one of our own to be in charge of the England team.

When I look at men like these I know I used to be as good as them, if not better, and I sometimes do think to myself, 'I pissed it all up against a wall.' I wasted it to some extent by retiring at the time and in the way I did. I know in my heart of hearts that if I'd been properly sound, physically and mentally, I could have been persuaded to carry on for another couple of seasons. It goes without saying that I would have won something in the process.

But it wasn't possible. While Muhammad Ali committed the cardinal sin of staying in boxing too long, taking one or two fights too many, I dropped my biggest clanger by getting into drink. On reflection, I'm sure the drink clouded my judgement during that final, fateful season in management. If I had not been drinking, if I'd been fully alert and clear-headed through-out, I'm convinced Forest would not have been relegated although I don't believe that was the one and only reason.

Finishing bottom absolutely devastated me. I couldn't face anybody I had respect for. I couldn't face the thought that I had finished rock bottom of the table, that my team had been chucked out of the Premiership, first time of asking, because our results weren't good enough. It still hurts. I didn't get over it in the immediate months after it happened and I still haven't got over it. I never will. I can shut it out of my mind occasionally but that nagging bloody reminder is always there ready to whisper in my head, 'You finished bottom of the table.' Well, I don't want to be remembered as a failure. I don't want to be remembered for getting relegated and I certainly don't want to be remembered just as a drinker because I think I'm entitled to a place a bit higher up the ladder than that. Aren't I? Just a little bit?

What caused that awful last season of my management career? Pride, possibly. Conceit. In the end, the inability to manage a football club. I've had time, lots of time, to reflect and I knew the booze was affecting me. I was spending time drinking when I should have been spending time thinking and working, at the club and away from the place. It was bound to take over, inevitable. If you eat, smoke, jog, hoover, collect antiques, drink . . . if you do anything to excess, something has to suffer somewhere. In my case, it was my body and my mind. I missed out on time, concentration, calculated decision-making. I possibly started looking for excuses. I lost the way. I was dogmatic and didn't listen to people. Mind you, I wasn't exactly surrounded by people who were prepared to say, 'Gaffer, you're wrong!' I had Ronnie Fenton and Alan Hill alongside me with Liam O'Kane as the coach. I'm not blaming them for failing to pull me up short. We operated in a certain way and had done for years, with me as the little dictator who always made the decisions and nobody could sway me.

My lovely wife Barbara – my God, how has she put up with me for forty-odd years? – was the one who did tell me I was getting things wrong in that final season but I would just shrug and say, 'Don't you start talking to me about football. You've got no idea. You don't even like the game.'

I don't know anybody in a responsible position, or your average working man, who doesn't have a drink, but I was drinking far in excess of what I should have been doing. I had become dependent. I couldn't win a match yet nobody believed we would go down. People were saying Forest were too good to be relegated. That's the oldest, most familiar but blatantly misleading phrase in football. I knew it every time I glanced at the league table – Forest were bottom. I had all the necessary proof right there in front of my eyes but I went into a kind of hole. It's not easy to describe now. I was looking for an escape because I could feel everything bearing down on me. I tried, or thought I tried, everything – the complete alphabet of remedies from A to Z. In the end, I didn't know what to do. The strain of that relegation season took its toll and I'm forced to say that drink advanced and contributed to it. I had done everything and yet it achieved nothing. Drink provided an escape and I wanted to escape completely. I wanted to get out.

I know now my judgement was impaired when I allowed Hill and Fenton to convince me of the ability of a young centre-half, Carl Tiler. I paid £1.5 million to Barnsley for him and I continued to play him in the side not only to justify the money I'd shelled out but because my pride seemed to be at stake as well. In the years before, given the way he was playing, poor lad, I'd have dropped him. I should have dropped him but here I was, the manager who left Martin O'Neill and Archie Gemmill out of the European Cup final when they both swore blind they were fit, sticking by a lad who I now believe was not right for the job I expected him to do.

I'm not blaming Carl Tiler for the fact that Forest went down; that would be cruel and wrong. I'm blaming myself because if I'd been totally with it I wouldn't have signed him. If I hadn't been boozing to excess already, Carl Tiler might have driven me to it. But I was worse than I thought I was. I suppose that can be said of all drinkers. I started missing things on the field. I was the one who used to take the piss out of managers who sat in the directors' box scribbling notes. What the hell were they scribbling? I was the one who used to brag that I never missed a thing and would leave players aghast, asking, 'How on earth do you remember that, Gaffer?' I remembered the lot. I remembered when they spat, when they kicked the ball away, when they didn't get back to defend, every single time they conceded the ball to the opposition – nothing escaped my attention. But in that last season, several things escaped me.

There was another particular blind spot – I fell out with Alan Hill, totally. I'm not in touch with him even now. He wanted me to play Steve Stone, who was eventually sold to Aston Villa and briefly made the England team, I seem to remember. Hill couldn't, daren't, insist that I put Stone in the side but he kept on suggesting it. I was loyal to Gary Crosby, Bing we called him, on the right wing. He played with such enormous courage and I suppose I remained loyal because I knew that only courageous players would get us out of trouble. Young Stone had had terrible bad luck with injuries, two broken legs, so I ignored Hill's well-intended advice. I was wrong. I should have listened. I persevered with Crosby for too long.

So I was stubborn on the one hand and made a beginner's error on the other – taking the word of my staff in the case of Tiler and signing him without personally watching him play. Had I gone to watch him, I'd have twigged immediately. He was over six feet tall but, despite this, I don't think he was strong enough in the air. He just wasn't the man Forest needed at that time.

I didn't drink in front of the players at the ground, but I did know I was drinking too much, drinking excessively. It was the same when I was on holiday in Cala Millor, Majorca – a favourite spot of mine and my family's, and of my Derby and Forest teams for years. I'll give you an example, an occasion when I was there with the Forest players on a short break at the end of the season. The players were off doing their own thing and I ended up in a little bar with a group of colleagues and friends – a place we have since affectionately referred to as 'Cosy Corner'. I drank whatever I drank; whether it was ten, fifteen, twenty, the number is immaterial – a few beers, champagne, who's counting?

We didn't move for a few hours and then, after a wander on the beach, I went back to the hotel for a sleep. When I woke up that evening, I fancied a drink. That's the drinker's drink, when you've been on spirits and probably been snoring and you need something to clear the throat. A beer usually did the trick. It was typical to meet up with my colleagues before having a bite to eat. I had a drink on everybody's round but I didn't mix them – it was wine, beer or vodka. Then it was dinner and a glass or two of wine, and a couple of liqueurs. After that I'd get off to bed. Of course it was too much, but I was off duty for heaven's sake. I was winding down on a well-deserved break in the sunshine.

Sometimes when I went to bed I would mull over the day and instead of counting sheep I'd count the drinks I'd had. If I'd had six drinks with somebody I'd call it five. If I'd had eight glasses of wine it was six, three Grand Marniers became two. I knew I hadn't had any coffee because I wasn't keen on it. It's a stimulant and keeps me awake and I had a saying that 'I go to bed already asleep'. So I kidded myself about the numbers, like all drinkers do, like all cigarette smokers do. But if you have five drinks before lunch, a few more with the meal, a couple of beers when you wake up at teatime and on to the wine later, that's when you realise you're drinking too much, whether you choose to admit it or not.

When I was a smoker thirty-odd years ago, there were two occasions when I longed for a fag – when I was having a drink and when I saw a woman with her legs crossed smoking a cigarette, like the female stars in the old films. I might be wrong in thinking that Marilyn Monroe was one of those stars but I'm prepared to be wrong. Something turned on when I watched them blowing the smoke from the sides of their mouths as they spoke – still does. I can see Marilyn doing it right now. Isn't the imagination a wonderful thing?

There are two legitimate reasons for drinking, it seems to me – celebration and pressure of work. I have always remembered, and generally carried out, what dear old Joe Mercer told me in the middle of my time as manager at Derby.

'Go and enjoy yourself – pour yourself a drink,' he told me after my team had beaten his.

'But I don't drink. Sometimes an occasional milk stout.'

'Enjoy yourself,' Joe insisted. 'Listen, you lose too many times in this game not to celebrate when you win.'

I took him too literally in the long run. I ended up drinking more than I could have justified if I'd won every trophy available in every season of my career. It was even easier to drink when you'd lost. Having drunk for joy, I had no bother boozing in sorrow. So there are the two totally opposite reasons – euphoria and the depths of despair.

I had a third reason, or excuse – flying. I hated bloody flying; it scared me stiff. The last time I checked I still hadn't sprouted feathers and as far as I'm concerned if you don't have wings and a full plumage you're not equipped to travel with your arse thousands of feet above the ground. I've stopped an aeroplane on the runway in my time. I sensed something dodgy; I wasn't happy at all, so I took my entire team off the darned thing. We got on the coach and drove back to Nottingham when we should have been travelling to the Far East! Flying was only acceptable to me as long as there were a couple of bottles of champagne to go with it. I suppose it was flying that gave me the taste. Well, it's as good an excuse as any.

So drink was part of my working environment for most of my time in management except at Hartlepools – we couldn't afford a glass of milk there. It was readily available and free for the most part, but it was never a problem for me until that awful final season when it was all going wrong and partly because of me. I misread the situation because I wasn't in the best condition to judge. I had been one of the best judges of a player and of teams but in that final year I deteriorated.

There were fewer reasons to drink once I'd retired but I didn't stop although my drinking didn't get any worse. Excessive drinking causes problems – that goes without saying – not so much for the one doing it but for those around them. All of my family wanted me to stop the habit. In fact, after I retired there was a time when my sons Nigel and Simon virtually disowned me. I knew what was happening but I couldn't manage that situation, either. I wasn't prepared or able to acknowledge the problem and face it. I wasn't prepared to concede and come to terms with the fact that I was harming other people's lives. Instead, I latched on to all the reasons why there was no reason for me to stop even though I recognised that I was drinking too much. Barbara reached the stage where she wouldn't go to Cala Millor for our usual holidays. Being a typical Spanish resort, it seemed as if every other building was a bar. Availability is essential to people who want to drink.

Availability became less when I was at home and retired, of course. Barbara didn't like me drinking in the house but I didn't reach the stage of hiding it in the garage, up a tree or under the lawn. If I needed it, I went to the shop and bought it. It upset my family – Barbara, my daughter Elizabeth, my sons and their wives. Even Stephen, the eldest of my five grand-children, seemed to be aware that all was not well.

When I say that Simon and our Nige disowned me it was a kind of cooling of the wonderful, natural relationship we had always enjoyed. It's a good sign when your sons want to be with you. I know sons who don't particularly want to be around their fathers. Well, my sons always wanted to be with me. I took them everywhere. I could always talk to them about what I was interested in and it never seemed to bore them. They were sufficiently educated and talented to enjoy our conversations to the full. Their mum brought them up well and I had so much in common with my kids. I suppose it says a lot for them and for our relationship that they were able to make their disap-proval of my drinking so clear, and so starkly that they refused to talk to me until I was making an obvious effort to leave the stuff alone.

Even though I had no more direct involvement with football, and despite Barbara being seriously upset and my kids not really wanting to know me, I continued to drink and, surprising as it might sound, to enjoy it. Drink became more important to me than the anguish I was creating for those I loved most.

Eventually, I found there were times when the situation became uncomfortable. I remember Stephen, the one I nick-named Jackie Coogan as a baby, saying to me, 'You're not having a drink, Granddad, are you?' Something had to be done.

I didn't take specialist advice but I did stop boozing from time to time. I regained full control. I proved I could do without it for a time. I've stopped drinking on countless occasions, sometimes for days, sometimes weeks, often months. I once went without a drop for more than a year although I did feel particularly weak and vulnerable over the Christmas and New Year period. I used to love a glass of champagne or red wine with my turkey.

I've had spells in hospital and owe particular gratitude to Dr Jan Freeman. He's not a 'drink' man but I've seen him on many occasions for my general physical health and he has tried to keep an eye on the drink levels as well, in the process. I had to stop driving a couple of years or so ago. A busted right knee ended my playing career prematurely and the left one was badly weakened by the strain it took from me trying to protect the other. I stopped driving not because of drink but because of the knees and the various medications I had to take. High blood pressure, for instance, was always something I had to be wary of.

Over the course of several months, I was in the Nuffield Hospital in Derby three times for three separate operations – on a finger, my knee and to have all my teeth whipped out. Because of tablets I was taking to thin my blood, operations were doubly difficult and Jan Freeman warned me.

'I'm not treating you if you're drinking because I would be wasting my time,' he said. 'Watch your drinking in the Nuffield.'

'What? It's like bloody Alcatraz in there. Every time you sneeze the door opens and a nurse pops her head in.'

'Don't laugh. I mean it. Don't try to sneak it in.'

'How the hell can anybody sneak booze into the Nuffield?'

'The last one I caught,' said Jan, 'smuggled it in his tooth-paste tube. He'd filled it with whisky!'

It was during those visits to hospital that the rumours started to fly. After the operation on my knee I was in a wheelchair for a while. People saw me being pushed around (the first time Cloughie's *ever* been pushed around) often by Elizabeth. I progressed from the wheelchair to crutches and then to a walking stick – all the genuine consequences of surgery to my knee. However, in some quarters I was either at death's door in hospital 'fighting for his life' or facing the remainder of my days as a cripple who couldn't walk unaided – and all because of the dreaded drink!

These recollections help to remind me, if any reminder is necessary, that I should keep off the alcohol. I recognise now that in the past I have not been able to control it. I don't know what normal is in a drinking sense. A normal drinker maybe has two or three glasses of wine a week. If I thought I could control it, if I thought I could do that, I would. I remember Jan doing a routine heart check on me, testing my blood pressure and saying, 'The next time you fancy a drink, have a Mars bar.'

'Blow me, I'm already as fat as a pig,' I responded. 'I've got the start of a beer belly and if I had a Mars bar every time I fancied a drink, I'd snuff it from a heart attack within a week.'

Reflecting on the periods when I was drinking excessively, I must admit there were bad times. On the other hand, I also have to say that drink, a little drink here and there, is associated with some of the best feelings of my life. I was with my closest family, Barbara, Simon, Nigel, Elizabeth and my mum and dad, on holiday in the Scilly Isles in 1972 when I heard that Wolves had beaten Don Revie's Leeds at Molineux. My Derby team, having already completed the season, were confirmed as league champions. If that wasn't a good enough reason to crack open a bottle of champagne or six then I can't think of one – unless, of course, it's winning a European Cup with Nottingham Forest in successive seasons. Aye, Sir Alex still has a little way to go if he wants to do what Old Big 'ead did!

You never know exactly when the drink problem sets in. Nobody can really put a finger on the precise moment. I could say to you that I only ever remember being drunk twice and you will say, 'The countless times you were most pissed you won't remember anyway.' Barbara says she can tell when I've had one drink and I'm sure she's right – despite the fact that when she used to think I'd had one I'd maybe had a dozen.

Drinking is a social thing. Ask for a scotch among friends and it's rarely measured. Only an optic in a pub guarantees you a minimum quantity – unless the bloody landlord's watered it down. I had booze sent to me from all over the place in huge quantities because I was successful, no other reason. I won so much champagne for being manager of the month that I think it almost dried up in France. If I'm not careful I'll be blaming somebody else; I'll be saying it wasn't my fault that I became a boozer, it was because of all those buggers who kept sending it to me. A drinker can always spot an excuse, remember.

I hate the word 'alcoholic'. For a start, I don't really know what it means or what qualifications you need to be one. I suppose the dictionary will say it's somebody who drinks to excess but 'excess' to a teetotaller is half a shandy. If he has one every week, he's an alcoholic. It's hard to define reasonably and sensibly. My eldest brother Joe, the head of the family, wouldn't have missed his Friday night out in Middlesbrough if somebody had stuck a fully armed tank between him and the entrance to the working man's club. He went to see his mates, for company, a hand or two of dominoes and a pint or two. That's the working man's vice, if there is such a thing – Friday night with a glass in his hand. If you didn't go to the club on a Friday in Middlesbrough, your mates would be round first thing Saturday morning to see what was wrong. You must be ill or dead. So his Friday night was a ritual for our Joe, a habit, regular as clockwork. He loves his pint but you wouldn't call him an alcoholic.

I object to clever buggers who are quick to brand somebody an alcoholic. The word and its inference annoyed me even before I drank. I detest the way it sticks. George Best, for instance, is for ever referred to as an alcoholic when our regard for him should be based on that handsome, athletic young man who thrilled millions of people with a talent that was as rich and vast as any we are likely to see. Besty has drunk too much. He knows it and doesn't need anybody to tell him. The last thing he needs is to have that word chucked in his face every morning when he opens his eyes. I have the greatest admiration for the way he has tackled the problem with some extreme measures, judging by what I've read. I don't know whether he ever visited Alcoholics Anonymous but I suspect he didn't last long if he tried. What that organisation does is admirable, incredible. They have helped so many, restored them to the straight and narrow and a good and decent life. I haven't been in touch because I've never felt the need, and because although I have no trouble with the word alcohol I think I might struggle with anonymous!

I did have a spell in a clinic once, in the recovery rooms of the Dove clinic in Derby. I don't know how long I was supposed to stay there, lying in bed with two drips attached to me, needing to ring a bell to attract somebody to help me to the toilet. I got so sick of it that I tried to make it on my own, dragging the drip with me, and didn't quite make it. I still shudder at the embarrassment. So I walked out after three days and they reported me.

'You can't stop me walking out of here,' I said.

'We can. We will have to phone Dr Freeman.'

'I don't give a shit who you phone,' I said. 'Have I punched anybody in the eye? Have I broken any house rules? Have I pinched anything? If I haven't done any of those things, you can't stop me walking through those doors.'

They got a bit shirty and eventually a doctor breezed in and asked me what was wrong.

'These walls are driving me round the bend,' I told him. 'First of all, the room's too small. Every time I open my eyes I'm having to look at that bloody wallpaper and it's sending me crackers. I've got to get out.'

And I did get out. I used a wheelchair, and I persuaded the family into a trip to Spain, wheelchair and all. That damned wheelchair! Can you imagine me having to rely on somebody pushing me around in a grown-up's pram? I swear the first thing I did each morning was give that chair a hefty kick, despite the iffy knees.

Nothing could have prepared me for the way it all ended at the City Ground, my eighteen years as gaffer at Nottingham Forest and forty-one years in professional football. The beginning of the end, in April 1993, was triggered by a story in the *Sunday People* newspaper. It was based on allegations from a Forest director, Chris Wootton, claiming there had been a plot to get me fired. He threw in allegations about my drinking, with suggestions that I had been legless well before lunchtime. Although I had discussed retirement with my family, I wasn't planning any immediate announcement. It all became rushed and frantic and badly handled in the wake of Wootton's piece. Wootton was immediately suspended by the club, but chairman Fred Reacher blurted out my retirement plan weeks before we intended. It all became a mess.

Wootton wouldn't have had his name in the paper unless it was associated with me. As far as I was concerned, he had wheedled his way into the football club. How dare he come into my company and my domain? How dare such a man believe he was entitled to share the adulation? Having once bought me a shotgun, he can thank his lucky stars that I didn't turn it on him at that time. Here was a man, a builder I think, who suddenly found himself sitting in the directors' box on a Saturday, watching football, able to drink and eat the excellent food and have access to the ground all week long and be able to talk to the manager who had been there fifteen years before he ever came on the scene – he should have gone to church not once a week but 365 days of the year to offer thanks for the privilege. But he chose to attack me instead. And you know what? After serving his three-month suspension from the club he was re-elected to the board. I remember watching on television and seeing their faces, Wootton and Reacher and the others, after the meeting. Nottingham Forest may have a stand named after me and a bust of me as you walk into the ground but when I look at them today, so far below the status they achieved in my time, I confess to thinking that they finished up with the kind of club they deserved the day they re-elected Wootton to the board.

I have to admit, here and now, that drink has had an adverse effect on my health. Drink took me over to a certain extent. I was sixty-seven on the first day of spring, enjoying the spectacle of the snowdrops. I still get up every morning, I'm still belligerent, I don't get headaches, I've got a home although I don't like the one we have now, in Darley Abbey, nearly as much as the big one a couple of miles away in Quarndon that we sold a few years ago. I've also retained what bit of money I earned.

Yes, there have been times over recent years when I've drunk to my own detriment and it has impaired my judgement and worried my family, and I have had medical attention. In fact, I'm still having ongoing treatment to sort out my damaged liver. Jimmy Greaves has long since packed in the drink altogether. The greatest goalscorer of his time is among those who have made the greatest comebacks from the drink. Nobody admires what Jimmy has achieved more than I do – setting about a completely fresh start to his life, leaving the bottle alone completely and achieving it in spectacular fashion. Fantastic!

I have to draw my inspiration from Jimmy. I have to do the same. I now know I must never touch alcohol again. It is no longer a matter of choice for me.

People shouldn't worry about me. They say drinkers have to stop like Jimmy Greaves has done and like Tony Adams has done and like so many hundreds of others have done. Never another drop shall pass their lips. Apparently, that's the only way. I have to join their ranks, to become one of them. I'm not being flippant here, but people didn't think Derby County could win the championship in 1972. People certainly didn't think Nottingham Forest would win the European Cup twice on the trot. It's not the same thing, I know, but you can draw a parallel. I'm dealing with my drinking problem and I do have a reputation for getting things done. Some people might claim I'm kidding myself. I hope I'm not.

CHAPTER 2

IF ONLY I COULD HAVE BEEN THE GREATEST

I'd have loved to be Muhammad Ali – that big, that quick, that fit, that talented, that famous. The word 'hero' means different things to different people. As a child your heroes are invariably people you haven't met. The first hero of mine, strange as it may seem, was Barnes Wallis, the bloke who invented the bouncing bomb, which helped to beat the Germans in the Second World War. As a ten-year-old when the war ended, that name had a mystique and a magic about it. I knew about him and how important he was to our country long before they made the film, 'The Dam Busters'.

To a kid, heroes were people we listened to on the wireless or, later, saw on television, which didn't apply in my case anyway. They were made of dreams and the dreams became your friends. Nobody likes to have bad dreams so you went to sleep thinking of things that made you smile or made you proud. I was luckier than most because I met my first and main sporting hero, Wilf Mannion. Just the mention of the name still makes me glow and feel envious of what he was. Wilf died a couple of years ago at the grand age of eighty-one. He was never truly rewarded for the extraordinary talent that brought so much pleasure, admiration, excitement and awe to so many people.

Like so many others of his generation, Wilf Mannion was robbed of part of his playing career by Adolf Hitler. If that little sod with the toothbrush moustache had had his way, maybe Wilf would never have played again – perhaps none of us would. Thanks are due again to Barnes Wallis and the millions of others who enabled our lovely little island to defy the clutches of the madman. Wilf played his part in the war, fighting with the army – the Green Howards, I think. He was at Dunkirk. But it was his football that made him my hero.

My dad, Joseph, was a fanatical Middlesbrough fan who worked quite close to the club's old ground, Ayresome Park. A sugar boiler originally, he became manager at Garnett's sweet factory. He would often tell us about the 'Boro stars of the time, including Mannion and George Hardwick, popping into the factory and how he would give them sweets. I've said before that times have changed. Nowadays professional footballers aren't handed fudge – they get Ferraris!

Dad idolised Wilf Mannion. That was clear to all of us at number 11, Valley Road, the end-of-terrace council house that my adorable mam Sarah turned into a little bit of heaven for my brothers and sisters and me. I was one of eight kids, sleeping three to a bed. Our family of ten lived together in a hard-working, happy-as-can-be environment in that red-brick house with Dad's vegetable garden tucked round the side. Why don't sprouts taste as good today as they did then?

Eventually, I fully understood what Dad meant when he drooled on about Mannion. Years later, thanks to Ray Grant, a teacher at Hugh Bell school who had spotted me playing and scoring for Great Broughton and tipped the wink to Middlesbrough, I was able to meet the great man. There were times when I got changed in the same dressing room as Wilf and I couldn't help but stare at him in his training kit in the mornings. He was skinnier than I was and yet there was no more meat on me than on a ninepenny rabbit. He was smaller than me – apparently he was only five feet five – but to see him out there on the football field in training, and particularly in a match, I felt as if I was watching somebody who lived on the moon. I knew where I was from and at that time I couldn't recognise that a young lad from Valley Road was of the same species as the footballer I saw doing things with a ball that I'd never thought possible. If he'd not been on the pitch he could have been on the top of a Christmas tree, or a birthday cake. He seemed that delicate and yet managed to dominate the surroundings totally. His hair, a glossy silken blond the colour of Father Christmas's wig, earned him the nickname 'Golden Boy'. He looked too fragile to cope with the physical competition of football but appearances can be deceptive. Wilf Mannion could cope with anything the game threw at him.

He played football the way Fred Astaire danced. He glided through every movement, every routine. He swept past centre-halves and full-backs without touching them and if they tried to kick him – no point, too late, he'd gone like a will-o'-the-wisp. He was a genius of his time but he wasn't alone, of course. England was well blessed with attacking footballers in those days. Wilf was one of the 'Famous Five', still the greatest forward line England ever fielded – Stanley Matthews, Stan Mortensen, Tommy Lawton, Mannion and Tom Finney. What would that lot be worth today? One thing's for sure, ITV Digital couldn't have afforded 'em. So I was lucky. My hero didn't have to remain tucked away in my imagination.

I'm not a Catholic but I've met the Pope and even been blessed by him. It was during a Forest trip to Rome and for our coach Liam O'Kane, who is a Catholic, it was one of the most memorable experiences of his life. We were in St Peter's Square among the nuns and priests, listening to choirs singing. I didn't know what they were singing but I am interested in music and can listen to anything. This sounded, well, heavenly. Barbara was with me, and more excited than I was at the prospect of seeing the Pope. She's a lot brighter than I am and the privilege of the occasion occurred to her far more readily than it did to me although I realised that these were special moments. When the Pope appeared among us he had six or eight people around him, like all famous important figures do.

I can only imagine that somebody, a member of his staff if that's the right phrase, had marked his card before he stepped out. I suppose the Pope asks something along the lines of, 'What have I got on today?' and somebody informs him, 'Well, from Asia we have Cardinal so-and-so, there are some sisters from Malaysia and the choirs from St Benedict's, if you can find time just to greet them.' I'll have been about 319th on the list – 'Oh yes, and there's a bloke called Cloughie. If you see him, perhaps you could have a word.' I'm sure it's not really like that but how else could he have known we were there? He blessed me. He made the sign of the cross and then he touched my shoulder. I think he might have said something but I don't speak Polish.

Liam O'Kane said that if he lived to be 500 years old he would never forget those moments. I was hugely impressed, awestruck and enthralled, but I suppose only a Catholic could fully appreciate the significance and magnitude of such an experience.

I've been close to that sensation once in my life and that was when I went to Jerusalem, taking Forest to play the Israeli national team. I still haven't got over it and I'm sixty-seven. Jerusalem – it's one of those names from childhood, a place you never dream of seeing first-hand. I have been all over the world but I've never seen buildings like those I gaped at on that guided tour – never, ever, anywhere.

I was taken aback by the narrowness of the streets, the cobbled stones, the houses that seemed to be built of sand.

Footballers and football people can be blasé, or pig-ignorant, about visiting historical places. No appreciation of what he is seeing, the average footballer. 'I'm not bothered about seeing that,' is a common reaction when they might be looking at something that has been there for thousands of years. They wouldn't be dumbstruck by the Grand Canyon or the Taj Mahal – just dumb. But there was none of that in Jerusalem. You could sense that everybody in our party was aware of being in a unique place.

One of the few ambitions I have left is to return to the Wailing Wall and show my three children the notes I wrote and left for each of them, the way people do according to tradition. You tuck them into the cracks and I know almost precisely where I left mine.

Heroes present themselves in various ways. Some fade quicker and further than others. I moved on from hero to hero, some musical, many from the sporting world. There were the fighters Randolph Turpin, Freddie Mills and, briefly, Henry Cooper when he put the then Cassius Clay on his arse. The legend might never have happened, you know, if somebody hadn't bought time between rounds, which allowed Clay to recover, and if dear old 'enry hadn't had eyebrows that opened up like zip fasteners. If the referee hadn't called a halt that night, Henry would have been in danger of bleeding to death.

I once had a horse as a hero but not for long. Dante won the Derby in 1945 and I heard everybody talking about it. There were countless reports on the wireless. I don't know whether it was true or not because I'm not into racing all that much, but as a little lad in Middlesbrough I had the distinct impression that Dante was the fastest horse that ever lived.

All of this brings me back to Muhammad Ali – it may be via Middlesbrough, Rome and various other places but that's appropriate because we're talking about a man whose fame is universal. Ali is, without a shadow of doubt, the most famous, the most recognisable man in the whole of the world.

I met him twice – in America and in London. I was taken to the States by the *Daily Mail*, I seem to remember, who obviously eyed a piece out of the greatest meeting the greatest or some such crap. For some reason, I ended up flying out on a charter trip with people from the old Victoria Sporting Club in London. They were said to include gentlemen from the criminal fraternity, and they certainly looked like it although they treated me to the best flight I ever had. The trip was for Ali's title fight with Joe Frazier at Madison Square Garden, New York – in those days *the* boxing venue.

The chaps from the Sporting Club organised my drinks throughout the flight. One of them, a whopping six-footer, treated us to his party piece of 200 press-ups, one-handed. I think a few bets had been laid, but it was impressive for all that. Somebody said he'd learned how to do it during a ten-year stretch in jail.

Our party included John Bromley, one of the dear friends who have recently died, and his wife, and Neil Durden-Smith and his wife, Judith Chalmers. We were among the earliest to arrive at the Garden. Once inside the arena I had an impulsive urge to do something curious. I don't know why but I just had to touch the boxing ring. I walked right down there to the front and put my hand on the canvas and I went round and touched the four posts. I suppose it was partly to convince myself that I was really there at one of the most famous sporting arenas on earth. It was like entering boxing's hall of fame and my little gesture was totally spontaneous. I suppose I wanted to feel where so many great performers had done their stuff – Joe Louis, Rocky Marciano, Sugar Ray Robinson.

Not for the first time, or the last, I was misunderstood. Some woman, obviously British, yelled out from the scatterings of the early arrivals in the crowd, 'What you up to, Brian? Want everybody to know you're here?' She had completely misinterpreted my actions. She seemed to think I was pretending to be Ali himself, strolling to the ring as if I owned the place, looking straight ahead and purposeful. I wasn't doing anything of the sort. I always walked like that in those days and people who couldn't acknowledge my desire to touch the ring that night have no understanding of the meaning of sport. I was touching the place where real warriors had been. I do have to say that Ali's walk to the ring was slightly more impressive than mine. You couldn't see a lot of him under his dressing gown and beyond his entourage, but I was immediately conscious of his size. We weren't in the best seats but we were within a spit of them, close enough to the action to hear and almost feel the punches thrown and taken by those two fantastic fighters. I wasn't a boxing fan, particularly, but I'm an admirer of talent and those two had it in abundance – Frazier the bull, Ali the matador.

There was blood and there was pain and there was something startling for a bloke like me who had never seen a big fight at close quarters – the force of it all, the power with which two big men struck each other. Even a simple jab seemed to strike its target with the impact of a ramrod being driven against a door. You can watch as many fights as you like on television but you don't smell it or feel it. Sitting at home in your armchair with a cup of tea and, apart from the voice of the commentator, in silence is not the same. Whether it's the body oils or embrocation they use or the resin on the soles of their boots, when you're ringside there is a smell about boxing.

Live sport does smell. Walk into a football dressing room and the first thing that hits you is the smell of Algipan. My missus reckons I smelled of the stuff for more than twenty years. She thought I bathed with it. I had to put her right one day and let her know I used carbolic. I don't know what Ali and Frazier used in the showers but it had to be something strong and soothing to remove the effects of the ferocity they displayed.

The following day we had to do the stunt that had been set up by the *Mail* – me being interviewed with Ali in the ring where he had fought the night before. It was like a king meeting a beggar. His face was puffed and he was sore but he was still incredibly handsome and elegant, majestic even. He didn't know me from Adam but he went through a little routine, grabbing the microphone the way he used to grab it before and after his earlier fights to remind the world, 'Ah am the greatest.'

When I told him I was the manager of a football team and he said I looked young enough to be playing, he was right again. I was still in my thirties. I spluttered on about the injury that finished me as a player and he mentioned some of those he'd had but I was completely overawed by the entire event. Ali's size simply overpowered me. I could have been in the presence of a dragon the like of which you come across in nightmares. I could have been in the shadow of Count Dracula himself with his cloak spread wide. But this was a man dressed casually in a T-shirt, smiling as best he could through lips that had been bruised in battle the night before. He was engaging and polite, charm personified.

The handshake took me by surprise. My hand disappeared into his. His grasp wrapped around not only my entire fist but seemed to reach well beyond my wrist. If he'd gone and waved to somebody, forgetting he was shaking hands, he'd have broken my arm! By the time we finished the chat and he said, 'So long and thanks very much,' the sweat was trickling down my back and I was shaking. I was supposed to be famous, good at what I did, a bit of a public figure, recognised almost wherever I went back home in Britain. In the presence of Ali, I was nobody, and rightly so. We're talking here about a man who was surely the very best at his chosen profession, a brutal game where the main object is to try to knock the block off the bloke in the opposite corner. Yet somehow this big, big man introduced new dimensions to heavyweight boxing. He brought the grace and agility of the ballet to the prize-fighting ring; he introduced beauty to the beast. What a performer, what an athlete, what a showman, and what a human being! If you could have elected a president of the world when Ali was in his prime, he would have topped the poll in every civilised country on earth.

The second time I had the privilege of meeting him was on the Michael Parkinson show in London. Parky wanted me to do a second appearance for him and asked me if I'd go on the same show as Ali. I didn't need asking twice, but I told Michael I'd do it on one condition – that he arranged for my two sons to meet the man himself. Sadly, Nigel missed out – something to do with school – but Simon met Ali. He ruffled Simon's hair and chatted for a few minutes to the little lad, who just sat there open-mouthed. There was not a sound out of him and his eyes stood out as if they were on matchsticks.

I am one of thousands, maybe millions, of people who have met Muhammad Ali and who refer to him as a friend. He's not our friend but we like to think he is. It might be my imagination but he has seemed to look better every time I've seen him these past couple of years. It wasn't all that long ago that he needed several helpers to ease him out of a car and walk alongside him as he struggled to place one foot in front of the other. Earlier this year I saw him walk on to a stage somewhere unaided, and I was happy for him. I hope I'm right. I hope the disability, which was surely the result of those last few fights he took, levels out and gets no worse. Long gone are the times when he floated like a butterfly and stung like a bee. What a great line that is and it described him perfectly – grace and delicacy, impact and pain.

I once borrowed the phrase, or part of it, to describe Trevor Brooking. I could be really cruel at times, couldn't I? On this occasion, I think it was in a column for the *Express*, I talked about Brooking being like Ali without the talent, floating like a butterfly and tackling like one. He was, quite rightly, upset and asked me on many occasions why I'd said it. 'Because it's true,' was my stock reply but it was an exaggeration. I tried to sign him from West Ham along with Bobby Moore so he must have been able to play. Brooking was stylish and honest and could play a beautiful pass, but he wasn't a tackler and he wasn't a header of the ball either although I do recall him scoring with his head at Wembley.

No disrespect but I've never wished I could have been Trevor Brooking. I've never wished I could have been any footballer, past or present, or any cricketer apart from Donald Bradman. I've certainly never wished I could have been Dante. But how I would love to have been Ali. You can't be better than the best, greater than the greatest, and who wouldn't want to be called that and to deserve it? Certainly not a conceited, self-opinionated beggar like me.

I've felt humble in the presence of some people, not least the Pope, to state the obvious. I've felt untold admiration, every time I saw Wilf Mannion with a ball at his twinkling feet, for instance. But Muhammad Ali presented me with something totally different and far more profound. He didn't need to bother taking time to meet me, some anonymous manager of a soccer-ball team, as the Americans call it, from the other side of the Atlantic; not the morning after the fight before, so soon after he'd finished working. I know I wouldn't have wanted the bother had the roles been reversed. But then, that's why I wouldn't have been worthy of being the man I would love to have been. I wouldn't have had his capacity to fulfil unnecessary engagements. They tell me that after one particular fight in which he had been badly cut, Ali insisted on fulfilling his obligation to attend a press conference before he went to hospital to have his handsome but damaged face repaired.

I'd known so-called stardom as a player with my record-breaking goalscoring exploits in the Northeast. (They're worth repeating – 204 goals in 222 appearances for Middlesbrough, 63 in 74 games for Sunderland. That's so impressive I'm likely to repeat them again before you get to the end of this book!) So I had something of my own to be proud of when I met The Greatest, but nothing to compare. That's why I was made to feel something I've never felt before or since. He is the only person to have made me feel insignificant. Old Big 'ead was reduced to the size of a pinhead and I'm not too conceited to admit it.

CHAPTER 3

A PLACE IN THE
PECKING ORDER

It was as if my life had been topped and tailed when I met Ali. Insignificant is not a word many people would choose to describe me but it applied to me in the early days of my childhood, which I adored in all its aspects. If anybody should be grateful for their upbringing, for their mam and dad, I'm that person. I was the kid who came from a little part of paradise.

Middlesbrough has never been the most attractive, picturesque place in the world but to me it was heaven. Everything I have done, everything I've achieved, everything I can think of that has directed and affected my life – apart from the drink – stemmed from my childhood. Maybe it was the constant sight of Mam, with eight children to look after, working from morning till night, working harder than you or I have ever worked.

It was inevitable, I suppose, that there had to be a kind of pecking order in the house. As the eldest, Joe was at the top and retains the status today as head of the family, never mind that I have made a bit of a name for myself over the years. Doreen came next, then Des and Bill, then me, Gerald, Deanna and finally Barry. Betty died before I was born.

If I have flashbacks to those days, as I do from time to time, the first picture reflects the warmth and comfort of our sur-roundings, the feeling of being wanted and safe. I'll say it again – no child can be given anything more valuable than that by his or her parents. I remember the scent of something good cooking in the kitchen at dinnertime – in the middle of the day, not in the evening. That was teatime, or supper. During my tougher times as a manager, particularly during that final season, or after a hard day during the best times, I was grateful for the same privilege. Maybe I didn't deserve it but the one, constant source of comfort was knowing that I could go back to a warm house, to Barbara and the meal that was waiting. She'll never know how grateful I am to her for making home the place I've always wanted to be more than anywhere else.

You always had to take your place in the order of things when I was a lad. A sign of progress was when you were allowed to go out with your older brothers. A kind of grading system was going on all the time. There was a two-year 'probation period' when we had to do the messages, running errands for our mam. On reflection, I suppose these were my first training sessions. I used to run everywhere – for the spuds, a bag in both hands to spread the weight and help the balance; for the faggots and pease-pudding; and for the herrings off a man who arrived every week with a horse and cart. Don't tell me that kids today are fitter and healthier than we were despite our modest lifestyle and finances. You don't get fit watching videos, gazing into computers or playing electronic games. Kids really ought to get out more but I don't suppose they will. These are the children of the satellite society.

Most influences came from mothers in those days, especially in large families like ours. The old man was out grafting and the mother was at the hub of the domestic operation. My mam was certainly the biggest influence on my life. She ran the show

– the cooking, the cleaning, the organising, the washing, cleaning eight pairs of shoes between her persistent headaches and her eagerness to make sure the front doorstep was scrubbed as clean if not cleaner than anybody else's in Valley Road. She was the one who applied the iodine when you jumped the fence coming home from school at dinnertime and grazed your leg or your bum. It was always my mother.

I lost count of the number of times she asked me to draw the curtains to ease those headaches and I was concerned if I saw her in any kind of distress. Only one thing gave me as big a kick, as much pleasure, as scoring a goal between the coats we used as goalposts in the park, and that was to see my mam's lovely, radiant smile. How on earth she and Dad managed to get enough money together to take us all for a fortnight's holiday to Blackpool I'll never know – a rigid regime, I suppose, with careful housekeeping, stretching the resources to the absolute.

An upbringing like mine, in surroundings and a situation like ours, demanded discipline – Mam, again. She kept a thin belt across the back of a wooden chair and could lay her hand on it without even looking. If I did anything wrong, something that really displeased her, I'd get that strap across my backside. You hadn't time to get out of the way. If you'd been careless and torn your best clothes through your own fault – that would be one reason. If you weren't home from school by quarter past four she would want to know where you'd been. It was only five minutes away, down the alley. 'And where do you think you've been?' – I got that after I left school right up until I was married.

I don't think Mam felt guilty about giving us the strap from time to time but when she did, when it had been necessary, she told Dad, every time. I'm sure it wasn't a matter of conscience but just her way of keeping everybody informed about what had gone on. She had a sense of right and wrong, a sense of order. I became familiar with the routine. Dad arrived home from the sweet factory, got off his bike at the front, wheeled it through the little wooden gate, walked round the back to put it in the shed, and then came in through the back door. He wouldn't have time to take off his coat before Mam, in the back kitchen where she did everything apart from sleep, announced, 'I've had to lay the belt on our Brian, today.' I don't recall the old man reacting with much more than a grunt or a shrug of acceptance because he knew I must have deserved it; Mam must have had good reason. For a start, it took something extreme for her to grab the belt because her hands were always involved in something far more important – they were covered in pastry, or the mixture that made her dumplings the crispiest, tastiest dumplings in the world.

Not that many people were allowed entry into my office when I was a manager. Even fewer – apart from the players of course – were allowed into our dressing room. Maybe that was a throwback to how Mam regarded what we called the 'other room', the front room I suppose you'd call it now. It was where we had the piano and on Sundays the whole family sat or stood around as Mam played and we all tried to sing along. We were allowed in the other room on Sundays only and Dad was never allowed to smoke in there. If he felt the need for a Woodbine, he had to 'gerrout' and have it.

It was best clothes for us on Sundays and no playing outside. I never longed for a game of football or cricket in Albert Park or on Clairville Common more than I did on a Sunday but there was no chance. The weekly walk to the Anglican church was as far as we got. We had best clothes for school as well. Our other clothes, the ones with a hole here and there, we wore for everything else and we were expected to change into them the moment we arrived home from school.

There weren't many artists in our house because there was only one paintbrush, the one used to re-coat the outside windowsills every year. You tried to duck that job if you could because it was more than your life was worth if you got paint on the glass. Mam did her own wallpapering. How the hell did she ever find the time? Out would come the trestle and a pasteboard and she worked at such a speed it was like watching one of those silent films in which every movement was carried out in double-quick time. A wrinkle in the paper was regarded as a crisis. Sometimes, tired and aching, she'd say, 'You paste and I'll put it on.' But if you missed an inch it was, 'Get out, get out of the way. I'm better off doing it myself.'

She had a short temper, which was hardly surprising. She didn't have time to look at you as she ordered, 'Get those shoes off.' She was always doing something else, at least two things at once, but it was, 'Out of those clothes and I'll get them washed straight away.' When you were old enough you were expected to help put the clothes through the mangle – the one I had renovated and which I have in my house. You were expected to carry the pegs while she hung out the washing before you left for school. If it wasn't out on the line before 9 o'clock on a Monday morning it was as if an earthquake had hit number 11, Valley Road – 'Half-past eight and I haven't got my sheets out!'

For a council house, we had the biggest garden you've ever seen in your life, or that's how it seemed. To a little lad it was like half a football pitch and Mam had two washing lines strung among three concrete posts. Isn't it funny but I still know that it was three pegs to a sheet. We slept on cotton sheets. We didn't need much in the way of blankets because, she told us, with three in a bed we would keep each other warm. I must have gone through the first ten years of my life thinking blankets actually provided the warmth. I didn't realise they were the insulation to keep the warmth of your body in. I regularly asked Mam, especially when we graduated to two in a bed and eventually progressed to sleeping on our own, 'Can I have a warm blanket on?'

'Lay still,' she'd say, 'and you'll get warm.'

It was the other extreme in the summer with sweat running off us, but it was the same advice – 'Lay still, don't be jumping around. That's why you're sweating.' She was right again.

It was inevitable that I gathered a little bit of leadership quality as a kid because, for a while, I had to look out for my two younger brothers, Gerald and Barry, and sister Deanna. That lasted for a year or so, maybe a little bit longer, until the graduation process took its course. It was part of my first taste of responsibility.

I was a conceited lad although I didn't know it at the time. I could do everything my mates could do but I could do it better. I was the best runner, I could kick the ball better and throw a tennis ball further than any of them. I was of average height but I was skinny, probably due to the fact that food was limited, except vegetables. It had to be. There was enough to keep us well nourished, beautiful food as well, but not enough to get fat on, and that was no bad thing.

Mam kept an eye on our size. She was keen on measuring us, marking the wall with a pencil. Getting measured was one of the highlights of the month because she associated height and weight with a fine-looking lad. No, there was no malnutrition in our house. We were brought up on vegetables from Dad's garden. We ate that many, that often, that they were coming out of our ears. Mostly, that was all we got. There was mince but no steaks, but we did have lamb on a Sunday.

A big family produces one. There's always one who is either a cheat, a thief or his nose won't stop running. I was the one in our house. I was the clever bugger. I was the one who could hold his own playing football with the lads a year above me. I was the one good at all sports. I was also the one who didn't bother with girls until far later in life than most. Cricket was my first love – I often dreamed about playing for Yorkshire – but I was berserk about football. I would sit for hours on end staring through the kitchen window waiting for the tiles to dry on the houses opposite. Once they had dried, proof that the rain had stopped, I was allowed out – another of Mam's rules.

I was a keen bird's-nester and became something of an expert on which bird laid which coloured eggs and how many – seagulls two, if memory serves, woodpigeons two as well. The wren's nest fascinated me most – tiny and built mostly out of moss, it's compact and cosy and protective with a minute 'front door'. I reckon that in the ornithological world, the wren's nest is the equivalent of my home as a child. Discovering the nests was an adventure. Knowing where to look was the art, collecting the eggs was the prize, and I collected stacks of them, learning how to 'blow' the contents before putting them in a box padded with cotton wool with all the rest. You never removed all the eggs from a nest. I was never a cruel child and we were told that to take one egg caused no distress to the mother.

Eggs were swapped among friends, a blackbird's for a thrush's, a wagtail's for a wren's. I never did get my hands on a cuckoo's. I'd probably have got thirty in exchange for one of them so you'd think I would have looked a lot harder!

It was an exclusive bunch involved in the swaps, a select few who had the courage, skill and inclination to climb trees. I climbed them for other reasons apart from bird's-nesting, mainly nicking apples and pears from the posh areas of the neighbourhood. I also climbed trees for conkers. We were careful not to do any damage. We didn't walk on the flower-beds. That group of ours sat for hours on the benches at the entrance to Albert Park. Those benches were so shiny from the seats of our trousers that men could have shaved in them. How I enjoyed life as a kid! I didn't have a lot of responsibility but responsibilities enough although I did shirk some of mine by neglecting my studies.

I wasn't a prodigy in terms of football at the age of fifteen or so. I was no genius on the field or off it. I was just a raggy-arsed lad, one of the gang, one of the Bowery boys who got up to everything that fell short of breaking the law. We had too much fear and respect for authority to break the law. We lived in the park up to around fifteen. The scenic railway was part of the funfair, there for the children's holidays, and the trick was to get free rides. Not a problem. Some lunchtimes or evenings when the ticket man went for his break, he'd forget to empty the container. We'd grab enough tickets to do us for a couple of days. I'm not sure many twelve- to fifteen-year-olds would get much excitement or sense of mischief from that kind of thing today. Some of them prefer to steal a car, spray-paint an old building or mug a pensioner; and they say the world has progressed, that times have improved!

Our Bill missed out on most things. He didn't have to do his turn with the mangle or the washtub and he was always immaculate. He was the studious one of the five boys and didn't swear. Sunday morning, he cleaned his bike along with the rest of us before putting on our best clothes. We'd whip through ours as quickly as we could but not our Bill. 'Ten o'clock to one o'clock, I clean my bike,' he'd say, and he did and probably still does!

Bill lives in the Lake District now, and our Joe and his wife June went to stay there a few years ago. Bill has been married twice, he was the only one to get a divorce – he was that clever. He needed a word with Joe after a while about June using the iron. 'When it's been used,' he said, 'you wind the cord around it clockwise, not anti-clockwise.' That's our Bill, bless him. Nowt to do with it probably, but where football was concerned, he was the only one of my brothers who couldn't play.

He could be hurtful without meaning it. I remember the day when I was standing at our little wooden gate having just heard that I'd failed my 11-plus exam. That was no great surprise to anybody, considering that my revision time had been spent in the park with the coats down for goals and a ball at my feet. He breezed in from his posh grammar school on his bike that had taken three hours to clean and shouted to one of my mates, 'See our Bri's failed his exam, then.' I was standing there and half of Middlesbrough heard him. It wasn't said out of malice, I'm sure, but he said it and just wheeled his bike through the gate and went past me as though I wasn't there. I'm glad I made something of myself in the end.

Bill went into the army to do his two years' national service. I joined the RAF, having served my footballing apprenticeship with the likes of Great Broughton, a local side run by Nancy Goldsbrough from the post office, South Bank, an amateur club, and Billingham Sinthonia. Billingham used to give me a bob or two for playing and I hoodwinked the tax people for the only time by not declaring it.

Bill finished up in Germany with the army and learned Russian, which must have been very useful in Middlesbrough where very few could actually speak English. He went to night school to learn German and eventually worked in local government. There was me, my arse hanging out of my trousers, and he used to come home wearing a white shirt. For some reason, he was Mam's favourite son. I never was. Perhaps it was because he won the teapot in a 'lovely baby' competition and I didn't. Still, it's nice to sit in my armchair, relaxed and retired, and remind myself that I had a reasonable consolation prize by winning the European Cup – twice.

Bill is a smashing bloke, the most placid of men, and he was probably just as likeable as a youngster. We shouldn't have been surprised that he was the favourite although, at that age, there was never a chance that we would agree – not least because he seemed to get more food than us. He was a big lad but I never recognised that as a reason for Mam offering him seconds at dinnertime.

Still, I had my moments as a schoolboy and not all of them were during the games lessons or on the sports field. The proudest was when they made me head boy at Marton Grove, my secondary modern school. I was the one who did worst of all at school in our family and yet they made me head boy. One of the teachers who was keen on football must have had something to do with it. I have to say that being head boy ranks alongside the Freedom of Nottingham, the Honorary Degree and the OBE – thick as they come but head boy and my mam was as pleased as it was possible to be.

She was not easily impressed, certainly not by my later success in life. Of course, she was pleased over there on the Scilly Isles when we learned that Derby had won the league title, but it wasn't the beginning or the end of the world in her book. She told me that my being made head boy at Marton Grove gave her more pleasure, pride and satisfaction. I knew what it meant to her the moment I saw her face light up with a smile.

I enjoyed being head boy because it gave me a certain amount of power. I couldn't get that power through academic channels, I couldn't get it by being a member of the smartly dressed group and I couldn't land it by being one of the best behaved. That power came from being head boy. There was one downside that I can think of. We didn't have a school uniform but a cap, a black and white ringed bloody cap, came with the job, and of course I was the only one in the school wearing one. That was the first cap I ever got – only one less than they gave me for playing for England. What a sight, though – the lad whose dad worked at the sweet factory walking round school with a humbug on his head.

I wasn't a belligerent head boy but I didn't mind telling another kid what he should have been doing. I actually enjoyed standing at the top of the stairs and warning the late arrivals – 'It's gone nine . . . you're late . . . and if it happens once more this week . . .' I wasn't frightened of being head boy. Some of my classmates would have been – frightened they were going to be resented, frightened of getting punched. I wasn't. I wasn't frightened of much at all that I can think of. I wasn't frightened on the range with a gun in my hand on national service – not because I knew how to fire it better than the bloke next to me, just that I felt comfortable with a gun in my hand. Anything I could shoot with I liked, a ball or a bullet. I was brought up on westerns, not on scientific magazines or *Mathematics for the Beginner*. I was brought up with cowboys who could shoot with both hands. I was thick academically, as I've said a thousand times. My education was in the park and watching the gun-fighters forty-three times a year at the Saturday morning matinee at the Scala.

Imagine my shock and horror when I had to leave school at fifteen and follow Mam's advice to go for 'a nice job' at the local ICI as a fitter and turner. I was fit and I could turn quicker than most but that had nothing to do with what they had in store for me at that place. Going through those huge gates with my sandwiches and bottle of pop in my pocket was like entering a different world. From the magic and the freedom of my childhood outdoors it was like being marched into a military establishment. They tried to explain what fitting and turning was but I was never cut out for it. They took me to an anhydrite mine one day. If I was to become terrified of flying in later life, this was the day I experienced terror at being below ground. They scared me completely. If I had one scrap of ambition when I walked through those gates, it disappeared without trace. There was no chance of passing my apprenticeship so I became a messenger. They call it 'junior clerk' but in my book a lad running around the place fetching and carrying notes is a messenger. That was before I was promoted to filling in overtime sheets. Oh, how I envied the Middlesbrough football-ers I watched so often on their way in or out of Ayresome Park, barely a quarter of a mile from home. Theirs was a dream I wanted to share and after Ray Grant's recommendation I was invited into their world at a quid a week plus £7 if they picked me to play in any of their sides.

Although Barbara also worked at ICI, I hadn't met her by the time I was called up to the RAF – square bashing at Padgate near Manchester, making sure to write home and tell my mam I was OK. Life in the forces, or accounts of it, were not new to her – four of the kids had done their time, including Doreen in the Wrens. Dad, a private in the King's Own Yorkshire Light Infantry in the First World War, had the worthiest story of all to tell. The wounds he suffered caused his return from the front and his discharge, and left him with a limp. He was still a single man then. He suffered deafness because of the explosions and heavy gunfire he experienced at close quarters. Years later, as we gathered in the other room on a Sunday, he would sometimes tell us how a German bullet pinged off a little part of his nose, and how he was hit in the ankle. He had two close calls but we always preferred Mam's version – 'The Germans shot him in the ankle when he was running away. He wouldn't have been hit in the nose but he was looking round to see if they were coming after him.' We knew it wasn't true and we heard it several times but it never failed to make us laugh.

I played a lot of football in the RAF but they couldn't spot real talent when it was right there in front of them, either. Leading Aircraftsman Clough was picked for the station but not for the national RAF side. However, I graduated from fifth choice centre-forward at Middlesbrough to the third team and occasionally the reserves so the £7 added to my £1.87p (or £1 17s. 6d. in those days) made trips home well worthwhile, when I was able to get there.

I graduated to something else, too – poaching. Not eggs, grouse. I got on with a lad called Brian Harrison who sold washing machines and who introduced me to a different game, the birds of a feather up on the moors. The wind made sure you put a coat on. Grouse aren't very big and slip neatly into a coat pocket. In those vast areas of open spaces on the moors, there were long periods when you wouldn't see a thing beyond the heather and the gorse. The odd skylark singing from somewhere high above was invisible but there was always the feeling that something was around and invariably it was the grouse. They are the most stupid birds imaginable. We would take an airgun and shoot the first one to show itself only for three or four more to look up to see where the noise had come from. They didn't fly away so you'd get at least one of those as well. Even on the wing they're not that hard to hit because they're usually low enough, skimming the surface like a seagull looking for fish.

It was the start of the good times again. I'd taken my first steps into the big wide world as they call it, into the misery of factory life as a messenger boy, and I'd done my national service. After leaving the RAF in the close season, it meant I had a three-month break before we began pre-season training at Ayresome Park – three months to spend outdoors again, a lot of the time shooting grouse. I was back in that little end-of-terrace palace that Mam had made for us and once again I had that wonderful feeling of being as free as a bird.

C H A P T E R 4

THE POWER OF FRIENDSHIP

The RAF restricted me more than I expected. I had applied to be moved from my posting in Somerset to Catterick so that I could get home to play for Middlesbrough on a Saturday, which made sense to me; it fitted my bill. But the warrant officer, a bloke named Stevenson, announced, 'You're going nowhere.'

'But I'm off to Catterick in two weeks.'

'Oh no you're not. You're staying put.'

He was an absolute football nut and he wangled it. He scrubbed my transfer, which meant I remained in Somerset for twenty months so that he could have me in the regiment team on Wednesdays and at weekends. That should have put me off drink for life. I was introduced to it for the first time prior to what they regarded as an important cup-tie – raw eggs and sherry. It tasted like poison. I was brought up on sennapods as a kid to keep me regular and I can tell you they were more palatable than raw eggs and sherry. It was supposed to be some kind of body builder – don't they feed it to racehorses on occasions? I don't know whether it made me run any faster but although I expected to be sick within seconds, I did feel a warm glow in my tummy after about a quarter of an hour.

A fortnight's leave was all you got in a year. There were twelve-hour passes, twenty-four-hour passes and forty-eight-hour passes but to get from Bristol to Middlesbrough and back took me longer than forty-eight hours in those days – or at least that didn't give me enough time to make it worthwhile. So I was rarely home apart from on annual leave and I had to find other things, as well as football, to ease the boredom of national service. My happiest times were in the summer, sitting on the grass listening to the Test-match commentary on the wireless. We were close to the Bristol Channel and it was a very beautiful place to be for a lad who came from our neck of the woods in the Northeast with its filth and coal and steel and steam.

Demob freed me from that institutionalised existence where every move you made was linked to the clock. We were being put through our paces in the early days, running it seemed until we dropped. After one such run a corporal called me over. You stood to attention when you were called by one of them because corporals were bastards, and this one told me, 'You'll look back on this and think it was the best time of your entire national service because the rest of your time will drag.' He was dead right. A week was a month even though I was playing football. The initial stretch, including the square-bashing, was best. There wasn't time to be bored because there wasn't the chance to think about it.

I went into football late because of national service. Obviously I would have preferred to start earlier but the introduction of youngsters to the professional clubs today has gone from the sublime to the bloody ridiculous. There's nothing wrong with competitiveness. All kids want to win and have to learn how to lose, but these days too many parents put too much pressure on little lads who should be enjoying every second on the football pitch. Our Simon used to run a team called FC Wanderers and I've never seen so many up-and-coming Alf Ramseys in my life – parents on the touchline thinking they were coaching their kids. There were about twenty of them, the same twenty every week, shouting their heads off. The mothers were the worst offenders and they hadn't a clue what they were shouting about. They'd heard some self-styled expert trotting out the same phrase on the telly.

Another thing that worries me, even at the age of sixty-seven, is the academy. The only academy I ever heard of as a child was at the cinema. It was a place where the Americans used to train their soldiers. Now we have a National Academy and every club seems to have one of its own as well; if it hasn't got one, it's regarded as a bit of a stigma. No academy? Can't be much of a football club then. What total, utter garbage!

They're grabbing kids almost before they've lost their milk teeth and although these places no doubt produce some good players at the end of the conveyor belt, I'm not sure they will produce enough to justify the investment and expense. Call me old-fashioned but I think some of those good players would emerge anyway without the need for such intense teaching processes. I'm scared the kids are being brainwashed and by the time they're eighteen or twenty they'll all be walking round in the same way, like robots. There will be nothing natural about them because their individuality will have been coached out of them.

You can suffer from coaching on two fronts – over coaching and no coaching. Either one is as bad as the other. It's finding the right balance that's important, the spice of life. There is something to be said for giving talented young players every possible assistance and facility. You can help them with their education, tell them how to behave and persuade them to eat good food rather than fast-food trash. You can give them encouragement, warmth and understanding, and provide the opportunity for them to fulfil the talent with which they were blessed; but you can't put talent where it doesn't exist, and you mustn't lose sight of the late developers. If the academies and their coaches had been the judges at the time, Jack Charlton would not have survived to become a World Cup winner with the Boys of '66. Jack was the classic late developer at centre-half for Leeds and was never the greatest in the business but Don Revie and Alf Ramsey saw enough to know he could be among the most effective.

Unfortunately for me, free as a bird and flying at Middlesbrough, Bob Dennison, the manager, didn't recognise an outstanding talent when he saw it. I was a centre-forward who scored goals. I scored them as a little lad in the park, I scored them at school, I scored them for every team that picked me and I scored them in the RAF. Goalscoring came easy – it was as if I'd been born to do it. I was scoring them at Middlesbrough, too, at various levels, but I remained their fifth-choice centre-forward until Peter Taylor stepped in.

People still wonder about Taylor and me, and how we became so close, best mates who developed into the best football managerial partnership of all time, even though I've tried to explain it on many occasions. Retirement offers time to dwell and I've dwelt on Peter for many an hour. I've thought about the good times and the way he made me ache with laughter. I've thought about our eventual break-up when I organised his retirement, his pay-off at Forest, and lost my rag when he returned to the game as manager of Derby and nicked John Robertson in the summer. I've thought about his funeral in October 1990 and the feeling of desolation that swept through me during the service at his little local church in the pretty Nottinghamshire village of Widmerpool.

I've wished over and over that I could have been big enough, man enough, to forgive and forget our fall-out. The reason seemed legitimate at the time but after all those years it was daft, stubborn and futile not to have made it up with Pete, put an arm around his shoulder and invited him to make me laugh again as only he could. I should have asked him along to

Wembley as Forest's guest and sat him in the royal box to watch us win the League Cup in 1989 and 1990. But I let the dispute simmer on. Time has helped to emphasise my guilt and the feeling of total regret.

Time to think has also convinced me that the first words Peter Taylor ever said to me had an enormous influence on my career, both as a player and a manager of some repute – not the greatest ever to tread God's earth, I have to concede, but somebody who made his mark and left a wee bit of an impression behind. As reserve-team goalkeeper, Peter was a good judge of players. He was a keen observer, especially where goalscorers were concerned. He took me aside one day and said, 'I can't work out what's going on at this place. You're the best player in the club.' I can hear him saying it now, his exact tone of voice, with no hint of a smile or kidology, and that curious little half-frown of his.

It gave me the assurance I'd longed for. It made me feel the same as I felt when they made me head boy at Marton Grove but this was even more important because this was at the start of the rest of my life. I knew I was good. I knew I could score goals more regularly than anybody else – mainly with the right foot but with the left as well if necessary and I was working on it anyway. I'd score them with my head, too, easy as you please. Goals were never a problem to me. Peter's words gave me confirmation and confidence. He gave me the kind of lift and boost that every footballer needs from time to time. I remembered that when I went into management. It was something that brought better things from players who had previously believed they were producing their best already.

That was the fundamental reason that Pete and I became friends. He had become an ally. He believed in what I believed in – my talent. There were other reasons as well. Neither of us had a car so we walked or travelled on the bus together. Pete was married and his wife Lillian made the best chips in England!

His belief in me left me even more frustrated. I should have been in the first team instead of a lad called Doug Cooper who was too heavy in the first place. But there he was with the number 9 on his back while I was carrying the reserve team on mine.

All good things come to the one who waits they say, but a goal didn't come my way on my first-team debut away at Barnsley. Again, with time on my hands to evaluate such things, I learned a lesson that day that all managers would do well to bear in mind today. Dennison didn't give me a boost on my way out of the dressing room for what was the biggest occasion of my life, or so I thought. 'It's up to you, now.' That's all he said. I might have landed myself a rise by then, eleven quid instead of nine, but the player trying to make his mark needs what Peter Taylor had given me with those first words of his – a boost. He needs to hear the manager express confidence, he wants an uplifting little parting shot with a cuff on the head or a friendly smack across the backside. I knew it was bloody well up to me without him saying so. I wanted to hear him say he believed I could do it.

This was the lad whose first football boots were hand-me-downs from my brothers, with big re-enforced toe caps that sometimes used to fall off. My first pair had been worn by our Joe, Des and Bill before me. If you opened the coalhouse door at our place there were maybe ten pairs of boots that had been handed down – you just grabbed the pair that fitted you. We seemed to do nowt else but put studs in. It was a regular job and a fascination. Boots were provided at Middlesbrough, as you might expect, but just the one pair, which was news to Bill Nicholson. Bill eventually became Mr Tottenham Hotspur, and produced such a dazzling team at White Hart Lane that they won the double and played the game in a way that was an object lesson to everybody. He was in charge of the England Under-23s when I was picked, and he passed around expenses forms at our hotel in London. Hardly able to write anyway, in those days I hadn't a clue what an expenses sheet was.

'Put everything down that it's cost you to come and play,' Bill told me.

'Including my boots?'

He clipped me on the ear and said, 'Boots? I'll give you boots, you little bugger.'

I spluttered and protested that I was telling the truth but he thought I was taking the mickey and trying to fiddle a tenner. Tottenham had probably been giving boots to their players by the boxful, but at Middlesbrough if we wanted an extra pair, we had to buy them for ourselves. The pair they provided was replaced only when they wore out – usually after a couple of seasons or so.

They were good days, those early days at 'Boro, despite the manager realising so late that I was as good as I thought I was. I had to clean the boots to start with – Saturday night after the match it was into the boot room, which was like a prison cell. We used scrubbing brushes and had to make darn sure we got every speck of mud off. We left them to dry, hanging by the heels on the wooden pegs, until Monday morning. Monday afternoon, after training and a quick sandwich, the boots had to be polished for the next match. We also had to treat the training balls with dubbin – a kind of axle grease that protected the leather and the stitching from the wet. I had to be told that was the reason for it. I needed to know because we used our fingers to rub it in and mine became red raw.

The pecking order had been apparent from the moment I joined Middlesbrough and got in to the A team before I went into the forces. It was a fact of life. You were one of the top men, the reserves or the A team – matter of fact, categorised, black and white. I was bursting for that chance in the league side but when it came, despite my self-confidence and, yes, even despite the boost Taylor had given me, I was awestruck, particularly playing at home. There was silence from my corner. I daren't say a thing and wouldn't have been allowed to anyway. The trainer had put the kit out – shirts 11, 10, 9 and so on, neatly in order. I was third in and just happened to be where the radiator was.

I wasn't to know it at first but where I sat was regarded as a privilege. It was right next to the space where Jimmy James, the famous old Northeast comedian, would come and sit with his pal and his stooge from the act, Ely. Apart from his humour, Jimmy James was well known for the way he smoked on stage – blowing the stuff from each corner of his mouth alternately. He was the same off stage and I often caught the full cloud. It must have been an odd sight in our dressing room on some occasions, that small group along the bench – outside-left, inside-left, Clough the centre-forward, Jimmy James and Ely. That was part of my introduction to first-team football. I'm sure they were there for my first match at Ayresome. They were there for most games providing they had no matinee to do at the Empire.

They were responsible for my stage debut, come to think of it. Perhaps it was for charity, I'm not quite sure, but they got me on at the Empire, playing head-tennis with team-mate Lindy Delapenha who became another good pal of mine. That was a claim to fame – I kept the bill for years and felt chuffed every time I looked at it, even though our names were in small print and right at the bottom.

It's strange, the things that come back when you have time to dwell. Bill Harris, a wing-half, always had to nip off to the toilet at a quarter to three for a smoke. It was his ritual, everybody knew he did it. Before every match, he just had to have a fag. Now I didn't always agree with Sir Walter Winterbottom. You can hardly blame me, seeing that he kept me out of the England side, apart from a couple of caps, when he was manager. But

Walter was a dear man for all that, a decent man and another whom we have lost in the last year or so. He did teach me something that was to be valuable when I became a manager. He said, 'If a player smokes all week, why deprive him of it at the time he wants to do it most of all – before the match?' Everybody had the shakes a wee bit. The adrenalin used to flow, although I was so thick I'd never heard of adrenalin and if somebody had mentioned the word I'd probably have thought it was a football team from abroad.

I often wonder whether modern players with their millions of pounds in the bank can possibly have the appreciation of the game that we had then. Of course, they'll enjoy the money and the independence and the security it gives them although some of them have more money than sense and don't know how to spend it. But does the privilege of actually playing the game for their living occur to them as it did to us? They certainly won't know the sheer joy I experienced walking or running through Albert Park on the way to training. We trained from ten o'clock till twelve, had a bath and I was back for dinner – always on the table for one o'clock.

They throw plastic bottles of Lucozade for footballers today, don't they? You see it when they're walking off at half-time and full-time – in fact, at any time there's a pause in the action and a chance to get the sponsor's name seen. It was a glass of water for us, take it or leave it. A treat, for me anyway, was a strawberry milkshake in a long glass with a straw, mixed with ice cream. I think I should have stuck to 'em!

Rea's caff was the place for milkshakes. When I became friendly with Lindy and knew I had been accepted into the players' circle, we would sit and talk for an hour or more in one of the little booths. He might have three milkshakes to my one because he'd been in the first team longer and could afford it. But Rea's caff is important to me for something far greater than a milkshake. It was where I spotted the girl with a smile that seemed to light up the entire Northeast. It was where I first saw Barbara and the rest, as they say, is my extreme good fortune.

People find it hard to believe that even when I was out of the forces, playing for Middlesbrough and courting Barbara, I still had to be in by ten o'clock at night. It was Barbara's one complaint (she must have had thousands since and a few more that she's kept to herself). We were never able to see the last five minutes of a film. Apart from anything else, I had to be back to catch 'Match of the Day' and the number 11 bus for Valley Road used to pass the Gaumont at ten to ten.

I read and hear lurid tales about the way some of today's young millionaire players spend their spare time. We had rebels in our day but I don't recall late-night drinking binges or footballers running riot in the city centre and getting them- selves accused of attacking people and ending up in court. There wasn't money to waste in nightclubs. I'm not sure there were nightclubs in the first place but I know from personal experience that even if there had been, we didn't have the money to waste in them. Obviously I didn't go out in the park at night. Still living with Mam and Dad, it was a case of waiting for the old man to come home from work, tea, fiddle about around the house, listen to the wireless, chop sticks and get the coal ready for the following day – anything to fill the time.

That was until I started going out with Barbara. We had about two of what I called the limbo years before we were married at St Barnabas' Church. It was 4 April 1959, the day I still regard as the most important of my entire life. We chose April to make sure we got maximum allowance from the taxman! I don't think David Beckham and his missus got married on a matchday but I did. We were married in the morning and had the reception at the Linthorpe Hotel. I gave Des twenty-five quid to buy a drink for everybody and the speeches were shortened to allow me to be at Ayresome Park in time to play against Leyton Orient. We won and I scored. Yeah,

yeah, every bloke scores on his wedding day but I managed it prior to the honeymoon. That had to be quick as well – a few days at the Russell Hotel in London where I spent a lot of the time kipping while Barbara went out and saw the sights. I had to be at Anfield to play against Liverpool on the Wednesday! I couldn't stop scoring on my honeymoon – two against Liverpool in the final two minutes. Those goals won the game and had Bill Shankly pointing in my direction and complaining to our trainer Harold Shepherdson, 'He's not had a kick!' Harold, England's trainer when they won the World Cup, was not renowned for his slick repartee but he produced a stunning reply to Shanks – 'He's had at least two to my knowledge, Bill.' It was back to training next morning, back in the old routine, end of honeymoon.

We moved into a club house in what I regarded as a rather snobby area of Middlesbrough. Next door on one side was a Catholic couple – smashing people – and a retired tailor and his wife were on the other side. Barbara was working at the building society until five o'clock so I had the afternoons to fill. I cleaned our neighbours' windows as well as ours and had Barbara's tea ready for when she got home.

With my ability to score goals it was inevitable that I would establish myself as a regular first-team player, but I was never conscious of being regarded as a star. Football was treated as a religion in the Northeast and that applied at Middlesbrough despite the fact that we were in the old second division. I was regarded as somebody who could play the game but the public, certainly those I came into contact with, never severed the umbilical cord that made sure I remained one of them. I'd been lucky and got on and didn't object when they reminded me, 'You're dead lucky, you are. I was a better player than you at school.' I'd smile and remind them, 'Well, you're not now.'

They weren't being nasty; they were being honest. That was the Northeast, that *is* the Northeast – straight people prepared to express an opinion and not be hurt by somebody expressing an opinion about them.

Three goals in nine appearances in the 1955–56 season followed by 40 goals in 44 the season after, 42 in 42 the season after that and 43 in 43 a year later. What would a striker like that be worth today? Never mind that Middlesbrough were in the second division, goals are goals and I kept 'em coming with 76 in 84 appearances during the next two seasons – and two full England caps to show for my trouble. Two bloody caps. If anything makes me bristle in my armchair these days it's that statistic. I must have another word about it with Walter Winterbottom when we next meet up, but I do hope it's not for a while.

On the promenade at Blackpool, aged ten. How my parents ever managed to save up enough money to take the whole family on a fortnight's holiday there every year, I'll never know.

The entire Clough family. *Left to right*: me, Barry, Doreen, Des, my mam Sally, Bill, my dad Joseph, Gerald, Deanna and Joe.

The most important day of my life: 4 April 1959. Barbara and I were married at St Barnabas' Church on a matchday. 'Boro played Leyton Orient later that day – and I scored!

Barbara and me with our three children Simon, Elizabeth and Nigel, in 1970.

I'm not sure if it was the diet of raw eggs and sherry that did it but RAF Watchet managed to win all four trophies we competed for in 1954–55. Unfortunately, being based so far from home meant that I could rarely get back.

Leicester's John Anderson can only look on as I score one of my first goals for Middlesbrough in October 1955. There were many more to come.

Not so lucky this time as the Huddersfield defence close me out.

The Sunderland team lines up at the start of the season. Manager Alan Brown was furious that I'd messed around in this picture by borrowing somebody's pipe. Ever since then I have always made sure that I take photographs seriously as they're such good souvenirs.

Once again the goal beckons. While at Sunderland I was to score 53 goals in 58 League matches before injury brought it all to an end.

A moment to myself in the dressing-room at Sunderland.

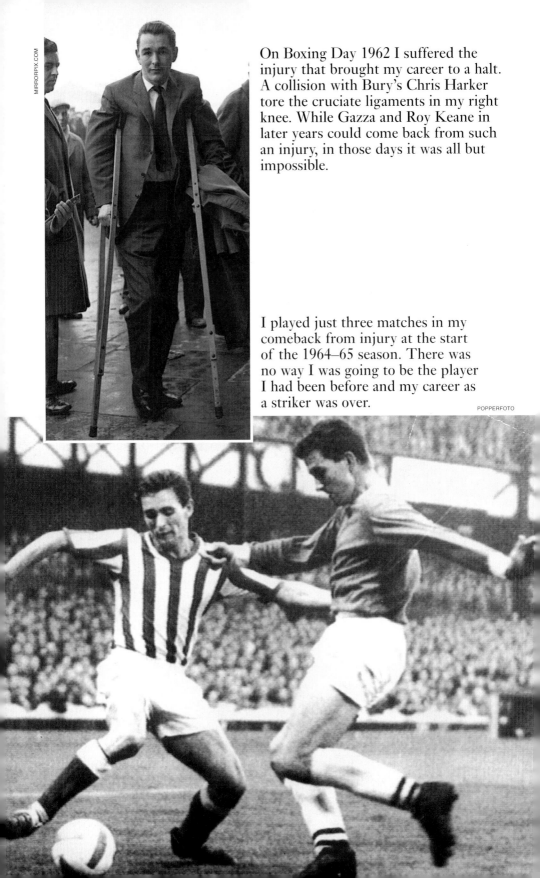

On Boxing Day 1962 I suffered the injury that brought my career to a halt. A collision with Bury's Chris Harker tore the cruciate ligaments in my right knee. While Gazza and Roy Keane in later years could come back from such an injury, in those days it was all but impossible.

I played just three matches in my comeback from injury at the start of the 1964–65 season. There was no way I was going to be the player I had been before and my career as a striker was over.

Harry Storer gave me some very good advice on management – not least on how to deal with football directors.

COLORSPORT

Sunderland manager Alan Brown was completely trustworthy and was somebody who instilled collective discipline in the side. From him I learned how players should not complain to referees and I always made sure my sides played that way.

EMPICS

Walter Winterbottom (left) addresses the England squad ahead of the match against Sweden in October 1959. As ever I'm keen to be the centre of attention.

Talking to Jimmy Greaves during an England training session. We were two of the most prolific strikers of our time, yet I got only two England caps for my efforts – something that still rankles to this day.

CHAPTER 5

GOALS THAT COUNTED
FOR NOTHING

I could never tolerate or accept anything I saw as an injustice. Conductresses who left people at bus stops insisting, 'Sorry – full up,' when there were empty seats drove me mad. I used to protest from the top deck every time that happened and tried to make sure at least some of those people got on to take up the empty seats around us. Peter Taylor and I always travelled up top, in the very front seats if possible so we could put our feet up on the ledge under the window as we chatted, always football, on the way into training or home from the ground.

I'm sure the television people have been preparing my obituary for several years. I'm also sure that at least one company became so fed up with waiting they used the material anyway, putting it out as a profile, a tribute, a kind of documentary, trying to suggest what made Taylor and me click. Taylor and me? It's simple – we were mates, the best of mates, both as players and later in management together. We were chalk and cheese in many ways and not for ever together, as a pair or with our families, but we did all share holidays on occasions and the bond between us was as strong as steel. When Pete and Lil had children I became a godparent. That's another example of how close we were and how big a mistake I made in not burying the hatchet and healing the silly rift between us long before Peter died.

His belief in me as a player was the start of it, as I've already explained. His judgement of a player was a vital ingredient in our management days together. Some reckon 90 per cent of our success was down to me. Bullshit. Pete contributed a far greater percentage than that but even if it had been 10 per cent, his input was just as important and effective as mine. I thought I could recognise a player when I saw one but I wasn't a patch on him. Nobody could touch him in his prime – in his flat cap and muffler, loosely disguised as a fan standing in the crowd. While other managers and scouts were watching the same player, the same would-be signing, from the comfort of the directors' box, Pete would be just another face among thousands of spectators. Those other club representatives would still be wondering about the merits of the player, possibly even discussing him after the match. How daft can you get? Taylor would be well on his way home by then. He might have gone at half-time – in extreme circumstances even before half-time. He would have seen something that convinced him the lad could play or that he couldn't. It might have been something that took a split second but Peter would know in an instant whether that player could bring something to our team at Derby or Nottingham Forest. An instinct, intuition, a gift – call it what you want but my God, without it we would not have achieved anything like the success we enjoyed together. I was full of myself, always have been, and I have to believe I would have made it in management but, once again, time to think has convinced me about the extent and value of Peter's influence.

He had something else that was almost as important to me as his judgement of a footballer. It was his humour, his ability to make me laugh, sometimes with no more than a single word. He was strong, too, one of the very few people apart from my wife who could pull me up short and steer me in the right direction at times when my impetuous, brash nature was leading me into trouble.

A manager needs an assistant, a number two, a right-hand man, you name it. He needs a prop, a support, somebody to lean on in times of uncertainty and doubt, who will also be a sounding board, a source of reassurance or correction. Believe it or not, there were times when I needed to be put right although I can't think of one off-hand. A manager needs a friend and that doesn't mean a yes-man. Peter Taylor provided the best possible combination of qualities, especially for me, such a big-headed sod from the time I scored my first goal. To be able to work with such a friend was ideal. For that friend to have the ability to make me laugh as well – hey, that was Utopia in my book.

Pete was a card-carrying communist when we first met. He changed his views eventually, or told me that he had, but when he got on the subject of religion he could keep us entertained for hours. He used to argue with John O'Hare, the centre-forward who was with me at Derby, Leeds and Forest. O'Hare was a devout Catholic and when he and Taylor got on to the subject of birth control, Pete's philosophies would have you in agony trying to stifle the laughter at what was supposed to be a serious, ideological discussion. They could make a flight to Hong Kong seem to last no longer than an hour and a half.

Taylor's presence and companionship were crucial to me in those early days as a player trying to find my way at Middlesbrough. I wasn't trying to find my feet, I knew where they were and they kept sticking the ball in the back of the net, but I was too long trying to find that first-team place – another of those injustices. It burned deep inside me and that resentment hasn't dwindled in my old age. If I lean back in my armchair and close my eyes, I can recall all those goals I banged in, season after season, once Bob Dennison recognised the obvious. I had been right all along and so had Taylor in the very first place – I had been the best at the club, at least the best at scoring goals, and they had been wrong to deny me my chance for such a long time. Barbara taught me to dance, transforming my footwork from a Norman Wisdom into a reasonable impersonation of Fred Astaire, but nobody taught me how to score a goal. When Brian Clough popped into this world on 21 March 1935, the knack of scoring goals came with him. When the midwife held me by the ankles and smacked my bum, I didn't cry – I yelled 'One nil'.

It became a familiar cry at Middlesbrough once I was established in the side. We were often in front, mainly on the strength of my goals – it had to be my goals when you look at that scoring record. But I sensed a nasty smell. There was something wrong, something obvious even to a blind man. It struck me as simple, straightforward incompetence at the time, but I came to wonder if it might be something sinister.

As a manager, if I'd had a striker coming to me and slapping in a transfer request because he thought our defence wasn't good enough, he'd have been given short shrift. He'd have got a bollocking and if he argued the toss I might have clouted him for his impertinence. But that sense of injustice had overtaken me, enveloped me, and I went to Dennison and told him I wanted a transfer. Probably it was that second season when I was to finish with forty goals from forty-four games. I told the manager I was fed up with scoring at one end then watching our defence conceding them at the other, match after match, in considerable numbers. It was happening on a regular basis and I was totally pissed off.

Middlesbrough, as I've said, were in the second division and that's where they stayed. Now it doesn't take a master mathematician to produce the theory that a team with a centre-forward as good as I was, scoring as many goals as I did, should have been promoted. Thirty-eight of my forty goals in that second season were scored in the League. My fury at the injustice of it was poured out to Dennison and the story made the papers. It was a mystery how it all came out but although the detail of it is a bit obscure now, I'm absolutely certain I let the press lads in on it. I knew how to use the media, even then.

The result was not a transfer but the captaincy. Dennison actually made me skipper, which was a popular decision with me but not with half the team – the half who resented my ability and the attention it attracted and who didn't like my self-opinionated personality and eagerness to express it. It might have been the half of the team who were conceding so many goals on a regular basis. The revolt was inevitable. Half the players sat on one side of Rea's caff and the rest, the Clough brigade, sat on the other. That was the scene after training. The other lot even signed a petition, a round-robin, protesting at my appointment, but it altered nothing. I carried on scoring goals and that bloody defence of ours kept on conceding them.

We went to Charlton on one occasion and drew the match 6–6. You tend not to forget a scoreline like that, not even me – a hat-trick to my name away from home and we still couldn't win. I'd been trying my darndest, busting a gut. I seem to remember scoring the last of our six just before the finish when there wasn't time for us to concede another, not even our defence. I was suspicious. I'd kept an eye on our defenders and to my mind something had to be wrong. Not even incompetence or crap players could explain the way Middlesbrough were letting in goals. I watched two of our lot in particular, Brian Phillips and Ken Thomson – poor lad died later while playing golf. I couldn't believe those two were genuinely as bad as they appeared to be.

A group of them were playing cards in the next compartment on the train back to the Northeast. It must have been a warm night and the doors were open so I shouted, 'If I can manage to get four goals next week, you never know, we might even win.'

One of them cracked back, 'Yeah, if we have a centre-forward who can move around enough for us to find him with the ball, we could have a chance.'

I kept mentioning our defence to Dennison, a bloke referred to by Don Taylor, Peter's brother, as 'the silent type'. He was six feet tall, maybe a little taller than that, with jet black hair and a strong build. He was quite a handsome man, an imposing figure in his own way. As a manager, he wanted no bother, no trouble whatsoever, and avoided it wherever possible. I suppose that's why he ended up getting the sack. Despite my protests and complaints about the quality of our defending, the way we seemed to be chucking matches away, Dennison believed I'd got it wrong. He let it out to me that Thomson had told him I ought to see a psychiatrist and that if I did, they'd cart me straight off to an asylum.

I'm convinced to this day that Phillips and Thomson had a bet on the Charlton game, backing Charlton to beat us. The whole thing disturbed me and I finished up losing the captaincy. The story made the papers for a week but that only increased my feeling of injustice, and once I get my teeth into something – aye, even my false teeth these days – I take some shaking off. Middlesbrough's defensive record was so bad and so regular, I didn't think it could be simple coincidence. It led me to go to see a director, Harold Thomas, a keen cricket fan and a solicitor. I can see his office as clearly today as I did then. It was like entering another world – wood-panelled walls, and him sitting in a vivid red leather chair behind a huge, cluttered desk. This was Rumpole of the Bailey decades before we were to set eyes on him on the telly.

It was a big thing for a young footballer to do. As a centre-forward, I was usually somewhere near the halfway line when the opposition were scoring against us so I didn't always have the best of angles to see exactly what was going on. But I did know how and when Phillips or Thomson should have been heading the ball clear and I did know there were times when they seemed to be missing it. I remember them doing it against Doncaster when Charlie Williams, who went on to become a well-known comedian, was playing directly against me. There was nothing funny that day.

Thomas, a rotund man not unlike Rumpole, peered over his horn-rimmed spectacles as I poured out my complaints and told him what I believed was happening in our team. Unfortunately, he was the same as Dennison – a nice man, I'm sure, but I'm absolutely certain he didn't want trouble on the scale I was suggesting. So my frustration went on and the goals kept flying in at both ends of the pitch. We scored eighty-odd in one season and still couldn't get promotion from the second division. That in itself should make any manager and his directors think. Time didn't heal the situation but it proved I was right. Proof eventually came to the surface. Brian Phillips, the one who had begun the revolt against me, was one of those sent to prison and suspended from the game for life for his involvement in the notorious soccer bribes scandal in the early 1960s.

I've gone over a bit of old ground but it's all part of the story I can now bring up to date with a better understanding than before. You can do many things when you're retired – walk Del-boy, the dog, as I did so often before he died a couple of years ago, see my five adorable, beautiful grandchildren, tend the garden, visit relatives, watch television and listen to music. It also gives a man time to look back and seek reasons for some things, if not all things, that have happened in his life. There isn't a logical reason for everything. Some of it has to be down to chance, luck – good and bad – or fate as some prefer to call it.

I've done a fair bit of analysing over the past nine years and there is a definite link between the various aspects of my life and career – explanations for the life and times of a bloke whose actions have sometimes bordered on the inexplicable. As I've said, my mam was the biggest influence of all with the way she ran her orderly house, overcrowded as it was. The routine and the pecking order established, it was an environment where we all knew our place and the expectations of us. We all grew up with that essential quality that seems to be missing from so many people in our country today, young and not so young alike – the awareness of what is right and what is wrong.

I scored so many goals partly because I followed my mam's insistence that whatever I did I should do to the best of my ability, and that I should keep trying harder and harder to be better still, even if I thought I had nothing more to give. That was what I instilled in my players when I became a manager, starting at Hartlepools United where hardly any of them could play in the first place, and money was in such short supply that if we'd needed a new shit-house door, I'd have been expected to provide it and fit it.

The injustice of it all at Middlesbrough, the good work I did that was so blatantly undone by others in the team, produced more than anger and resentment. I realise that now with time to think and analyse. It has dawned on me that those days, that experience, had a profound effect that was to play its part in the remarkable success I enjoyed in charge of those relatively unfashionable football clubs, Derby County and Nottingham Forest.

I had at least two things in common with Bill Shankly. I don't know if his mum was like mine, I suppose she must have been similar, but Bill used to say that a man should always do his best at whatever he attempted. 'If you're going to sweep the street, then make sure your street is the cleanest in town,' he'd say. He also believed that good teams were built from the back. That was my philosophy and I believe that the experiences at Middlesbrough helped form it. There's no point in having the best and most prolific attack in the League if you can't keep the ball out of the net at your end. That doesn't mean a team has to be destructive. It is the easiest thing in the world to destroy – you can do it by putting your foot through a Picasso canvas. I could have had a destructive team, or a totally negative team, with a couple of nuns in my back four. That's not the point. The Middlesbrough episode taught me a fundamental footballing fact of life – defenders need to be as good at their jobs as any forward. They are not there to clatter the opposition, to kick people, to destroy. Their job is to protect their own goal with skill and intelligence. They should have the ability to recover and retain the ball and deliver it to the feet of the creative players in the side. Whether that registered in my subconscious as a wasted goalscorer at Ayresome Park, I don't know. I suppose it must have done because it was the first intent I carried into management. Look at my record in the job and you will see that I always made sure I had a good goalkeeper and a good centre-half – oh aye, a good centre-forward as well but, with me, you could always take that for granted.

I was nowhere near ready for management by the time I left Middlesbrough in 1961 (36 goals in 42 appearances, sorry for going on about it but it's worth repeating) and joined Sunderland, but it was to happen far sooner and far more cruelly than anybody could have imagined.

I wasn't that chuffed at the idea of a Mediterranean cruise in the close season of 1961 because sailing is like flying to me – something I can well do without. But Barbara relished the prospect so who was I to argue? In the event, I loved it, but I wasn't prepared for the welcoming party that greeted us when we returned to Southampton. Alan Brown, the straight-backed guardsman who managed Sunderland, was waiting on the quayside.

I'm known as the one who speaks his mind, who gets to the point without fuss, but Browny was the master at it. He tipped the porter a couple of bob, heaved our luggage on to a trolley, looked me straight between the eyes in a way that made lesser men freeze to the spot, and asked, 'Would you sign for Sunderland?'

I presume David Beckham was asked to re-sign for Manchester United and, if you believe what you read, you have the impression that, after prolonged negotiations, his wages are in the region of £100,000 a week, give or take a few pence here and there. That's daft money, crazy money, even for a player with that talent in his right foot. Times change, they say. Well, times haven't just changed since Browny met Barbara and me on Southampton docks; times have been contorted beyond reason, out of all proportion. One day it's going to end in an awful lot of tears and bankruptcies.

Would I sign for Sunderland? Done! 'Yes,' I blurted out without the need to be asked again. Brown said he'd see me at Roker Park in a week and assured me I would be on top money at Sunderland, whatever that might have been at the time. We're back to good solid standards here. I didn't know Alan Brown personally, but I knew of him. I was aware of his reputation as a strict and honest man. I took him at his word. He went back to his holiday in Cornwall and I agreed to see him at the ground in a week. I'd been to Cannes and back and suddenly gone from Middlesbrough to Sunderland in the time it takes to say 'Yes'. The best goalscorer in England had been sold for £42,000 – by my reckoning, still a lot less than some players in the Premiership make in a week, and I'm including inflation!

Still the goals came my way, 34 of them in 43 matches in my first season. I had 24 to my name from 24 league games, plus four more in the Cup, by the time Boxing Day arrived in 1962. That was the day that changed my life because it changed the knee joint in my right leg. We faced Bury at home on a bitterly cold, snowy, sleety day on Wearside, the kind of day when seagulls flew backwards to stop their eyes watering and made sure they kept their tail feathers well down. That day the Clough playing career effectively ended in its prime – done and dusted, dead and Buryed. There were to be three more appearances, my only ones in the then first division, and one goal. That was in the 1964–65 season – a desperate but futile attempt to hang on and prolong a career that perished as quickly as it suddenly went dark that Boxing Day afternoon at Roker. Bury goalkeeper Chris Harker's shoulder slammed into my knee as we challenged for the ball, my head hit the ground and everything went black.

I came round soon enough and knew immediately that this was no minor injury, no simple sprain. Instinct demanded I get up but I could only crawl and I'll never forget the voice of Bury's centre-half, Bob Stokoe – who somehow managed to win the Cup as manager of the Sunderland side that beat Leeds against all odds in 1973. He moaned at the referee, telling him to get on with the game, accusing me of play-acting. I'll never forgive Stokoe for that. I had a torn cruciate ligament, the Gazza injury as they call it today. Thanks to improved surgical techniques, Paul Gascoigne's knee was repaired and he was given the chance to continue his career. His problems turned out to be in his head as well, but in my case the knackered knee put paid to my playing days.

I'd encountered an injustice or two already but nothing compared with this. It wasn't the £45 a week I was earning although in those days that was a decent wage. When the end of my playing career was confirmed, having missed the entire season when Sunderland were promoted, I suddenly knew the meaning of the word desolation. Happily married, with sons Simon and Nigel both born in Sunderland where Barbara and I had so many good friends, life had seemed so good and so promising. Suddenly, I had nothing but worries. I was finished, an ex-footballer who knew how to do nothing other than play football.

I was totally unaware that Sunderland had me insured for £40,000 or so, but I believe they were more concerned with getting the money than with my continued belief that I could keep on playing. They got it in the end. I got about £1,000. Alan Brown had gone to take over as manager at Sheffield Wednesday so it was a different regime at Roker from the one that took me there. Thankfully, George Hardwick, the new manager, gave me something far more important and useful than a few quid. Dear George. I went to his eightieth birthday party in Middlesbrough in 2001 and needed no reminder from him that he launched my managerial career by giving me the chance to work with the youth players at Sunderland.

I bowed to the establishment, so to speak, when I agreed to pack in playing. They told me, 'We don't believe you're going to make it back to the player you were,' but I still think I could have gone on for a little bit longer, maybe in a lower division. Perhaps it was, and is, wishful thinking but to this day I wish I'd tried. I wish I'd given it another whirl. It was my life and at twenty-nine, I knew I was good at it.

I accepted the decision too easily. I didn't know where to go or who to go to. Although our Joe was head of the family, once you reach a certain age you have to stand on your own feet and get on with your own life. I felt like the cub that had just been kicked out by a pride of lions and made to fend for itself. Alan Brown, I suppose, would have been an appropriate counsellor but he lacked two things – warmth and the ability to communicate in some circumstances. He could sympathise but he wasn't the kind of man to put his arm around somebody in trouble. For instance, if a player had ever gone to him and said, 'I've got a girl pregnant,' he wouldn't have been the man to go to a doctor and ask for an abortion as I once did for a player of mine. No, I'm not saying who it was.

Assumptions were made about me when the end came at Sunderland. It was assumed I would stay in the game in some capacity, at some level. It was assumed I would pass my coaching badges with no problem whatsoever. Everybody else was convinced I'd be fine but, deep inside, I felt vulnerable. Suddenly that world out there seemed a hell of a lot bigger. For weeks I wished the injury hadn't happened; every time I was nodding off to sleep I wished that something magical might cure it during the night.

There is nothing like playing. You've heard it a million times from many sources but it remains the irrefutable truth. There is nothing like putting on that pristine kit and tying on those immaculate boots, nothing like the smell of the dressing room and the adulation of the crowd – particularly when you were as good as I was at doing the thing the fans want to see most. There is nothing to equal the ecstasy of putting the ball in the net.

Looking back I can think of clouds and silver linings and that type of thing. Thanks to George Hardwick's generosity – and it was generous because neither he nor I knew whether I could coach – I was given a head start on others of my age. I was able to take the first tentative steps on the road to a managerial career five years ahead of schedule. That was some compensation at least for having to draw a line under my playing career so prematurely. It set other wheels in motion. I never got over finishing so soon, never recovered from the blow of that injury (in fact, the knee still gives me unmerciful gyp) but I was on my way. Management, here I come – with another chip on my shoulder to go with the rest.

A HARD LIFE AND A SOUND SENSE OF VALUES

I didn't go into coaching with any particular preconceived ideas or theories. I didn't go into it convinced I would become one of the best managers who ever drew breath. I went into it as a former centre-forward with one of the best goalscoring records of all time who was scandalously disregarded and under-used by his country – two bloody caps for a lad who was totting up goals like telephone numbers. I was overlooked mainly because Walter Winterbottom preferred a player called Derek Kevan, a big, bruiser of a player from West Brom who scored a goal or two here and there but wasn't in my class, nowhere near it.

Apart from the two full caps, this is my international record: one England B cap and one goal; three appearances for the Under-23 side and another goal; two games for the Football League representative team – six goals; one game for an FA XI – five goals. That's right, five in one game for the second time in a representative shirt, and I'd achieved it once for Middlesbrough as well, against Brighton in my fourth season.

I didn't go into coaching because of my record as a player but because I needed a job, needed the money and needed a future.

It was the past that armed me. I wasn't aware of it then, but I'm sure now. The sudden and premature end of my playing days had an important subconscious effect. I would make damned sure that every footballer with whom I came into contact made the most of whatever ability he had. If he didn't, he wouldn't remain in my company for very long. The ability to play football for your living, or any sport for that matter, is a gift that should be cherished and relished by those who have it. Those who abuse it to the extent that they reduce their capacity to perform at their very best are guilty of a criminal waste.

I knew how much I was envied by the supporters of Middlesbrough and Sunderland. First I was the local lad made good and when I moved from one to the other I was still aware of the warmth and friendship despite arriving at Roker from one of their fiercest rivals. I would have hated to be transferred further afield. I couldn't have gone to a London club, for instance. That would have been like moving to a different country. It seemed so far away, and struck me as a vast, impersonal place, too big to be intimate and cosy. Of course, people who were born there and who live there will probably argue the opposite, but I would have been homesick within days.

The Northeast was home to me, an area that still regards itself as out on its own as far as football is concerned. The people have a parochial mentality, in the nicest possible sense, and their love of football is more intense than it is anywhere else in England. If one of the three major clubs, Newcastle, Sunderland or Middlesbrough, had had the success of Manchester United, Arsenal or Liverpool, they wouldn't be playing to crowds of 67,000 nowadays; they'd need grounds big enough to hold 167,000.

I was just like the fans who paid their hard-earned money to watch – consumed by the game. Other places didn't interest me, apart from their football grounds. Every city seems pretty much the same to footballers. There's not much difference between a trip to one railway station and hotel and a trip to another. Playing was everything.

There were a lot of northern clubs in the second division. We seemed to be playing in Rotherham, Barnsley, Huddersfield or Doncaster every other week. For a while, the furthest I travelled was Nottingham. I scored my first hat-trick at the City Ground in 1956. These days in the Premiership, there are plenty of foreign players with glamorous names – Laurent Blanc, Thierry Henry, Dennis Bergkamp, Juan Sebastian Veron, Jimmy Floyd Hasselbaink, Kanu, Ruud Van Nistelrooy. There was something so much more homely and comfortable, simpler and more straightforward, about the names of those we played against, Barnsley's goalkeeper Harry Hough, for instance. You can't go wrong with a Harry Hough. You don't expect any more than he can give from a man called Harry Hough. As you might imagine, he was as tough as a tree, solid as a rock – that I can vouch for because, as a centre-forward, I know that when he clattered you there was no room for doubt; you had the bruises to remind you for weeks.

Charlie Williams is another name to conjure with. He might not have had the style of a Laurent Blanc but as one of the first coloured players in our game, he had more to prove than the Frenchman who joined Manchester United so late in his distinguished career. Charlie inevitably attracted a lot of attention well before he went on stage as a comic. He wasn't a bad player, either – a terrific athlete and game as a pebble. On one occasion when we played Doncaster, Charlie didn't give me a kick – apart from the ones he landed around my shins and calves. 'I'm going wherever you go,' he said. He stuck so tight that I told him, 'If you come any closer to me we might as well get into the same pair of shorts and save a few bob on laundry.'

Doncaster's goalkeeper Harry Gregg, another good, solid name, was an international with Northern Ireland. He later joined Manchester United and was among the lucky ones to survive the Munich disaster. In one game at Ayresome Park I'd stuck a couple past him and he was frantic. He charged out to the edge of the penalty area, foaming at the mouth, and screamed at me, 'You come anywhere near this box again and you'll not get out alive.' He'd completely lost it, couldn't take it, but his Irish charm was never far below the surface and after the game his was the first arm to be draped around my shoulder in friendship as we left the pitch.

Football was such an important part of the lives of people in the Northeast that even amateur football was renowned. Bishop Auckland used to win the Amateur Cup at Wembley season after season. In their way, Bishop Auckland were as famous as the rest of the Northeastern teams, and I'm including the times when Jackie Milburn was a folk hero at Newcastle and when Wilf Mannion was regarded as a god at Ayresome Park. They used to talk about 'hotbeds' of football, the areas of the country where young talent could be found in abundance. South Yorkshire was one but no bed was hotter than the Northeast. We regarded ourselves as the Mecca of the game and allowed the Londoners to delude themselves by thinking they were the important ones who ran the show.

Home games in the Northeast – and at most other venues – were staged in front of a sea of flat caps. Look at the pictures from those days. I can imagine local papers running a competition – spot a fan without a cap and win yourself ten bob. We didn't mix with supporters on a regular basis apart from on matchdays. We bumped into them in the street or the local caff from time to time but we didn't booze with them. We didn't fight with them either, which might be a surprise to some young footballers I could mention today. Football was a way of life, almost a branch of religion, in my world. Supporters would forgive you almost anything just as long as they saw you working your balls off, prepared to sweat blood for their team.

It might sound like a statement of the obvious but I was at

home in the Northeast. The feeling of warmth and comfort and being needed was a continuation of the security I experienced at number 11, Valley Road, I suppose. I didn't go sightseeing before away games. For a start, there was never time and I was not one for the cultural things in life. When I was away there was only one place I wanted to be – back at home.

That pull was never greater than during an England Under-23 trip abroad in 1957. Moscow was part of the itinerary, and a conducted tour of that imposing, historic city was included. It was a privilege, of course, although few of us in the party appreciated that side of it. Bobby Charlton, my roommate, had warned me in advance that I wouldn't fancy the food in that neck of the woods and told me to pack a lot of chocolate. I soon found out what he meant and was grateful. They might have learned how to goose-step in Russia but they had nothing to touch my mam's stew and savoury dumplings. I'd shown Bobby all about bird's-nesting in the grounds of the hotel in England before we headed for the Iron Curtain. By coincidence, the first thing I ate in Moscow was a clear soup the colour of washing-up water with a raw egg in the bottom of the bowl. I don't know what bird had laid it but at a time like that, a bar of chocolate sounds like a bloody good idea.

Not many things about Moscow registered, not the famous things that attract so many people. But I do remember being struck by the sight of so many queues. People queued for everything. They were still queuing to take a look at Lenin and he'd been dead for years. They left me out of the side to play Russia so I wasn't the happiest tourist anyway. My thoughts didn't turn to the Kremlin or anywhere else in the eastern bloc. I was fed up and wanted to go home.

They say home is where the heart is and mine was steeped in the Northeast. They made sure you kept things in perspective there. At Middlesbrough, one player had a car when Barbara and I got engaged. Lindy Delapenha was the star with the Ford

Anglia and it wasn't just a gesture when he offered to take us to Stockton-on-Tees to buy the ring. It was the equivalent of giving me a knighthood, even though as I got out of the car to head for H. Samuel's, one of the doors fell off.

David Beckham, Steven Gerrard, Michael Owen and the rest of them have their cars, their 'image rights', their agents and investments, and I'm glad the game is rewarding its top performers well – but it's too well by a mile in many cases. That's not the players' fault. It's down to the chairmen and those who run the clubs who think they can keep on paying out more and more. One day soon they'll have to put a lid on it. I look at these talented and extremely fortunate young men and wonder whether, somewhere along the line, they were denied the chance to develop a proper sense of values. They can't know what money is worth because they have too much of it. You need to be a very level-headed young man indeed, or to have enjoyed a sound and secure upbringing, if you're to cope with millionaire status before the age of twenty.

You see many leading young players on television these days and I don't mean on 'Match of the Day' or 'The Premiership'. You see them in commercials for which I assume they're paid another fortune. Whether they're advertising shampoo, sunglasses, cars or frozen peas, there's rarely a hair out of place. I don't think we were quite as fussy about our image in my day. I was a big name at Middlesbrough and at Sunderland – goalscorers always were and I did it as well as anybody ever had – but the sea-coal still had to be gathered. I used to cycle down to Seaburn with a sack and a rake to collect coal that had been washed in by the tide. It was a cold job when that east wind blew through to your bones, and hard graft. But the coal was free and available, and the knowledge that once it was dry it would keep my mam and dad warm was incentive and reward enough, never mind the image or the reputation. Such trivial things never dawned on us. Life was harder then, the basic essentials not easy to come by or taken for granted, but it seemed so much more fulfilling on the strength of it.

This was the background, the life and the learning process, that swept me into the coaching side of football. Now I can see that I was a young man who, in the words of John Osborne, looked back in anger – a lot of anger and good reason for it. I needed a job. I had to work for a living. As my mam had instilled into me, I would make the best of it and do the job to the utmost of whatever ability might be in there, but I hadn't a clue whether I'd be good, bad or a complete and utter failure.

In quiet, reflective moments, I wonder what experiences I drew on and relied on, what lessons I'd learned from other managers that stood me in good stead and I have come to realise there were a few. I certainly learned something from Bob Dennison at Middlesbrough. It wasn't what he had or hadn't said or done; it was that he'd been hopeless – couldn't have spotted a diamond in a diamond mine. He was surrounded by jewels in the dressing room and on the training ground, international players with a lot of caps and others who were good enough to be internationals but were never given the chance – and me with my forty goals a season, regular as clockwork.

It wasn't as if he had to go out and test his judgement with a few signings – a part of the job that often dictates whether you succeed or fail, and nine times out of ten is the main reason for managers getting the sack. The talent was there for Dennison, give or take a transfer here and there. I doubt if the entire side cost anything like £100,000, but he didn't do anything with that squad of players because he didn't bung up the leaks. He needed to stop up the great big hole he had in his bucket. Points were flooding out of it. We had the ability to score goals by the boatload but Dennison did nothing about our serious problem of conceding just as regularly. No matter what was poured into that bucket of his, it was all allowed to gush out at the bottom. We couldn't defend to save our lives.

Dennison had been a defender in his time. You'd have thought he would recognise the problem, and even if he didn't know the underlying reason, it was his duty as manager to try to put it right. The need for a team to defend effectively was like a message imprinted on my mind from those infuriating days. Dennison taught me by accident, through incompetence. I learned what not to do.

The first lessons I absorbed came from Harry Storer. Anybody who knows me or has read about my career must realise how much I valued the words I heard from him. Pete Taylor, who'd had him as his manager at Coventry, introduced us when we were at Middlesbrough. A wiry little bugger he was, with a tough reputation. Most people refer to me as a talker, somebody who never stops going on. Well, I've got news for them – I was always a good listener, still am. I was a wee bit apprehensive about Storer, realising that with him it was better to be seen and rarely heard. I was awestruck but fascinated as old Harry reeled off home truths about football: 'Once you're a manager, if it ever happens, do a quick check before away games. Look at your players prior to the coach leaving and count the hearts. If there are less than five, don't bother setting off. A team's no good without courage.

'Something to remember about football club directors – whatever you do for them, as a player or a manager, you'll be lucky if you ever hear them say thank you.

'Once you're a manager, everything lands on your doorstep. If a fan trips up on his way into the ground, if a player gets barracked from the terraces, if a seat doesn't work properly, if a season-ticket holder can't find a programme seller, if the postman brings a sackful of letters saying the team's no bloody good – it will all end up in the manager's office. You can stake your life on it.'

Every word Storer said to me was eventually borne out in

reality. He managed Birmingham in his time and was at Derby prior to my predecessor, Tim Ward. He might have been of the old school but former players going into management would do well to bear in mind the philosophies of Harry Storer, even today, because they still apply. Some things never change. Good advice is always good advice.

Alan Brown taught me about discipline. I knew plenty about that from my mam, of course, but Browny's discipline was applied to the team as a whole as well as to the individual. It was collective discipline. If you need an example, remember how my teams at Derby and Nottingham Forest went about their work – not by effing and blinding at match officials, not by intimidating referees or hacking the ball away in disgust at free-kicks given against us. Referees regarded my teams as their favourites because we simplified their jobs. We made refereeing easier than it was with other teams. We didn't antagonise them or chase them with angry words and gestures. That seems to be a lesson Arsene Wenger's Arsenal side has yet to learn. I don't care what they've won – they'd be respected a great deal more if they'd won it with an attitude and level of behaviour in keeping with their undoubted talent. As far as I'm concerned, they leave a nasty taste.

Brown was totally in charge at Sunderland. The first day I turned up at Roker Park, I realised he ran every aspect of the show, morning till night, top to bottom. This really was the boss at work, the gaffer who left nobody in the slightest doubt about who was in charge. I don't scare easily and never did but I remember times when I was frightened of Alan Brown. A bollocking from him was like ten from anybody else. When he dressed you down you stood there feeling totally naked. Talk about tearing you off a strip – he could tear off your entire shirt.

I often think of Browny. He's dead now, God bless him. I can be in the garden or sipping a cup of coffee or looking for relief from the boredom of a televised match when nothing is happening. Whatever the moment, I can catch a glimpse of him standing there, his back as straight as a goalpost. I can remember, as if it was today, looking at him at Sunderland and thinking to myself, 'This is the way I'll do the job if the opportunity ever comes.'

I'd seen both extremes – Dennison, easygoing and negligent when it came to repairing the suspect department of his team, and Brown, the rigid disciplinarian who allowed nothing and no one to escape his notice. Browny struck me as a fifty-year-old who wanted to be twenty. He'd been in the Guards and it showed in his magnificent physique, hard as nails and without a sign of fat, and his short, military haircut. He was not outwardly compassionate at all. He had what I had but couldn't recognise in myself at that time – terrible conceit. He used to stride down the corridors thinking he was the most important man on earth. I used to do it not realising I was doing it, but he was well aware of himself. He meant it.

Then he went to a real extreme. He introduced the entire dressing room to a man with glorious silver-grey hair, a former cricketer. He was Browny's new friend and mentor, apparently. Our gaffer had gone religious. He'd joined up with an organisation called Moral Rearmament. He wanted to get me involved and the three of us met on a couple of occasions but their jargon had me nodding off within minutes.

Browny took it seriously. Once you joined up you had to purge yourself of all your sins – confess to everything you'd done wrong in your life. I gather it took him quite some time! They used to insist they were not a religious sect but that's how I regarded them. It left the Sunderland dressing room aghast when he told us he had enrolled. Suddenly the Iron Man, as he loved us to call him, had begun to bend. Somebody once told me, 'Don't be fooled by Browny. He'll give you all the stuff about living right and not stepping out of line but he's been knocking off his secretary for eighteen months.' I'm told he admitted it when he joined MR.

Maybe a touch of compassion did enter his life once he'd joined the gang. After treatment on my injured knee one afternoon, he offered me a lift home. He installed me and my plaster cast across the back seat of his car and when we arrived at my house he just said, 'Get on my back.' He piggy-backed me to my front door and told me to stand on my good leg and lean against the wall while he fetched my crutches from the boot. 'See you tomorrow,' he said as he handed them to me. Nothing else. Alan Brown was not one to talk a lot.

I'm grateful to him because, without realising it, he sent me into management with his conceit and arrogance and the highest possible regard for discipline in a football club. I never found out anything about his background, his childhood, his mother and father. He lacked that human touch that warms a man's personality. I used to think he was someone who hadn't been conceived – he'd been constructed.

Taking those first steps up the coaching and management ladder, I knew I wanted to be strict. I wanted to be arrogant and by then I knew I was conceited because I was born conceited. I thought that was normal. Knowing nothing about Brown's early background but being so proud of my own childhood, I felt equal to his strengths in a peculiar kind of way. So although I was dipping my big toe into unfamiliar waters that first morning George Hardwick let me work with Sunderland's youth players, I had an air of confidence about me. It was well founded because, would you believe, the moment I got out the practice balls and gathered those young footballers together and started to talk, I discovered straightaway that I had another ability to my name. I could teach.

CHAPTER 7

HEY, I CAN MANAGE

It's only when you get on in years that you fully appreciate how it all happened – in my case, how a raggy-arsed slip of a lad from a big family in Middlesbrough, with a big head and talented feet, made it and became a name known to millions. Bad luck, or fate, put paid to my playing days before I had the chance to do full justice to myself but nobody needs reminding of my achievements in management with Derby and Nottingham Forest. They are there for all to see. They are in the record books, in black and white, and I've talked and written about them often enough to make sure nobody forgets.

It's why I was so successful, how it happened, that intrigues me, and it should intrigue every young man who fancies his chances as a manager and every manager already working but still wondering why he's not succeeding. That's why I've dwelt so long on my upbringing and playing career because that's where it came from. I learned things along the way as a manager, obviously, but there were things inside my head, often little things that stuck for years. These were the roots of my managerial success. There was never a book to explain how to go about it and how to succeed, not until this one.

I had an immediate effect on the youth side at Sunderland. I was with them for just one season but they started winning matches virtually straightaway. There are two things to say about that. Firstly, they all looked up to me as the best centre-forward, or former centre-forward, in the country, so I was given instant and total respect. As you might imagine, that appealed to me. Conceited men like to be looked up to. Secondly, I changed the training. They didn't spend their time jogging lap after lap around the training ground; they spent almost all the session with a ball.

Training was regimented, predictable and boring when I started out as a professional player. Maybe that was another reason why Middlesbrough couldn't win owt. When we arrived at ten o'clock, the favourite occupation of the coaches was to sit on the radiators. If they were seeking inspiration, all they got were warm bums. 'OK, come on, let's go. Remember, it's ten, five and twelve' – same orders, same start to a session, day after day. It was an unnecessary reminder that we would be expected to run ten laps followed by five half-laps and twelve sprints. You did it in your own time and the lazy buggers would cut the corners and run on the grass. Only occasionally would they toss us a ball for a bit of a knockabout. How on earth could a training regime like that possible help a group of blokes whose job demanded that they should manoeuvre a football better than the opposition, under the scrutiny of thousands of paying spectators, every Saturday afternoon? It struck me as barmy then, and any manager or coach who pays scant respect to the constant need for practice with a ball is barmy now.

It was Lindy Delapenha who eventually broke the monotony of it all by asking for volunteers to come back and play head-tennis in the afternoons. I was probably the first volunteer. We strung a rope from a drainpipe at the back of the stand to the fence of the factory next door – a span of about twelve yards. It was six a side with a shilling to the winners – 5p in

today's money. They could play for five grand a man nowadays
but it wouldn't be any more competitive than we were. In time,
because it became the most popular part of training at Middlesbrough, we marked out the court with whitewash borrowed
from the groundsman. Once the game was under way, you
weren't allowed to let the ball touch the floor, and there were
times when it would fly at you like a bullet. It didn't take a
genius to work out that this was more closely related to the
action of a Saturday afternoon than jogging and sprinting
without a ball in sight.

For all the positive lessons I learned from Alan Brown, he
had some peculiar training methods. At least we had a ball, and
we wore our match strip and lined up as a team, but we played
against nobody! Browny was a Lilleshall man – one of the
managing and coaching fraternity who swore by the so-called
education they gathered at that training establishment in
Shropshire. It was regarded as a footballing university by the
theorists, the fancy-dan coaches who had a thirst for what they
called technical knowledge but who hadn't got the first idea
about the way football really worked.

It was at Lilleshall that Bill Shankly, invited to give a talk, I
suppose, became so frustrated and angry about some demon-
stration they'd laid on that he left his seat, walked on to the
pitch, grabbed the ball and half-volleyed it into one of the
goals. 'That's better – it's safer in there,' he said, or words to
that effect. Bill couldn't tolerate people who insisted on complicating the game. To him, that Lilleshall lot would have been
talking in a foreign language.

Alan Brown believed and followed their theories. He became
a fanatic about what he called shadow training – the first team
against nobody. Word has it that after moving to Sheffield
Wednesday he developed this form of practice match so that his
team were confronted by eleven dustbins. At Sunderland we
were confronted by nothing more threatening, challenging or

realistic than an empty opposing half of the pitch. We played against invisible men and we usually won! Even though we did have a ball to work with, it was the most boring and meaningless activity I was ever involved in. I don't know whether it was intended to improve our understanding and vision, or whether it was just a matter of confidence in knowing that, eventually, we would have the satisfaction of putting the ball in the net. Whatever the intention, it was totally false, right down to Brown's instruction as he barked at us, 'Just do what you would do if there was an opponent standing in your way.'

'I would try to go round him and stick it in the net,' I told him many times. 'But there's nobody here. There's no bugger to go round so what do I do, just roll it in?'

'No,' Browny snapped, 'you smash it in.'

So I did. I finished up smashing them in from well outside the penalty area, from all parts and all angles, but I'll be blowed if I know what good it did because come Saturday Browny's theory went out of the window. Every time I looked up to take aim, or just hit the ball instinctively, there was some bloke, usually wearing a green jersey, hanging about between the posts trying to make bloody sure he kept it out. Shadow training? When did you last hear of shadows benefiting anybody's work – apart from the lads who backed Cliff Richard?

Working with the youngsters at Sunderland brought me into close contact with Colin Todd and John O'Hare, talented young men who were a pleasure to work with. Getting to know them as I did proved very useful when I came to sign them a little further down the line. The youngsters responded because my emphasis was on preparation for matches, working with an objective, a purpose, striving to make them as comfortable as possible with the ball. They would see little enough of it on a Saturday so it was common sense to make sure they had plenty of it during the week. It was during the matches, though, that they learned whether I was right or wrong in what I'd told them and asked them to do from Monday to Friday.

It's no good training to a peak if you reach that peak two days before the event. You don't have to be at your peak all the time to play well, either. I'd say there is a margin of roughly 15 per cent and a player can still perform well providing he doesn't drop any further than that.

A good coach or manager can't walk out there cold on a matchday; he has to be as worked up about the game as his players. You could call it fanaticism, and I know I had it. At the end of most matches as a manager, even as a coach with L plates at Sunderland, my shirt used to be as sweat-stained as any of the players'. Total involvement is what you must have. You must be on the same wavelength as the players, share their emotion whether that's elation or disappointment, and always believe you know why and where it has gone right or wrong.

After a few months, George Hardwick gave me a title, youth-team manager, and told me it would be to my benefit to take my coaching badge. It was on that FA course at Durham that I met Charlie Hughes who was to become top man in our game, Director of Coaching at FA headquarters. On the rare occasions that I can't get to sleep it's usually because somebody or something has reminded me that Charlie Hughes was on the short-list at the time I was interviewed for the England manager's job. What an insult! This was the man who argued that the quicker and more often you landed the ball in the opposing penalty area, the likelier you would be to score a goal. Some believed it. Some managers had their teams bouncing the ball off clouds to get it in the box, and their players piling in. I wonder what happened to the word 'creativity' in the Hughes approach.

You might argue with a certain justification that Wimbledon flourished from Charlie Hughes football. Their rise from the bottom division to the top and their FA Cup win over Liverpool in 1988 – one of the biggest Wembley upsets of all time – was fairytale stuff. It was an extraordinary feat for them to make it to the old first division and to survive for so long in the Premiership, but there wasn't much sophistication about them. They pushed the rules to the limit and on too many occasions overstepped the mark. They were not an easy team to admire, compensating for lack of talent with an overuse of intimidation and brawn.

I'm sure that wasn't the kind of thing Hughes had in mind when he advised haste and distance in shifting the ball from A to B. Wimbledon took it to its extreme. Nevertheless, I don't think the man had any idea about the way in which football should be played. That's why I defied him at every twist and turn on that coaching course. I just had to tell him that, no, you didn't always have to head the ball with your forehead. You could stick it in with the side of your head or the back of it, your kneecap or your you know what, just so long as you stuck it in the net legally. Of course I was aware that the forehead is the largest part of the head. I didn't need him or anybody else to tell me that. It was all part of the theory and might have been accepted together with the rest of the bullshit by the accountants and clerks and other non-football blokes 'studying' with me at Durham. It didn't fool me and it didn't stop me from trying to prove Hughes wrong time and again. I kept telling the others in the group that there was an alternative to his way and they, like the youth players at Sunderland, listened to me.

That was further proof that I could get my point across. This was football, my subject, after all. I'd been a player and a good one; most of them hadn't. They were entitled to listen and I don't suppose any of them were surprised to learn that, despite Charlie Hughes, I qualified. I became one of the youngest in the country to get my full coaching badge. It didn't mean that much to me, bits of paper never have. On paper, Nottingham Forest shouldn't have been relegated. On paper, Wimbledon shouldn't have won the Cup. It's on the pitch that the truth comes out.

The truth was that I'd developed an instant liking for being in charge. The challenge of management was not just to my liking, it was one I knew I could meet and conquer. A coaching qualification hadn't proved anything like as much as the reaction of those young men at Roker Park, the ones who put into practice what I'd been telling them all week. They were the ones who convinced me I could be a manager. I was beginning to think I could be one of the best ever and it didn't take as long as I thought it would to prove it. George Hardwick lost his job at the end of the season and the bloke who took over, Ian McColl, did what most new managers do – he gathered his own staff around him.

My testimonial match at Roker Park did me two huge favours. A crowd of over 31,000 provided me with a windfall of approximately £10,000, and later, a word or two in the board-room put me in the big time. Well, to a lad who had just had to finish as a youth-team manager, Hartlepools United *were* big time. Their chairman, a little bloke called Ernie Ord who turned out to be an absolute shit, offered me the job. Suddenly, I was the youngest manager in the Football League. The English game hadn't a clue about what was in store. The old fourth division had just been blessed with genius. I'm kidding, honest, but I'm not far wide of the mark.

I became the youngest manager in the League with exactly the right motivating forces in my head and in my heart. The chips on my shoulders were as hot as any you could find in a pan of boiling fat. I knew I should have had more recognition as a player. I was only really known and appreciated in Middles-brough and Sunderland. England didn't seem to want a prolific goalscorer, and all those I scored for 'Boro had been wasted because of a rotten defence. It hadn't been my fault that they failed to get promotion to the top division. Then came the killer-blow – the injury. I could have disintegrated then. I was in my prime and anybody who could score twenty-eight goals in twenty-eight matches by the time Boxing Day came around – well, he couldn't have been far short of his peak, could he?

Beneath the brashness and conceit, and the feeling that I could be one of the best managers ever, there was fear as well – just a touch but enough to make sure I worked hard and took nothing for granted. It was the fear that had been instilled by my mam constantly reminding me that I didn't have a trade at my fingertips. All I had was a spell as head boy at school, eighteen months running messages at ICI, two years' national service with the RAF, and football. In other words, football was all I had. National service had taken two years out of a crucial stage of my life. I always envied lads who had a trade because some of them either avoided national service altogether or joined up at twenty-one once they had finished an apprentice-ship. The difference between eighteen and twenty-one was massive, one a child, the other a man, with uncertain years in between. When that knee buckled underneath me, I could have been on the way to the scrapheap. That was when the fear crept in. Thank heavens for luck and for friends.

The legendary Len Shackleton is dead now, but never to be forgotten in my house, not only because of his dazzling talent with Sunderland and, staggeringly, only five times for England, but for the fact that he helped launch me into management. He'd had a word at Hartlepools, which was why they approached me on the night of my testimonial. Good old Len later had a word with the people who ran Derby County, easing my way in there, too. I had reasons to be thankful but those chips on my shoulder did my management prospects no harm at all. They taught me that I hadn't really appreciated what I'd got until it was denied to me, taken away completely.

You need friends in this life and I needed one in particular at Hartlepools. Peter Taylor had gone into management in his own right – ironically, with Burton Albion where our Nige has been cutting his teeth as a manager these past couple of years. He's doing extremely well so you never know, it might not be too long before another member of the Clough dynasty is continuing the tradition in the League.

A chuckle is the first thing that springs to mind whenever I think of Pete and that's the nicest legacy any man can leave. I've chuckled countless times at the recollection of our get-together in York. He'd have to take a cut in money to join me as assistant, of course he would, but I knew he was keen, if not desperate, to get into league football. I helped him make up his mind by giving him two hundred quid. I made many great signings in my time – Dave Mackay, Kenny Burns, Colin Todd, Peter Shilton, Garry Birtles, Roy McFarland, Trevor Francis, if I continued the list it would just about fill the rest of this book. But the best piece of recruitment I ever achieved was getting Peter Taylor, my mate and Uncle Pete to my kids, to join me in trying to make something out of a ramshackle, failing, totally skint football club called Hartlepools United.

Never was Pete's dry old sense of humour needed more than at Hartlepools. Never was his talent for spotting poor players and good replacements more of a priority. I can see him sitting there now, thinking, tongue in cheek, having slipped the *Sporting Life* from underneath his arm and flipped it on the table. 'Something's got to be done about this lot – and quick,' was his opening address. 'We're in the shit, good and proper. We'll be asking for re-election at the end of the season with this team. They're bound to finish bottom unless there's a place even lower in the bloody table.'

They had less than ten points and it was October. We were bottom of the entire Football League with defenders who couldn't defend, strikers who couldn't score, apart from a lad called Ernie Phythian who bagged a few, and the only thing the midfield could create was confusion among themselves.

Our first thought was that they might respond to a bit of encouragement, but reality screamed at us that, overall, we'd been lumbered with a crap side. There were other important things to establish in those initial stages and I knew I would be at my strongest during the first three months. A manager always is – anybody starting a new job should make emphatic decisions in that time if they want to establish working conditions to suit them.

To my knowledge, Pete was the first number two in the game, or at least we were the first proper partnership. Chairman Ernie Ord and the directors needed convincing about Pete's role and seeing that we were going to have to do everything between us, including painting the stand and the barriers in the summer, Pete had to be the trainer as well. He was the bucket and sponge man on matchdays and there was nothing funnier than that. He knew nothing about joints, ligaments and tendons. If it couldn't be cured by sploshing a cold sponge on it and telling the injured player to 'gerrup and gerron wi' it', he had no cure at all, and I certainly didn't.

But we learned at Hartlepools. We learned how to ship-out the deadwood and bring in better players. We learned how to lift a team from bottom in October to the safety of eighteenth place by the end of the season. We learned where to place buckets to catch the rain that leaked through the holes in the roof. We learned how to sign a youngster from grammar school whose headmaster wanted him to go to university rather than to Hartlepools United, which wasn't an unreasonable point of view, I suppose. I persisted, arguing that surely the lad should have the choice, already knowing the boy wanted to sign for me.

So John McGovern became a professional footballer instead of a university student. He, Taylor and I were to have good reason to be thankful for the day he put pen to paper at the scruffy little club that gave us all a start. John McGovern of

Nottingham Forest was to hold aloft the European Cup on all our behalves, not just once but in two consecutive seasons. Not many players, captains, have done that. People still ask me about the secrets of football management. How do you manage a football club? Read on . . .

CHAPTER 8

GOALKEEPERS, CENTRE-HALVES AND CENTRE-FORWARDS

Len Shackleton left an entire page blank in his book, reserved for what he believed directors knew about football. If I'd had my way there would be a blank chapter in this book dedicated to the same subject. I have never understood why men with such poor knowledge, or no knowledge at all, insist they know about the game in general and the needs of management in particular.

The vast majority of them knew nothing in my days as a player, nothing in my time as a manager and the modern lot still know nothing today. Yet I continue to see them quoted in the newspapers and droning on in television interviews, trying to convince the public and themselves that they have the faintest idea of how football works. It makes my blood boil; it makes me want to put my foot through the television screen and I'd have done it long before now but I have a dodgy knee to look after.

Football club chairmen and directors are still so barmy, so naïve, so thick and so stubborn yet full of themselves that they continue to make stupid decisions when it comes to the appointment of a manager. That is one of the reasons why there is such a turnover in my industry, so many sackings, resignations and departures explained by that cosy little phrase 'by mutual agreement', which I have never understood for the life of me. Many of the casualties are the victims not only of their own failure – they are the victims of chairmen and directors who shouldn't have given them the job in the first place.

Look at a couple of my former players, defender Colin Todd and Stuart Gray who used to do a job for me in midfield. Toddy, you won't need reminding, was a wonderful player, a brilliant defender who should have eased himself into the England side and stayed there for as long as he wanted. He did get twenty-seven caps, which is twenty-five more than I got, but there was a major difference between us. In my opinion, he didn't possess the same ambition I had to go along with his outstanding talent. I knew when I had Colin Todd playing for me at both Derby and Forest that it was highly unlikely he would make a top-notch manager.

I can sense it in people if I have enough regular contact. For instance, I always thought Martin O'Neill was cut out for a future in management because he was bright and sharp, a right smart-arse who was fully prepared to stand his ground and answer back when he believed he was right. He was also bursting with enthusiasm for the game.

It was not quite like that with Toddy. He managed Bolton for a while, twice relegated from the Premiership unless I'm wrong, so his track record wasn't that clever. Another example of a manager whose talent didn't meet the demands of the game at top level. Getting out of the first division is one thing but keeping a club in the Premiership asks even more of the man in charge. But in 2002, the directors of Derby, my club, decided in their wisdom that a change was needed and dear Jim Smith had to be replaced if the team was to survive among the top sides in the country. Todd was already at Pride Park and he was their man. They put him in charge. I could have told them they were taking a huge risk. Everything at a football club – success or failure, the sale of replica shirts, filling the executive boxes, and a million other things I could think of – is dependent on the performance of the man who creates and selects the team.

Do you think for a moment that Manchester United would have become the richest football club in the world without the expertise of Sir Alex Ferguson as manager? If you do, you're as daft as the directors who appoint managers who have no chance, absolutely no chance, of doing much apart from struggle. The Old Trafford empire, if that's what they call what is now one of the big financial institutions in our country, would not have developed the way it has without Fergie. Those who support United, those who direct it, those who buy shares in it and those who are paid such ridiculously high wages to play for it, they should all be eternally grateful to Sir Alex Ferguson and the ability he brought down from Scotland sixteen years ago.

It's not a coincidence that he has turned out to be United's most successful manager of all time, and I'm not underestimating what Sir Matt Busby did for them. Alex had done his time, served his apprenticeship, learned the ropes north of the border. He'd even known what it was like to get the sack before he emerged and blossomed with Aberdeen, and steered them to a European trophy. It hasn't been all plain sailing for him in Manchester, but his background means that at least the thinking in the United boardroom was sound. For once, directors, unless they've been extremely lucky, paid attention to the candidate's qualifications. Those who don't shouldn't be anywhere near a football club, but the game is littered with them.

I was at Pride Park in April 2002 and it was painful to watch my old team lose to Newcastle – a defeat that virtually sealed their relegation from the Premiership. They'd been two up with little more than a quarter of an hour to go – two up and they couldn't keep a clean sheet. That wasn't a mistake in my day – it was nothing short of a disgrace and a bloody crime. It was too late by the time John Gregory moved in from Villa, even though he won a game or two immediately after Toddy lost the job. Derby paid for bad judgement at boardroom level. You can't blame Colin for accepting the job; I believe you must question the men who made the appointment.

Similarly, I wondered about Stuart Gray being given the manager's job at Southampton when Glenn Hoddle answered Tottenham's call 'home'. I'm not sure what job Gray had with the club, whether he was coaching the reserves or helping out with the first team. What I do know is I don't think it sufficient to qualify him for the job of manager of a team in the English Premiership. He couldn't have been right for it in normal circumstances because he had no experience to fall back on, but they weren't normal circumstances at Southampton – a club well acquainted with the struggle against relegation seeing that they've been involved in one for most of the seasons I can remember. Season 2001–02 was going to be one of the most important in the entire history of the club. They had left The Dell, their tight little ground that was worth several points a season to them because every other team hated playing there, and moved to a new home at St Mary's, one of those so-called state-of-the-art modern arenas. It was Mary, Mary, quite contrary as far as I was concerned when I heard young Gray had been made manager. It made no sense at all to me. He was a nice lad, I'm sure he still is, but wet behind the ears in management terms. Unless he was a genius so far undiscovered, he hadn't a prayer. If ever there was a season when survival in the Premiership was absolutely vital, that was it. Yet Southampton's directors, surely realising the team had lost the distinct advantage of playing home games at The Dell, chucked all that responsibility into the lap of an untried manager. He didn't last long. He couldn't last long, but when he made way for Gordon Strachan's return to management, why weren't serious questions asked of those who shoved Gray in at the deep end? Why weren't any of them held responsible? Why didn't any of them pay the price of losing his own position with the club? Why? Because they rarely do. Football chairmen and directors at any club you care to look at are among the great survivors in life.

Perhaps I was prejudiced against directors once I found myself working for that horrible little bugger Ernie Ord at Hartlepools. I suppose I do have to give him some credit for choosing me and hiring Peter Taylor as well. Hartlepools, a little club fighting for their existence at the wrong end of the entire League, was the ideal place for any ambitious young manager to learn to walk. Ernie Ord hadn't a clue what Pete and I were about, what we were doing on his behalf as the owner of the club. We not only won him a few matches and kept him in the League but we got his club in the newspapers on a regular basis, helped paint the ground and, all right, on occasions did threaten to sling him out physically.

Hartlepools suddenly found themselves getting more publicity, relatively, than some of the top clubs in the country – not as much as David Beckham's left foot when he injured it in the spring of 2002, but the game's even dafter now than it was then. Ord, having informed us that his son was going to deal with publicity all of a sudden, and having contemplated sacking Taylor, announced at a meeting of the directors that we had both been fired. Now there are two things you can do as a manager if you're sacked. You can go, hopefully with the necessary pay-off, or you can stay! At least you can if you're Clough and Taylor with the public support we had at a little club like Hartlepools almost forty years ago.

Ord couldn't have been the big man if he'd tried. As a bloke who was hardly tall enough to peer over the steering wheel of his Rolls-Royce, he was at something of a disadvantage. But like so many of his ilk, and so many in the game even now, he wanted to be seen as the man who ran the place and he wanted to be sure he took the credit. I spotted that early on and made sure the press were there when I learned to drive the team bus. It was made very clear to the supporters of Hartlepools that if this club was to go places, even by their modest standards, nobody would be left in any doubt about who was doing the steering.

Once he sold his drapery business Ord immersed himself in the club. I detested his interference, the way he insisted on knowing what Taylor and I were up to and he resented me telling him to keep his nose out. I was getting his little club in the papers on a regular basis so there was no need to have his son dealing with publicity. He was critical of Peter and we both felt he was trying to drive a wedge between us. He wanted the credit for the fact that all of a sudden his club was doing pretty well. I suppose it was Ord who made me wary of football club chairmen, right from the start.

It was no surprise that we saved them from the humiliation of finishing bottom and having to apply for re-election; no surprise, either, that we finished eighth from top in our second season. It wasn't my personal highlight of the year, though. That was the birth of our daughter Elizabeth, completing the threesome with Simon and Nigel. Married with three kids now – for me it was a big responsibility, those mouths to feed. I knew I could manage a football team. I knew I could be among the best in the business if somebody would give me the chance. I'm sure there are some today who believe they're entitled to their chance at a higher level, especially when they've put in their time lower down and achieved a level of success that should register in the boardrooms of bigger clubs.

The only thing I knew about Derby was that the town had a reputation in the locomotive industry and for building Rolls-Royces – aye, even though some of them ended up being driven by nasty little men like Ernie Ord. I also knew that Derby was one of the country's traditional football towns, steeped in the history of the game. The club was in the second division. It had been dozing for too long. It needed reawakening. Somebody had to set the alarm clock. When Taylor and I took over, the bells never stopped ringing.

Len Shackleton put us in for the job. Actually, Taylor and I had seen off the chairman at Hartlepools, somebody else had taken over from Ord, but Pete's feet had started to itch. He was convinced we'd done enough to earn our big break, and put Shackleton in the picture. It was Shack who arranged for me to meet Derby's chairman Sam Longson and I'd landed the job before I met the directors at the old Baseball Ground later that same week. I left Barbara and the two elder children in a nearby park and told her to expect me when she saw me. It might have been the quickest interview of all time until I told Longson and his cronies that I'd be bringing Peter Taylor with me. If they were hiring me, they were hiring him. We were a twosome, a partnership, a bit like Morecambe and Wise with me as the straight man. Yes, I know all about those who later enjoyed referring to us as the Kray twins!

My side of the meeting went swiftly and easily. 'My injury finished me as a player but gave me an early start to management at Hartlepools,' I told them. 'As you know, applying for re-election had become an annual event for them but we changed all that, left them in the top half of the division. We built them a new stand and we've left them solvent.'

Some words impress directors more than others. Solvent is one of them. At least, the Derby lot sat up and took notice at the mention of the word, and I can think of about forty clubs today the directors of which would be impressed by any prospective manager who used it. I had Derby's directors shuffling uneasily in their seats one minute and smiling the next when I told them, 'I cut the playing staff down. I got rid of the players who were crap and brought in one or two who were just a bit better.'

I told them I wanted their job even though I knew little about the place other than that Harry Storer had been their manager five years earlier. I told them if they had any doubts they should look at my record at Hartlepools. I knew I had caught them at their weakest moment because the team was having a bad time. They'd had to fire their manager Tim Ward and, most significantly of all, they were getting stick from the public. If there's one thing football directors cannot stand, it's the kind of criticism managers have to face on a regular basis. I knew I was on solid ground, not just because they needed help in their predicament but because Sam Longson had already promised me the job when I met him with Len Shackleton at Scotch Corner. By the time I rejoined Barbara and the kids in the park, Taylor's appointment had also been rubber-stamped. Those directors had just made the best decision they were ever likely to make but they hadn't a clue what they'd let themselves in for. There were to be some fantastic times to enjoy but there was also trouble ahead, trouble that would cost me the England manager's job, to name but one thing.

They made their decision for two main reasons – they'd had enough of Tim Ward and the crowd were spoiling their week. They worked in and around Derby and life was being made uncomfortable. Once directors feel uncomfortable, they shift responsibility to somebody else. I'm sure some of those on that Derby board must have gone home to their wives that day and said, 'We've got a right big mouth coming to work with us.' Now those ladies wouldn't have known who the hell I was but after a couple of weeks they knew right enough because one of the first things I did was to introduce myself to all of them. They loved it. Within days, their enthusiasm had been rekindled to the stage where they were competing with one another for the prize of being in charge in the tearoom.

I didn't haggle over money. I didn't haggle with Longson at our original meeting and I didn't make an issue of it when I met his colleagues at the Baseball Ground. I settled for my £100 a week or whatever it was at the time. I told them I'd be buying a house and reminded them that they'd just hired a former centre-forward who had more than 30,000 people turn up at his testimonial, just in case they weren't aware of how good a player I'd been.

Once the meeting was formally closed I told them, 'Right, now we can talk football. I don't know what's been going on at this club but I do know that you've got a part-timer playing for you and that's no bloody good to me for a start.'

'What do you mean, part-timer?'

'Ian Buxton, your centre-forward.' You have to spell it out for people like them. 'The lad who plays cricket for Derbyshire and is given time off and doesn't join up with us until September. I can understand him needing the break but by the time he's available to me, your team could be at the arse-end of the second division.' They looked aghast – the perfect situation for me to press my point. 'I love cricket but I love this job even more at the moment, and I'm telling you that if Buxton doesn't turn up for pre-season training, he doesn't play for me.'

'But he has an agreement in writing,' one of them protested. He had – their blessing for a two-week holiday after finishing with his cricket.

'Good for him,' I told them. 'I'm sure it's a beneficial agreement from Ian's point of view but if you've got twenty players on your books at Derby, I'm down to nineteen before I've even arrived.' I could sense that uneasy shifting and shuffling of backsides around the boardroom table. Perfect. 'It's not on. It's no good to me. I'm rescinding that agreement here and now and I don't care whether it's in writing or not – on headed notepaper or daubed all over the dressing-room wall.'

Mission accomplished, first job done. I didn't know whether

they were going to like me. I didn't know if they would always support me although the likelihood was that they wouldn't. But what I did know as I walked out of the ground and went to rejoin Barbara and the kids was that those directors knew exactly who would be running their club. If they were uncomfortable and longing to shift responsibility, they'd picked the right man. Needless to say, one of the first tasks Taylor and I carried out was transferring Ian Buxton to Luton. He wasn't a bad player but he would have been a non-playing centreforward for at least two weeks and I think that's crackers.

Centre-forwards, centre-halves, goalkeepers, in that order or in reverse order – you've heard me mention them umpteen times and the system applied at Derby as much as anywhere else in football in England, Brazil or Outer Mongolia. That was the system we used from the very beginning at Derby. On Taylor's recommendation, or instruction, I returned to Sunderland and signed John O'Hare for £21,000, so Buxton was replaced by a young man with tremendous ability.

We persevered with the goalkeeper for some time because, even in his late thirties, Reg Matthews was 'the bravest player on the staff', according to Peter Taylor. Eventually, though, he had to go and Pete brought in his man, Les Green from Burton Albion. The centre-half, Bobby Saxton, had shot it and his replacement became key to just about everything we were to achieve with Derby. Everybody knows about our late arrival at Roy McFarland's front door on Merseyside and us asking his dad to get him out of bed. Some managers might have agreed to Roy's request to sleep on the prospect of a move from Tranmere to Derby but some managers don't have any idea. I knew Liverpool or Everton or some other club would sign him if we didn't – he had so much potential. It must have been gone midnight but the instinct was still sharp. I had to clinch it somehow. I told him Taylor and I were going to turn Derby into one of the best teams in the country and that if he insisted on sleeping on it I'd still be there in the morning, offering him the chance to be a part of something big. He signed and went on to become the best centre-half to play for England for many a year, arguably the best ever.

People began to sit up and take notice of Derby County despite the fact that we were crap in that first season, conceding seventy-eight goals, seven more than we scored, and finishing in eighteenth place. The changes had been gradual, John McGovern arriving from Hartlepools, Alan Hinton switching from Nottingham Forest's left-wing to Derby's and the introduction of other new faces. In fact, we changed almost the entire side apart from the good players already on the books – Kevin Hector up front, Alan Durban in midfield and Ron Webster at the back.

Taylor and I were in our element. We were never more excited or effective than when we were building teams from basics, getting rid of the dead wood and planting fresh new saplings. I was talking a lot, making the back pages a lot, attracting journalists like flies. Suddenly Derby were news again. A pressman loves nothing more than knowing that when he takes the trouble to go to see a manager, he'll come away with a worthwhile piece to write. When they came to see me, they usually left with enough copy to keep them going for a week. I had been used to publicity throughout my playing career because I scored goals and goalscorers are guaranteed a mention. I wanted publicity at Hartlepools because it served my purpose – it reminded people that the town still had a football club.

I think those Derby directors had a few doubts in that first season when we finished lower than Tim Ward had managed the season before, but they changed their tune a year later. They were all there to be seen in the front row of the stand, no longer uncomfortable, no longer worried about the crowd on their backs. They wanted the lot. They were revelling in it, lapping it up. That's how directors re-emerge when the good times come to call, and for those at Derby there had never been a day like the one when we celebrated winning the second division championship.

Clough and Taylor had arrived on the scene and shaken a few egos in the process. We had transformed an ordinary, small-town club in the space of two seasons and there were many, no doubt, who believed it had been done as much by luck as by judgement. I don't think they were saying the same thing three years later when we won the league title. True to form, I was sitting on the beach in the Scilly Isles the day the championship was confirmed, relaxing in the grand manner, having no doubt been for a nice long walk on the water.

How did it happen, why did it happen, what is a good manager or management partnership and how do they pull it off? How *do* you manage a football club successfully? I will get round to explaining, honest. It's the most common and fiercely burning question in football because good managers, great managers, are like the best diamonds – rare and priceless. All I can tell you is how I did it, how Clough and Taylor did it.

CHAPTER 9

HOW TO MANAGE A FOOTBALL CLUB

What I'm about to say should interest all managers and would-be managers, all those who think they can do the job and all those who might be planning to have a crack at it in the future. Coaches in particular, those people who prefer to be called a coach rather than a manager, might just learn something.

Some will appreciate the value of what they're about to read, others will say I'm stating the obvious and that the job can't possibly be as simple as I make it out to be. Those who can't see the point in what I say and those who continue to insist that football is far more intricate and complicated, technical and sophisticated – whatever phrase or description they prefer to justify their own opinion – well, they are too thick to become good managers anyway.

Talking came naturally to me, even though I was a late starter. I was around five before I could string plenty of words together. I had no trouble talking to schoolteachers, head-masters, other parents and their bairns. I had no trouble talking to the policeman or the bloke who used to come to Valley Road selling his herrings. I had no problem facing microphones or television cameras. I opened the first sports programme they had on Tyne Tees Television and I also presented a programme for the BBC. I was pleased but not surprised when I discovered that football management also came naturally to me.

If you could wander into a public library and pick up a foolproof guide on how to manage a football team, everybody would be able to do it. But you can't. That's why I'm considering opening the Brian Clough Academy of Management – only kidding, but it couldn't fail. They'd be queuing overnight, those budding bosses and all the failures and even some of those who think they can do it already. Kevin Keegan might just learn something about how to get the best out of the best players in the country. I never had the opportunity but I think I might have done it just a shade better than he did.

I used to play at centre-forward, as you might have gathered (267 goals in 296 appearances for Middlesbrough and Sunderland – go on, digest the figures again). I knew that goals won matches, which told me, as a manager, that I needed somebody who could score them. Then I thought, 'Who is the one who stops the other team from scoring?' The centre-half – two centre-halves these days but the principle is the same. Any team of mine would need a good centre-forward and a good centre-half. In our time together at Middlesbrough, with a first-team defence leaking like a rusted bucket, Taylor convinced me about the true value of the goalkeeper; hardly surprising, seeing that's where he played.

'No point in you scoring three if our bloke's letting three in,' he'd keep saying, time after time, day after day. 'There are key positions in any side where real talent is vital. If necessary, you can fill-in everywhere else.'

So I signed good goalkeepers. In fact, I've never fathomed why top keepers don't cost as much as top strikers. A save can be as important as a goal but a mistake by a keeper is often more costly than a miss by his team-mate at the opposite end of the field.

One of my earliest worries at Derby concerned the keeper. As I mentioned, Reg Matthews was getting on in years and I was convinced he was well past his best. He was good enough to play for England on five occasions but it had been ten years since his last cap. Taylor insisted that 'Matthews might have "shot it" but he's the bravest player on the staff.'

That immediately attracted me to him and convinced me I should persevere with him for a while. No matter how good you are as a footballer, if you're frightened it is a big minus, a big handicap. There are many players who can get away with a certain lack of ability because they are particularly courageous. Very few, if any, can get away with not being brave at all, however talented they might be. Ability will never blossom if a lad is too frightened to have the ball.

To have possession of a football generates a kind of fear in itself, an apprehension, concern about being able to control it and find a team-mate when you decide to let it go. But physical fear is a player's worst enemy. Some players used to study match programmes to see if an opponent they'd faced before was playing. If the programme was available on a Friday night, they'd look at it then. If not, it would be on matchday. If a player's thinking, 'Bugger me, that's the same fella who kicked me last season and I can still feel it,' he's going to be second-best before the teams reach the pitch so there's no earthly point in sending him out in the first place.

So Reg Matthews's courage kept him in my Derby side for a while, despite the fact that he couldn't always get to the shots that were flashed at him because the old reflexes had gone a bit; either that or, as a heavy smoker, his eyes were still watering from the fags he'd had before the game.

I tried to make sure of one basic thing in management. Educated people would call it a fundamental but I'm not sure what that means. I know what basic means and my basic was that there should never ever be the slightest sense of complication in my dressing room. Footballers, by and large, are not academics. They are people who realise from an early age that, with any luck, they will be playing for their livings. I'm not saying they all abandon their education but I know from my own experience that once I realised I was a bit special at football, geography and history never grabbed my attention anywhere near as much as the games lessons!

I would far rather have my players rolling about the dressing-room floor laughing than have them trying to fathom a list of instructions and tactics before they went out to play a match. In fact, Taylor had them laughing like that on countless occasions, in training, on the coach, around the ground and on matchdays.

Discipline was crucial. Without discipline you have no team, or at least you don't have a team that will do itself full justice and operate to its full potential. I could never have players who set out, or were even prepared, to make life more difficult than it already was for referees and their linesmen. I couldn't abide players being late for training. Alan Brown, I'm certain, would have liked nothing more than to fine me for turning up late at Sunderland. He'd glance at his watch every single morning but he never caught me out and my money was safe in my pocket.

Discipline was no great issue, no big deal, at Derby or at Forest later on. It was routine. They knew that I would be the same bloke every day – awkward, inevitably bad-tempered and for ever talking, reminding them that this was the good life. Playing for your living, being able to look forward to your work every day, was a great privilege afforded to very few people. I suppose it was only when we'd won or when the close season arrived that I was totally relaxed and liveable with.

One of the first things I'd hear when I arrived at the ground in the morning would be somebody whispering, 'I wonder what kind of mood he's in?' The moment I heard it I'd shout, 'I'm in a rotten mood. Start off believing that and you won't go wrong. Believe I'm in a rotten mood every time you see me and you'll be fine. On that basis, I can only get better.'

Yes, of course we had a laugh as well. That was just as important – part and parcel of the variety required to relax those involved in a high-tension industry. I'm not sure how often top footballers laugh today but I don't see many smiles on the pitch or in front of the television cameras afterwards. Priorities seem to have gone wrong with the modern bunch – over the edge in the sense that everything they do, every aspect of the game that makes the papers, is dominated by the mention of money. Players have always wanted to be paid well; it was no different in my day although we were never paid well at all. It was right that footballers should be awarded salaries in keeping with their value as entertainers, packing the stadiums and generating so much wealth for their employers, but money has become something of an obsession. I get the impression, looking at some of them, that all they do every day is go home and count their cash. Security is a wonderful thing in anybody's life. Today's footballers are financially secure virtually from the moment they make the first team. There's not a lot wrong with that but I'm sure that, like me, the general public must be sick and tired of hearing how rich they are.

People continue to wonder whether I would have been as successful as a manager in today's climate of multi-millionaire players and their interfering agents. Well, whatever the money and the drastic shift in the balance of power, it would have made no difference to me whatsoever. There is no doubt that players have become more powerful than they were, more independent, more capable of calling the shots if weak managers allow them to. That's what money does. But the principles of management remain the same. Ground rules apply just as much to millionaires as to those who can hardly afford to pay the mortgage. I applied them from the start, telling my players exactly what was expected and what would happen if those rules were broken, and I always ended by asking, 'Have you heard everything I've said?'

It usually met with the stock reply, 'Yeah, yeah, Gaffer. We've heard it that many times we know it off by heart.'

'Right, then,' I said. 'And do you agree? Is there anybody who wants to say anything? If you all agree to a fifty-pound fine if you're late, then that's the rule. No point in cribbing when I demand the fifty quid.'

Somebody would say something like, 'But what happens if we get caught in heavy traffic on the way or we're involved in an accident?'

'An accident, that's different. That's exceptional. But busy roads? Don't give me that. We all have to contend with traffic and if it's that bad where you live, set off a bit earlier. What do you want – a ten o'clock start for training or ten thirty? And don't tell me ten thirty would have your missus complaining it made you late for lunch. It's up to you.' It usually became ten thirty on a majority vote. That became the rule and they'd laid it down themselves.

I wasn't programming my players or turning them into robots in any shape or form. I was simplifying their lives, spelling out with their agreement what would happen in a given set of circumstances – lateness for instance, failure to dress properly when required, getting booked for things that could be avoided such as kicking the ball away in disgust or anger and mouthing off at a referee or a linesman. It was easy enough to get booked anyway, and it's a darned sight easier in today's football, so what was the point in adding to the risk of suspension just because you couldn't control your temper? I saw many things in my time as a manager, many changes along the way. What I didn't see was a referee change his mind and his decision after a player either effed and blinded at him or whacked the ball into the back row of the stand.

I wasn't being heavy handed or dictatorial although, yes, I was a bit of a dictator in my time. Had to be. But in laying down the rules with them, I always had their interests at heart because whatever else I might be, I'm a players' man. After all, they're the ones who win matches for you. On the other hand, they won't win as many as they should if half of them are getting themselves banned through their own stupid irresponsibility.

Little things mean a lot in management. Take Fridays at Nottingham Forest when we were playing away next day. Inevitably, we had to travel on Friday nights. You couldn't risk going reasonable distances on Saturday morning because of the traffic. For another thing, a long coach journey on the day of the game isn't conducive to fitness and the right frame of mind.

'So we'll all come in at three o'clock Friday afternoon and do some training,' I told them at Forest. I'm sure I did something similar at Derby because that was the way I worked. 'And when you come in, make sure you're ready to leave. Have your smart gear for travelling. You know the drill. We'll train, have a bath and I'll get a meal laid on for us at the restaurant up the road.'

Common sense told me that if you travelled at five o'clock on a Friday afternoon, you'd cop for all the traffic. We'd leave the restaurant at half past six or so. Then it was on the coach, game of cards, in London or wherever we were going by half past eight. By the time we'd checked in, found our rooms, come down, read a paper, it was time for bed and 'See you all at eleven o'clock in the morning.' They loved it. It saved their wives cooking for a start, and they knew I'd have everybody back home by half past eight on the Saturday night. We might have Sunday, Monday and sometimes even Tuesday off as well.

Do you know why they loved it? It was because I was doing the thinking for them. It suited them not to have too many decisions to make. Some players don't like making decisions and when I made them, I did it in the interests of their families as well. It suited the wives because they were not being messed about with silly times. It suited the bairns because they were seeing plenty of their fathers rather than an hour here and half an hour there. The players had the opportunity to stay in bed if they wanted – Archie Gemmill, for example, would go to bed on Sunday and stay there all day. He'd get up for a meal and then go back. Those days off, sometimes three in a row, were good thinking on my part because it was like a holiday, and when the players came back to work, they wanted to be there – either to escape from the wife and kids or to avoid the washing-up.

It wasn't the same on the pitch. You still have some thinking to do with a ball at your feet. It's the feet that hold the key. If you can control a ball, you are three-quarters of the way there. With most footballers, it's a natural thing and it reduces some of the need to think on the field.

I was for ever reminding them how much I sweated on matchdays, like them. 'But do you have to shout all the time?' they'd protest from time to time. They always received the same reply. Yes, I did have to shout – not all the time but most of the time. I'd shout reminders, adjustments when they occasionally got themselves out of position, which is easy to do in the heat of the moment. I'd emphasise the need to keep the ball and to pass it forward whenever possible. I had to shout to tell them they weren't tired when sometimes they thought they were. Contact was vital because it made me one of them, part of the team. It was the same with discipline and those all-important rules. Footballers are normal people with normal emotions and they need a bit of help and reassurance from time to time. They need to feel a sense of familiarity and comfort in what they are being asked to do. Being high-profile doesn't make them any less normal than a bricklayer on a building site. It just makes them richer. If ever any of them showed signs of getting carried away, I saw it as my job to keep his feet on the ground. They were never in any doubt about who was boss because I told them myself – 'There's nothing the matter with a place being run by a dictator – as long as that dictator is me.'

It's a good job talking came easily to me because talking is a major aspect of the job. I don't care if you're a manager, a coach, a university lecturer, an orchestra conductor or the bloke who sold his herrings in Valley Road – if you can't get your message across, you might as well pack in and do something else. When my players reported back for a new season, they heard a familiar theme: 'It's now July and we're working again. Two plus two equals four and, come next April, it will still equal four. Nothing will have changed that drastically and nothing is going to change drastically with your game, either. We hope you've all got a bit richer, we hope you're more content, we hope you're more mature and we hope you won't run foul of the rules we've laid down. It's going to be a tight ship because, as you well know, that's the way I believe it should be done.' And they'd take my word for it.

I took charge of pre-season training because I believed it to be so important. It's like taking the first steps on a long military campaign. Make sure you've got your helmet on securely in July and it will keep you safe right the way through.

A team that has sound discipline will always have a greater chance than one whose players don't know how to behave in a decent manner. Pre-season was the time to remind my lot, 'Do things properly and we might all achieve what we have in common, the desire to succeed. We all want to be able to look back, have a medal to show to our kids, raise our standard of living and pay off the mortgage. We want to finish in May and say it's all been worthwhile. And during our break next summer, we want to be sitting on a beach or climbing a mountain, maybe riding a bike, with satisfaction and pride in what we've achieved. Believe me, you'll feel in better nick if you've achieved something that makes you proud. There is no greater satisfaction in life than doing your job well. If we all do that, everybody benefits.'

As far as timekeeping was concerned, I'd tell them, 'I started at twelve minutes past seven when I had to work for a living as a messenger boy. Don't ask me why it was twelve minutes past but it was. It meant me getting up at six in the morning and riding five or six miles on my bike whether the sun was shining or it was snowing or pissing down, all for a couple of quid a week. You lot don't have to be in until half past ten. You've got swanky cars and nice houses. You can get up, have a bite of breakfast while watching TV, read the paper and come in to a very pleasant working environment. You don't have to go down a coalmine and work in the dark for eight hours and you don't have to put up with a lot of noise apart from the occasional shout from me.

'You've got yourselves a good job. Don't you dare dissipate the advantages and privileges a good job gives you. If you can't get into work by half past ten in the morning, you're not worth bothering about and I certainly won't waste my time on you. It is natural for a man to come into work, it's not natural for him to want to sit in a chair all day long – there are enough of them having to do that through no choice of their own.

'Go down to the local infirmary and have a look in Ward 7 and then try feeling sorry for yourself and telling me you've got a rotten job. Go and hang the washing out for the entire family by nine o'clock in the morning like my mam had to do.'

The rules are the rules. We all have to abide by them, on and off the field, because somebody has written them down. They might be good or they might be bad but the rules enable us to have a game. Without them, there is no game at all. Everybody makes mistakes. I haven't seen a goalkeeper yet who hasn't let a ball slip through his hands when he should have stopped it with his eyes closed. I've never seen a centre-forward who hasn't missed a simple chance to score. I've never seen a perfect referee, either. In fact, I've not seen a perfect anything in life (apart from me!). My players learned to understand that referees were doing their best, honestly and in keeping with whatever talent they had for the job. It developed into a kind of mutual respect for one another – my lot made life as comfortable as possible for match officials, and they were quick to appreciate it. I lost count of the number of referees who came to me both at Derby and Forest and said, 'I'd just like to express my thanks. I love matches involving your team. We never have any trouble with them.'

It worked to our benefit. A team of mine was the referees' best friend. It was only human nature that they should have a sympathetic outlook towards us. They wouldn't bend the rules or do us any particular favours but they knew that my players were not cheating or taking liberties. A mistimed tackle was exactly that and nothing more sinister. When a player of mine stayed down with an injury, no one was in the slightest doubt that he was genuinely hurt.

I made a point of going to talk to referees at their meetings. Inevitably, I was asked about the badly behaved sides and I told them, 'That problem could be eliminated overnight. If a team persistently has players in trouble, especially for dissent, arguing and cussing and swearing, they should fine the managers concerned – a month's wages. If a manager was hit in his pocket, he'd be quick to get rid of the rotten apples in his barrel. He wouldn't stand for some yob or thug costing him his wages.'

I think Arsene Wenger should have been fined several times for his team's behaviour – forty-odd sendings off in his first five years as manager is nothing short of a disgrace. I don't care how successful he's been, how many trophies Arsenal have won – the shine on those trophies has been tarnished as far as I'm concerned because they have been won by an extremely talented team who have devalued their own achievements by often behaving like brats. No, Arsenal have not been a dirty team but they have been a bad-tempered, bad-mannered team and as far as I can see Wenger has either done little to change it or has failed to have much of an impact.

He comes across on television as a polite, charming, kind, intelligent man with an accent we all fall for. He speaks English better than they do in Hartlepool. Then we analyse the situation. He's with one of the biggest clubs in the country but he cannot justify the number of players Arsenal have had booked and sent off. I think it's no good him (like so many managers) saying he didn't see the incident in question because if his eyesight is as bad as it seems to be when an Arsenal player lands in trouble, he couldn't be the talented manager he is.

I've heard and read so much rubbish over recent seasons with players, managers, so-called television and radio experts complaining about bad refereeing. I can't believe they stop to think about the reality of the situation before they open their mouths. Referees are no worse than they ever were. The chances are that they're even a wee bit better. Their problem lies with players who make their lives a misery, kidding about injuries, diving for free-kicks and penalties, trying to get opponents booked or sent off, arguing with linesmen as if the award of a throw-in is as important to them as the size of their wage packet. Referees are being conned right, left and centre and then taken to task by people in a television studio with every electronic gadget technology can produce. The referee has no chance. Of course he makes errors of judgement but not as many as the player who is only too eager to chase him half the length of the field to tell him that he's dropped a clanger.

Scrutiny is the referees' greatest enemy. Their performance is watched and recorded from just about every imaginable angle. Eventually, after as many re-runs of the slow-motion replay as it takes, the experts make up their minds and declare whether the referee was right or wrong. Would you like to have your every move at work recorded and analysed by some smart-arsed expert who hasn't a clue what it's like to do your job in the first place? Of course you wouldn't and neither would I. The only thing that surprises me about modern refereeing is that so many people volunteer to do it.

I was lucky in being allowed to run the show. There's no doubt about it, in the early stages at Derby and nearly all the time at Forest I ran the show lock, stock and barrel. I had some players with strong personalities over the years, including Dave Mackay, Kenny Burns and Larry Lloyd to name just three, but they all toed the line. I didn't need to tell them I ran the place – they could see it. I think players need that; they prefer to know who is boss, how far they can go in a given situation and where angels fear to tread. I suppose, with me, they were never quite sure. Oh they were well aware that they had to stay within the rules, but they could never be certain how I was going to react from one day to another. They knew I would be striving to help them be part of an extremely successful team – what they didn't know was exactly how I would go about it, how today might differ from yesterday. Uncertainty is a good thing if you apply it properly.

What I set out to do – and this was a natural thing, an instinct rather than a planned philosophy – was to embrace the particular strengths of my players. Kenny Burns joined me with a reputation for being a dirty so-and-so as well as having a lifestyle that, well, let's say didn't portray him as a model professional. Reputations can be misleading. He turned out to be as nice a lad as I have ever managed – the opposite of his image. No, I'm not forgetting that he was a fierce competitor on the field, a tough Scot capable of cutting you in two. He deserved his medals, including the European Cup, and he deserved his honour as Footballer of the Year.

Lloyd was Lloyd. Some people thought Pete Taylor and I were barmy when we signed him but Taylor particularly knew he had what we required from a centre-half. Larry was a big lad. When he finished playing he went into the licensed trade and became the only landlord I knew who was bigger and wider than his own pub. I think his size, well over six feet, gave him a feeling of grandeur. We knew that he could give our team a sense of stability providing we restricted him to the simple things he could do well, and jumped on him if he attempted anything that was beyond his capability.

Dave Mackay was the total professional from start to finish. He was set to leave Tottenham, where he won the double, and go back to Edinburgh to become assistant manager of Hearts. Bill Nicholson, the Spurs manager, made it clear to me when I turned up in London that I had no chance of signing him for Derby, but I had to have a crack at it. I was in awe of Bill Nicholson because he was one of the game's legendary figures, a great manager and a great man. But if you are to have the slightest chance of succeeding as a football manager, you have to pursue your instincts and your judgement all the way. Bill was a bit dismissive on my arrival at White Hart Lane. Sign Dave Mackay? I got the impression I'd be better off turning round and driving back to Derby.

Mackay himself was just as dismissive. He was going to Hearts to be an assistant manager, no arguing, no move to Derby, no chance. Forget it. This was Dave Mackay I was talking to, one of the real greats as far as I was concerned. Taylor and I had agreed that he was just the man we needed to complete our team at Derby, to turn it into one with the potential to be really outstanding. I had to talk this man into joining a team he knew next to nothing about. So I talked. You can't teach that kind of thing at any academy or on any coaching course. I talked about wanting to build a team that would beat every other. I talked about how I wanted that team to play. I talked about generalities and specifics and soon I had him talking as well.

Timing is as important in negotiations as it is with a ball at your feet. Bang! 'What would it take to get you to Derby?' I hit him with the question the moment his dismissive mood seemed to mellow just slightly. When he said he'd consider £15,000 I said I couldn't raise that much and he said he'd be on his way to Hearts then. 'I think I can raise fourteen thousand,' I said, instinct again. Mackay didn't hesitate – 'Done.'

It had taken a good couple of hours at White Hart Lane to sign the player I had no chance of signing. He was going to transform my team and I was going to give Dave Mackay his second lease of life. He was disappearing from the English game but I brought him back from the brink to discover that, given the right setting and the right players around him, he could still win championships. He was on borrowed time with fourteen grand spread over three years. I never did a better piece of business in my entire career although the man himself had serious doubts the minute he arrived at the Baseball Ground.

It had been Taylor's original idea that we try to sign him, Taylor at his very best, doing what nobody ever did better – assessing a team, deciding what it needed most of all and knowing precisely the best man to provide that key element. It was Pete's suggestion – my job to do the rest. That was the way it worked with the Clough-and-Taylor partnership. And when it came to convincing somebody he could do something he'd never even considered, we had a technique.

'Better get him in here so you can talk to him,' Taylor told me next day when Mackay arrived to complete his move. 'Er, Dave, I think you'd better listen to what the Gaffer's got to say. He's got a new job for you.' Mackay's eyes switched from Taylor on one side of him to me on the other, and they kept switching their line of vision like a spectator at Wimbledon's Centre Court as we employed the technique that became our speciality.

'We're going to play you as a sweeper.' He protested, of course. He wasn't a sweeper, never had been, never would be, never could.

'I've covered every blade of grass on every pitch I've ever played on,' he said. 'That's my game, that's my style. I can't play as a sweeper.'

I told him he could and that once he'd seen our centre-half Roy McFarland (nineteen years old) and full-backs John Robson (eighteen) and Ronnie Webster who was still a young man but hadn't fulfilled his potential or ambition, he'd know he could. I surrounded Dave Mackay with young talent who would do the running and the donkey work and allow him not only to give our team the perfect finishing touch but to make them better players in the process. I said a few pages ago that I'd never seen anything that was perfect – Dave Mackay playing in that Derby defence was as near to perfection as makes no difference.

People who can't manage a football team would never have seen the reason to change the role of a man like Dave Mackay. Coaches who might have thought of it in the back of their cluttered and complicated minds wouldn't have had the guts or the way with words to put it across to the man himself and get him to agree. Taylor's idea, my persuasion – once it was put into practice it all made perfect sense. Not a lot alters in football when you think about it, apart from the number of noughts on the players' wage slips. The dimensions of the pitch remain virtually the same and the goalposts are where they've always been, even though some strikers still have a lot of trouble hitting the target that's never been known to move.

The skill of good management lies in assessment, judgement and motivation. It lies in knowing what your team needs, recognising the player or players capable of providing it and making bloody sure that every single one of them in your dressing room gives absolutely everything, match in match out, in the interests of the team. Defenders defend, midfield players provide the link and create and, if you're lucky, strikers score goals. It never ceases to amaze me that so many people have so much difficulty in assembling a good football team. How can they make such a simple job so complex?

C H A P T E R   1 0

COACHES GET FOUND OUT

Some people can do it, some can't. I know that's a statement of the obvious but football is full of individuals who think they can be managers when they haven't a cat-in-hell's chance. In fact, a cat would have a better chance than some of them.

It can be learned if you are prepared to start nearer the bottom of the scale than the top. It can be learned day to day, striving to improve a smaller club with limited resources. But it can only be learned by those with the capacity to take it in, who can use the knowledge they gather in those lower divisions and put it across at a bigger club once they are given the opportunity.

There are a few who have had the extreme good fortune of ending their playing careers and going straight into the top job with a top club. Liverpool made Kenny Dalglish manager while he was still in the team. I've never gone along with the idea of the dual role of player-manager, not at a major club, not at the highest level of the game. It worked for Liverpool and Dalglish for a while, but he was fortunate enough to inherit an extremely good team to begin with – Dalglish was one of the finest players ever to wear the famous red shirt – and good teams continue to do well for a time. When things started to get a little tougher, when changes had to be made, it got to him to such an extent that he had to pack it in.

Looking back, I feel sure that terrible day in April 1989 had a profound effect on him. The Hillsborough disaster. The FA Cup semi-final in which my Nottingham Forest team faced Dalglish's Liverpool on what should have been a glorious day en route to Wembley for one or the other. Instead, it became the blackest day in the history of English football when so many innocent people lost their lives. It affected everybody. But for Kenny, surrounded by the sadness and despair that engulfed Liverpool, it must have been particularly difficult to deal with while trying to continue to do his job as manager. Throughout the weeks and months after the disaster, Kenny Dalglish's dignity and understanding shone through the darkness but only he could know the full effect that it had on him inside. We should not have been surprised when he eventually stood down at Anfield because, although he was having to make changes to the team, bringing in fresh faces, no manager had had to endure the strain and emotional trauma Dalglish needed to contend with in 1989.

I'm sure Dalglish learned a lot from the experience because later, helped by the late Jack Walker's fortunes, he was able to buy good enough players to win the league championship with Blackburn Rovers. Whether he was truly cut out for management, whether he might have benefited from an initial period spent learning the ropes with a smaller club, we'll never know. But he didn't exactly set the world alight or Tyneside dancing during his time in charge at Newcastle, did he?

Some coaches think they can make the step up to manager without a problem. It has worked in a few cases although I'm struggling to think of one, but by and large these are men who tend to drown in their own self-delusion. Number twos tend to be brilliant at being number twos, a job that varies in its nature and responsibility from club to club. There are some coaches with mouths so big that if they had their teeth taken out you could put seats in and save a fortune in travelling costs on matchdays. Coaches tend to talk a wonderful game.

Harold Shepherdson, Bob Dennison's right-hand man at Middlesbrough, was the equivalent of today's number two or coach; we called him the trainer. Harold was a lovely man. It wasn't possible to dislike him. He probably knew he would never make a manager in his own right. He worked alongside Alf Ramsey as part of the England backroom staff when the World Cup was won in 1966, a valued member of the set-up although I'm not sure exactly what he did. What I do know is that he enjoyed a long and illustrious career in the game – and winning a World Cup is illustrious, you know – with a minimum of responsibility on his shoulders.

I think of Harold Shepherdson every time I see that a coach has accepted a job as manager. The game might have changed, Harold might never have regarded himself as one of the great technicians or innovators on the training ground, but the difference between coaching and managing, moving from number two to the biggest job of them all, remains a massive leap. Too many don't look before they take that leap and the majority of the rest just leap anyway. They leap in the dark.

A coach works to the requirements and instructions of the man in charge, the manager. He might have an idea or two of his own when it comes to training routines, little games to break the monotony and liven up the morning. It's up to him where the cones are placed before they start work. He can feel like one of the lads. He can be pals with everybody in the dressing room, going round ruffling hair or patting heads – 'All right, big man?' 'Had a good day off, son?' – all nice and cosy and friendly and unthreatening. Those players might have got done three nowt at home on the Saturday but he can still smile come Monday morning. He might believe and argue that part of the responsibility lies with him but we all know, chairmen certainly know, that the real responsibility lies elsewhere.

You can't afford to be everybody's friend as the manager. There are bollockings to be handed out; there are players to be told their performance was unacceptable and that any repeat will be the last. There are some who need cuddling and reassuring, of course, but there are those who have to be dropped as well. Always there is the need for improvement, the necessity to be constantly striving to make the team a better team, however successful it might be already. You can't be totally pally with footballers you are secretly trying to replace.

Recruitment, the signing of players who will improve the side, is one of the key components of the manager's art. We all drop clangers, some of them mighty ones as I discovered from time to time with the likes of Carl Tiler and Justin Fashanu to name two of a few, but you can't afford too many. That's another shock in store for the coach who becomes the manager. He knows it's part of the job, he knows he'll have to commit the club's money on his own judgement – if he's lucky enough to be with a club who have a bob or two – but knowing it and doing it are two different things. As a coach he was safe, shielded and protected, going about his job mainly in the background. Once he becomes the manager he is on his own, totally exposed to public scrutiny. All the responsibility is his and it can weigh extremely heavily. It can leave a man feeling he has the loneliest job in the world. So he'd better be able to cope.

The 2001–02 season provided a classic example of what I'm talking about. It's ironic that the man in question should be called Peter Taylor. Peter and I were twenty years ahead of our time when we took over at Derby County. This Peter Taylor was ahead of himself when they made him manager of Leicester City. I do hope they paid him the compensation he was due when he parted company after a handful of games in his second season.

Taylor was a coach, a pal of Glenn Hoddle's – that's how he ended up working for the FA as coach to the England Under-21 side. I'm not sure where he'd worked before that but somebody said he'd been at Southend and at Dover. Some people come from nowhere and get management jobs with England, don't they? I believe this man's reputation was in part a product of the media. If they didn't make him they certainly sang his praises and elevated his managerial prowess out of all proportion. When news leaked out that Howard Wilkinson, the man in charge of the coaching set-up at the FA, was planning to take charge of the Under-21 team again, there was a big reaction. Not all the main football writers, the London lot, get on with Wilkinson. It's not stretching the point to say that some of them don't think he's got a clue. Yes, we are talking about the bloke who won a league championship with Leeds.

It's only my opinion, looking at things from afar, but I believe there was a lot of anti-Wilkinson propaganda behind the incredible support and projection Taylor was given not only in the newspapers but on radio and television. It was as if the nation had made an astounding discovery, one of the greatest managerial talents of all time. How could the FA get rid of a man who had done such a wonderful job for them, hadn't lost a match since God knows when?

I'd just like to remind you, and them, that Peter Taylor was coach of the England Under-21s. He met up with them once in a blue moon and has always professed to be at his best on the training ground. I'm telling you that as the man in charge of those youngsters – call him manager or coach or whatever he wanted to call himself – he had one of the best jobs our game has to offer because the responsibility, the comeback if things don't go too well, is negligible.

He had the cream of the crop apart from the kids who would have been available to him had they not already made the full England side. He had the best youngsters the country could offer and if you can't do well with talent like that, you want locking up. If he was without some of his first choices because of injury, it didn't matter much because he wasn't under the kind of pressure club managers endure, results weren't that vital. He was running a team that was part of a process, familiarising them with the kind of football Hoddle preferred his teams to play. It was all part of a theoretical production line, an attempt to establish continuity so that youngsters moving up to the first team would feel comfortable when the call came. If they won matches at the same time, smashing. If they lost a few, I'm not sure too many people noticed. What a position to be in! What a job! I know one thing, though – it wasn't a job to equip anyone for the demands of club management at top level.

Taylor had a successful spell at Gillingham, achieving promotion from the second division, but I don't think it was long enough to make him a prime candidate for the job at Leicester, let alone the actual choice of the people who run the club. He would have learned something working with the Under-21s. He had a group of youngsters still at the starry-eyed stage, most of them untainted by the lavish lifestyle of the modern professional, some of them just grateful to be able to tell their mums and dads, aunties and uncles, grandmas and granddads that they'd been picked to play for England. Youngsters have such a fresh outlook on life. He must have gained something from the experience.

He possibly made the mistake of thinking that a bit of success with Gillingham meant he'd cracked it sufficiently to go to Leicester and take over where Martin O'Neill had left off. If he was ever going to meet the requirements of that particular job, he'd have needed at least another season lower down, preferably two or even three. The Leicester board believed what they'd been reading and hearing, all the accolades he'd received from the media during his time with those England kids and particularly after he'd finished. They were over-blowing the reputation of a man who was about to undertake an extremely difficult proposition. Following O'Neill at Leicester was not too unlike following me at Nottingham Forest – a prospect that did not appeal to O'Neill, and I think was the main reason why he rejected the chance to be my successor.

As I said, a good team that has been soundly managed will continue to function for a while, but there comes a time when the new manager has to make his own decisions. Changes are necessary; new blood is required. Suddenly, the coach who turned into a manager finds his judgement is well and truly on the line.

O'Neill and his mate John Robertson had performed wonders at Filbert Street, not only by getting Leicester into the Premiership and surviving without too much trouble, but by winning the League Cup, the Worthington to bring it up to date, and taking the club into Europe. They'd done it by exercising good judgement, signing talented players for far less than the fortunes others spend on inferior ability, and excellent motivation. They got the very best out of whomever they had at their disposal. Some say they learned it playing for me. I don't know about that.

What amazed me in particular about Taylor's ill-fated time at Leicester was that he thought he could do two jobs at once. They put him in charge of the England team for a little while prior to Sven-Goran Eriksson's appointment, and he is still being congratulated for what was described as his inspirational move in awarding the captaincy to David Beckham. I don't know whether it was inspirational or not. I can't honestly remember what alternative skippers were available at the time. What I do know is that the choice of Beckham was guaranteed to be a popular one so it was hardly the most stressful decision a man could ever make!

Taylor, of course, continued working with England as one of

Eriksson's coaches. This, remember, was a bloke new to Premiership management. He was trying to preserve and improve the team O'Neill had left him and yet he believed he could afford time away from the club to work at international level. As a candidate who didn't get further than an interview for the full England job, I despaired every time I read that Taylor was among those being groomed or regarded as a possible England manager of the future.

I don't hear that mentioned quite as often now, not after some of the signings he made at Leicester and the money he spent in the process of creating a side that was struggling when he left and surprised nobody by being relegated months after he'd gone.

I'm glad to see that Taylor thrived in his new job at Brighton. I believe they were top of the second division, or as near as damn it, when he joined them and I'm absolutely certain that the Leicester experience helped him maintain their promotion challenge and pull it off as champions. Had he learned all his lessons at the lower levels in the first place, maybe he would have been more capable of fitting the bill at Leicester. Maybe he would have known that Ade Akinbiyi was not a top-quality Premiership centre-forward instead of paying Wolves £5 million for him. Hey, are we sure that's true? If so, it was as unsuccessful a buy as when I took Justin Fashanu to Forest. Mind you, I did sign a few strikers who could actually do the job. Akinbiyi couldn't, no matter how hard he tried. If he was supposed to be the new Emile Heskey at Filbert Street, it was one of the worst impersonations I've ever seen. He wasn't to blame, poor lad. Whenever I saw him on television he was doing his level best to put things right, to score the goal that was as elusive as a butterfly to a man without a net. He was genuine, never shirked it, never hid and continued to want the ball at all times, even with the crowd on his back. That's a great credit to him. That takes moral courage, you know.

But he struggled to score goals. Like one or two others, he couldn't give the team the qualities he was bought to provide. When that happens in too many areas, a team begins to decline. That's what happened at Leicester. It was inevitable that Taylor would depart to continue his managerial education elsewhere. It was inevitable, also, that some idiots would say he was given a raw deal, losing his job so early in the season. It wasn't those few matches that cost him the job. He'd had a bad time towards the end of the season before and there weren't many signs of marked improvement. It was an accumulative thing. He lost the job in my opinion – and possibly the opinion of Leicester's directors now – because he wasn't the right man for it in the first place.

He'd been given a false impression of management, working with that young England side. I have never professed to be Einstein. I have never claimed to have the ability to fix a car engine. The closest I've come to knowing anything technical about the motor car is that after retiring from football management I actually reached the stage where I had to put petrol in it for myself – not my subject, not my field. Why do some coaches believe they can slip into management with no problem? And why do so many directors still seem to think the same way?

With Taylor, the rise to sudden prominence began when Hoddle took him into the England set-up. Seeing that I don't rate Hoddle as much of a manager himself, I suppose we shouldn't have been too surprised.

I was surprised, in fact I was staggered, when David Platt was put in charge at Nottingham Forest. He was given the seat I occupied for nineteen years, possibly even the very same chair, after a few weeks as a coach in Italy. They're a bit strict about qualifications there, I gather, so Platt didn't last long at all as the man in charge at Sampdoria. He finished up at Forest, a club steeped in tradition – not because it was a big club but

131

because of what we won while I was there. By the time Platt left, Forest were virtually on their knees. They were stopped from trading during the 2001–02 season though many of the problems were there before he arrived. They are skint and, like all clubs in trouble, need to sell their better players, leaving the latest manager, Paul Hart, with a thankless task. Hart is a pleasant young man who used to play centre-half for me. He has worked very effectively with young players at Forest and at Leeds. He's done some kind of an apprenticeship and worked for good managers. With a reasonable crack of the whip I believe he could make a manager of some repute, but to ask him to build a team from the situation he inherited at the City Ground is asking a hell of a lot.

I blame David Platt for much of what went wrong. He spent several million pounds on easily forgotten footballers. There were Italians among his signings but I don't remember their names because I don't remember any of them making an impact. I'm not sure if any of them are still there. When I took part in a local radio discussion, I gave David Platt some real stick on air. I couldn't help it because I meant it, and if ever he makes contact with me, I'll give him some more. As far as I'm concerned, he left my old club in a terrible state.

Platt was another with a reputation – a charming man, possibly, who seems to be on good terms with so-called important people. He is a former England captain who made the most of a talent to get forward from midfield and score a few goals; and he's a good talker who took the trouble to learn the language thoroughly when he went to play in Italy. But he is another who believed he could run before he could even crawl as a manager. Where is he now, the manager who left Forest in such a state? Blow me if he's not doing the job Peter Taylor used to have. He's in charge of the England Under-21 team. From what I read, Platt is a good friend of Eriksson. They met when Eriksson was in Italian club management and Platt was playing. That's fair enough. So is Platt's admiration for the man who has such a fine record in club management, but it is no reason for his appointment to a job in the England regime.

Rumour has it that Platt's appointment is part of a policy of stability and continuity at the FA and he is being groomed for the top job, possibly even as Eriksson's successor. If that happens, I'll know I'm going mad. My insanity will be official because, based on the management skills he showed at Nottingham Forest, I am better qualified for the England job now at the age of sixty-seven than Platt will ever be.

CHAPTER 11

TWENTY YEARS AHEAD
OF OUR TIME

No, you can't buy a manual on management and sorry to all those who think you can learn how to be a manager simply by copying the exploits of others. Nobody can do the job in precisely the same way as someone else. But anybody who wants to know about management at its best, the effects of a partnership working in perfect harmony, should make a close study of what happened at Derby County from the moment Peter Taylor and I arrived in the summer of '67 to the time we stupidly walked away from it all in the autumn of '73. That period in Derby's history, and in my career, was the definitive example of football management in all its aspects and all its glory.

Taylor and I built two teams in that short time. The Mackay side won the second division championship, and we reshaped, refined and improved it so thoroughly and effectively that we won the league title three years later.

In many ways, football management is an instinctive process. I was blessed with an assistant of Peter Taylor's calibre, providing the elements of the job that I didn't have. In fact, Peter was in his element at Derby, coming up with the right names at the right time – as I've said, he told me to go and sign Mackay, believing in his own mind that I had no chance of pulling it off.

I can't overstate the impact and influence Mackay had at the Baseball Ground. Our self-belief – mine, Taylor's and the entire team's – stemmed from the confidence of Mackay himself. It won him the Footballer of the Year award and it won us that second division title. Mackay taught my two boys, Simon and Nigel, how to kick a football. He would spend hours on end with them, practising in what we called our shooting-box – a little wooden target area under the main stand at the Baseball Ground. It was sad when his playing days ended. He was what I had always believed him to be before I knew him and came to admire him so much – a man of immense talent, hard as nails on the pitch but with a gentle and pleasant nature off it, the consummate, complete professional. It was Dave Mackay who not only took over from Taylor and me, but led Derby to another league championship in 1975.

When Mackay stopped playing, we were faced with the problem of replacing him. How do you replace a legend? But we were full of ourselves in those wonderful days at Derby. Others would have been daunted by the prospect but we knew exactly how to go about it, who to get. 'You know everything there is to know about Colin Todd so you'd better get up to Sunderland and sign him,' was Taylor's solution, and no sooner said than done, as usual. The chairman? I never felt the need to ask Sam Longson. It never dawned on me because I was running the club. I felt totally in charge and success or failure was down to me. I was happy to have the buck firmly in my grasp.

Toddy cost us £175,000 which was an absolute fortune in those days – and far too much in the eyes of men who didn't understand management and never would. Longson was probably telling the story until the day he died – how that young bugger Clough took it upon himself to go and sign Colin Todd without a word until he sent a telegram to say he'd done it and that he'd virtually bankrupted the club. It wasn't big-headedness on my part although, aye, it was a wee bit cheeky. I saw it as my job to sign the best talent. Our judgement had been proved to directors who couldn't tell a good player from a bad player in any case, and as far as the money was concerned I knew we could afford it, if only just.

Few managers enjoyed that kind of freedom; even fewer would be given such privilege these days. But that was management as I saw it and, after all, few were as good as I was at the time. Nobody was as good as Taylor.

Many clubs had watched Archie Gemmill, the little Scots-man who was running Preston's midfield. Many scouts and managers had watched him several times but Taylor needed no further confirmation once he'd cast that expert eye of his. Gemmill was the one, Gemmill had to be signed. Get off your arse and get it done, which I did, even though the awkward little sod said he wouldn't sign. He insisted on thinking about it overnight, unlike Roy McFarland earlier. I'm always amazed when managers allow players to go away and consider a proposed transfer. Let them out of your sight or your grasp and the chances are they'll sign for somebody else, especially nowadays with an agent on the other end of a mobile phone telling him he can always get him a better deal. If Gemmill was going to sleep on it, I was going to sleep alongside him, or at least in the spare bedroom. Funny, looking back – his wife Betty was pregnant with Scot who was later to play not only for my Nottingham Forest side but for Scotland as well.

After a hearty breakfast and helping with the washing-up, I signed Archie Gemmill. Once again, he was among the finest of our signings. Of all the footballers who have played for me, including Martin O'Neill, Gemmill was one whom I believed would turn out to be a successful manager. He was to play or work for me until I packed in as a manager and his knowledge of the game is second to none. He had a crack at management but it didn't work out and I can only assume it was a problem of personality rather than ability. He was always a bit dour, miserable-looking. It must have given a wrong impression because Archie had what it takes to be in charge of a football team.

It is no exaggeration when I talk of Taylor and me being twenty years ahead of everybody. We were fortunate to have the ability to recognise who could play and who couldn't. You'd be amazed at how many people who earn their money in football don't know that. It's the secret behind everything. Peter could spot them, I could sign them, and I knew how to handle the lot of them. I didn't recognise danger. I was like the twenty-year-old pilot in the war who went up in a Spitfire to take on half a dozen German fighter planes. I didn't know the meaning of fear. I thought I could shoot down the lot. I had age on my side and that was a big advantage. You don't see the possible pitfalls when you're thirty. When you get into your fifties and sixties, you see nothing else.

I reached the stage where I got away with everything. I was good value for the newspapers because I blew my own trumpet – too often and far too loud, I now realise – which made good copy for journalists. I was the bloke who brought some welcome fresh air to a game that had been draped with cobwebs, run by men who, if not exactly of the old school tie brigade, had become far too comfortable and smug with their routine. I regarded the game as a business and I was the first one to use the word 'industry' to describe professional football. It was an industry then and it is even more of one today. Now it's huge – possibly too big for its own good, too big to last.

Chairmen remain a major problem. We've gone from the butchers and bakers and candlestick makers to the so-called high-powered businessmen. Some of them seem to have the philosophy that says: 'Just a minute, if I'm going to put substantial money into this club, I want some credit and I want my face on television and in the papers.' Some of them pay themselves fortunes and believe that one of the ways of justifying their existence is to assume a bigger profile and have almost total involvement in the day-to-day operation. I know Leeds United have had their problems over the past couple of years with the court case involving Woodgate and Bowyer, and that the chairman, Peter Ridsdale, has had some public relations work to do.

Sam Longson and the chairmen I worked with in management used to pay for their own petrol but I'd be surprised if today's chairmen do that. They may be somebodies in their business lives, they may be known to people in the commercial and money markets, but if you took away the passes that get them through the front doors of the football grounds, if you removed their status as figureheads of football clubs, they would be nobodies. They could be buskers or vagabonds but football makes them believe they're kings.

Generally speaking, certainly at Hartlepools, Derby and Nottingham, I gave my chairmen fond memories. I made them popular with the public because their football clubs brightened up the lives of everybody in the community and, when you boil it all down, that's what football clubs are for. I did it in various ways. I introduced daft games in training – games from my schoolboy days, passing a ball by hand down two lines of seven players. I won't bore you with the details but cheats were made to run half a lap or do a dozen press-ups. Everybody hated press-ups, especially when he was made to do twelve of 'em with everybody else taking the mickey. Believe it or not, those daft games became as competitive as any match on a Saturday afternoon or a Wednesday night. So was the heading game. Again, Dave Mackay was best of the lot but everybody benefited; they were all slightly better at heading a football by the time we'd finished. Time passed so quickly because the level of enjoyment was so high. There was no routine as such but lots of variety. Only one aspect remained the same – whatever we did, we did it with a ball.

Tactics played very little part in my method of management. I concentrated 90 per cent on how my team played, in preference to wondering about how the opposition would set out their stall. In other words, I worked, taught, coached, cajoled – call it what you want – all with the aim of getting the best out of my lot because, provided I achieved that, I knew that the opposition would have too much on their plate to surprise us. I didn't watch our opponents especially but I had a rough knowledge of them from seeing them on television. I believed in getting the absolute maximum from those in our dressing room. I didn't collect dossiers on opponents like Don Revie did at Leeds. It might sound as though I was lazy, possibly I was, but I had enough on, coping with my team, and wasn't prepared to waste time worrying about anybody else.

For instance, I can't see what difference it makes whether a goalkeeper clears the ball with his left foot or his right. He usually kicks it up into the air, which means one of your guys is going to have to head it. I made sure I had good headers in my teams. Obviously, if we were playing Liverpool, I would know their strengths. I knew their coach, Ronnie Moran, as well as I knew anybody. He had a favourite phrase that he shouted twenty-five times in each half of a match. Over a period of twenty-odd years or more, that's a long time yelling one instruction – 'Keep the ball rolling.'

I knew exactly what he meant – once you stop a ball you invite the opposition to take it off you. A team blossoms only when it has the ball. Flowers need the rain – it's a vital ingredient. Common sense tells you that the main ingredient in football is the ball itself. Common sense told me that, as a manager, you need somebody to get the ball, somebody to keep it, somebody to play it, somebody to put it in the net at one end and somebody to keep it out of the net at the other. Now doesn't that sound simple?

We didn't practise free-kicks in training. We just used the best man for the job depending on where and at what angle free-kicks were awarded during a game. 'Get in on it, a couple of you. Have a look at how the other lot have positioned themselves and if they've lined up badly, use your loaf.' That was about the sum total of my coaching on free-kicks. I signed players who were bright enough to work out those things for themselves. I did like to eliminate some things – particularly shooting at goal from a distance of thirty yards or more. There are very few players who can score from that range. David Beckham has done it a time or two and Stuart Pearce did it for me on several occasions at Forest, whacking in free-kicks with his terrific power. But goals from thirty yards or more are the exception rather than the norm.

I was not in favour of practising our defence of free-kicks, either, but if we conceded a goal from one on the Saturday, first thing Monday morning there would be a familiar to and fro.

'And where were you when that ball went in?' was my first question to the centre-half and back four.

'Well, the centre-forward ran there,' our centre-half would protest, pointing, 'and I went with him.'

'So if he goes for a piss, do you go with him to pull his pants down?'

'What do you mean, Boss?'

So I'd have to explain, spell it out to the lot of them. I know some would call this coaching but I call it management and still do. It was usually the central defender I aimed at.

'You couldn't get to him on the near post because he's quicker than you. So you stand in your patch and if he comes into your patch you deal with it. If he goes ten, fifteen, twenty yards beyond you, it's not your job. It's a full-back's job, somebody from midfield will deal with it.' Football really is a simple game if only people didn't insist on complicating it.

It's the same with crosses from the flanks. Peter Taylor, as a former keeper, used to drum it into me and I used to drum it into the players – the longer a ball takes to come into the box the easier it is to deal with. It's the one that's driven in that does the damage and we had that off to a fine art at Derby and then at Forest with wingers Alan Hinton and John Robertson. Robbo was the complete master. He didn't float crosses very often but if necessary he could float the best crosses known to man. My word, how he could pick out a team-mate! He combined precision with pace.

I prepared my teams almost identically, week in week out, no matter whom we were playing against because, providing we were at our best, I wasn't the slightest bit interested in or concerned about the opposition. My team at its best would be able to deal with them at their best, whomever they might be. I relied on my best wherever possible – the best keeper, the best left-back, the best centre-half, the best centre-forward, the best left winger. You can only have one 'best' in each position, so what was the point in picking anybody else?

I didn't ask any of my players to mark an opponent out of the game, not once. I would give them the instruction, 'You look after your own patch no matter who comes into it.' Obviously, if the other manager told six of his team to play on the right wing, I couldn't leave our left-back to cope with half a dozen, but I'd always tell our right-back, 'You stick to your position whatever the circumstances. I don't care if nobody comes near you, if you don't have a kick all afternoon. You hold your position because one ball will come across at some stage of the ninety minutes and if you're not around it will be the one they put in the net.'

Sometimes one defender would come in at half-time without a bead of sweat while his mate's tongue was hanging out. We weren't influenced by that, we weren't bothered about it. Bear in mind, it works two ways. If the opposition decide to attack one area, it leaves them vulnerable and weak, and open to exploitation. So if you have a good all-round side, a nicely balanced side, you've half a chance. I always had to have a good left-footer somewhere. It meant that however we played and whomever we played, Brian Clough's teams never looked ragged.

All these things slipped nicely into place at Derby. The players learned and I suppose I learned as it all progressed, the promotion to the first division and the walking off with the title three years later. One of my most vivid and satisfying memories of that championship season was my decision to solve the right-back vacancy by chucking in a lad called Steve Powell in the crucial game against Liverpool. He was sixteen years old. We had to fill the gap somehow and Taylor and I took no time at all in deciding the kid should play. 'He's good enough, he's not inclined to freeze or to panic – gerrim in.' That was our attitude and the youngster strolled through the match. We won by the only goal.

If I get angry during these quieter days of my life, it is usually when I'm reflecting on the championship we won at Derby. We were not given the credit we deserved. The same thing applied at Forest to a certain extent, but there was just some grudging recognition given to our achievement at the Baseball Ground. I'll remind you again – we finished our season before Leeds, who won the FA Cup and would have done the double had they won at Wolves on the Monday after the final. We had our feet up by then. Taylor was in our favourite resort, Cala Millor, with most of the players, and I was in the Scilly Isles with Barbara and the three kids and my mam and dad. If I could take a break during the season, taking time off to be with the family during school half-terms (and I made a habit of it), I could certainly be on holiday while Leeds were trying to fix themselves up with the league title at Molineux. Fix is at least the allegation. There were questions raised about that game, and allegations of attempted bribery, though some of the claims were legally disproved later. However, the outcome was a defeat for Revie's side – and the opening of a lot of champagne in the Scilly Isles and in Majorca.

Nearly everybody said that Derby won that championship by default, we hadn't won it as much as Leeds had lost it. Now that still rankles with me, still makes my blood boil because, unless the rules had been changed for that season, they give the championship trophy to the players whose efforts leave them at the top of the table. That's the way it was and that's the way it will always be, and the fact that Leeds didn't finish their fixtures until after ours were complete is a minor and irrelevant detail. Taylor and I worked extremely hard to create the team that ended the season higher than all the rest. It was a genuine and worthy triumph, of as much merit as any that went before it and any that followed it.

I was in the perfect situation to enjoy that incomparable glow of satisfaction – on a beach with my family. Mam was never carried away by what she considered to be the unimportant things in life. She probably got more satisfaction from seeing her washing blowing in the wind before anybody else's in Valley Road on a Monday morning than she got from the championship pennant fluttering above the Baseball Ground. But I think she was pleased that day I became manager of the English League champions. I think I detected an extra little sparkle in her eyes as we sipped the champagne and enjoyed the moment.

Personally, the league title was the ultimate. It was the supreme test of management. Anybody could win a Cup, given a fair wind and a fair slice of luck over a few matches, but finishing top after forty-two games, as it was in those days – that was indisputable evidence. That proved the pedigree of both team and management. They've devalued it in recent years with the top two or three, or even four, qualifying for the

Champions League but it is still the competition that singles out the best team in the country. There can be no argument – just as there should have been no argument or protest or grudging acknowledgement when we won it at Derby.

I didn't lose a wink of sleep, mind. I dropped off thinking of the next stage of our development – competing with all the champions from around Europe for the European Cup when it meant far more than it does today. Now as many sides as possible are involved in order to generate as much money as possible, fat cats getting fatter and fourth-placed sides being involved in something wrongly called a Champions League. I don't suppose you could call it a Champions, Runners-up and Third and Fourth-place League but that's what it amounts to. It's a joke and not very funny but it makes money so they're all happy with it.

It was a genuine competition in the seventies. There was no league format to start with. You were in the hat among the very best and you survived or were knocked out with no second chance in the next stage. You sank or you swam, and our lot at Derby just couldn't wait to get in the water. I certainly couldn't – I immediately became obsessed with the European Cup, as obsessed with it as Sir Alex Ferguson could ever be. I wanted to rub shoulders with the likes of Juventus, Real Madrid and Benfica. I'd come a long way from Valley Road but I knew I wouldn't feel out of place in the slightest.

CHAPTER 12

THE BIGGEST MISTAKE OF MY LIFE

They say that time heals but it doesn't, not entirely – it just helps you put things into some kind of perspective. I've had nearly thirty years to think about the events of 1973 and time has not eased much of the pain. If I live to be a hundred, I don't suppose it ever will.

Derby County were equipped, capable and ready to take Europe by storm. All time has done has been to convince me that we would have won the European Cup at the first time of asking but for the distasteful events that occurred in Turin during the first leg of our semi-final against Juventus. It wasn't that we lost 3–1 although, obviously, that was bad enough. I believed then and still believe that, one way or another, the match was bent. My immediate reaction on the night has been well documented, with my quote about 'cheating, fucking Italian bastards' – no, I'm not much calmer when I recall that night, even now.

Nothing has been proved despite the official investigation that took place later. It wasn't established whether or not the German referee had actually been bribed. It was never established, as far as I know, why one of our opponents had apparently been into the referee's room prior to the match and during the interval. Something else I'll never know is why Roy McFarland and Archie Gemmill were booked before we got to half-time. The offences were seen by the referee but they were by no means obvious to anybody from Derby. What we did know was that both had been cautioned earlier in the tournament and would therefore have to sit out the second leg against the Italian champions. As far as I was concerned, the entire episode stank the place out. We had been done but not fairly and squarely by a team worthy of a 3–1 margin – I could have lived with that. Defeat is never easy to take but I have always been able to accept it providing it's been inflicted legitimately. To name just one rotten aspect of the game, it is corrupt in my book for players to dive like dolphins at the slightest pretext. I close my eyes and think of that bloody awful night in Turin and what I see is the majority of the opposition flinging themselves all over the place and conning the referee time after time after time. It might have become a little exaggerated in my mind but the overall picture hasn't. The effect has lasted as long as the pictures from the match itself.

Peter Taylor was just as incensed as I was and as a result he had his collar felt by the local police. Fortunately, his arrest didn't last very long. If he'd managed to get hold of that referee, the consequences might have detained him in Italy for the rest of his days.

A night like that one in Turin could sour you. It could destroy your belief in your own industry. Thankfully, my belief in the integrity of the English game – despite what happened with those two defenders at Middlesbrough – and my belief in myself and my team was too strong for one evening of skulduggery to harm it for long. But the heartbreak was to become even more intense, unbearable, by the time the second leg came around.

It just happened to be on the night of my birthday. Hope didn't spring eternal exactly, but we still had hope enough of turning things round and making it through to the final. No team liked coming to the Baseball Ground. Tight, intimate and intimidating, with the crowd so close to the pitch, the unique atmosphere we created was worth a goal at least to Derby. It could be hell on earth to the opposition and I don't care how experienced they were. But time can't alter the facts – our centre-forward Roger Davies was sent off and Alan Hinton missed a penalty. Of course we were dejected at being knocked out of the competition but it was fury at what happened in Turin rather than frustration at what happened in the second leg that dominated our mood.

Just when you think things can't get worse, they invariably do. We'd been knocked out of the European Cup on my birthday but a phone call reduced all that, even the things that occurred in Italy, to meaningless trivia. The late-night call was from our Joe breaking the terrible news that Mam had died. We had all realised that she was dying from cancer but it was still a devastating blow. You don't need reminding yet again about my feelings for my mam and the influence she had on my life. Knowing all that, you still can't begin to imagine how I felt when I picked up that phone and heard our Joe's voice. I was empty – thankful, oh so thankful, that Barbara and my family were around me but I still had a feeling, strangely, of being alone. Your mam is someone who's always been there and should always be there. She's a guide, a reassurance, your best friend and the finest teacher you'll ever come across. I know mine was. I also know I haven't always lived my life in the way she showed me I should. She was seventy-three at the end. Dad was eighty-one when we lost him four years later. Time doesn't end the sense of loneliness; it just helps to make you a little less lonely.

It was a sad, tragic end to that European adventure of ours;

sadder, in personal terms, than I could ever have expected, but sad, too, from a professional point of view. Derby had been capable of going all the way, as we proved in the early stages of the tournament. We were getting through without a problem, we were cruising past the opposition, we were doing it with our eyes closed – or I was, literally.

We liked a soft pitch at our place. It wasn't soft enough for my liking the night before Eusebio came to town with his Portuguese mates from Benfica. I knew what was needed to get the likeliest winning performance from that team of ours at home. Those were the days when Brian Clough took more water with it! I used to water our pitch more times than the groundsman did. Half the time nobody knew I was doing it because I went back at night. I had the keys to just about everything and everywhere at the Baseball Ground. If I needed to see in the interests of accuracy, I knew how to switch on the floodlights, but the night prior to the Benfica game I did it in the dark. We didn't have sprinklers; we had two big hosepipes that were equivalent in power to the ones firemen use. I would switch them on, sit back on the terrace steps and let them do their job. Usually, I'd leave them for no longer than twenty minutes because the pitch couldn't take any more water than that so quickly. Unfortunately, or fortunately as things turned out, on that night I dropped off. Hey, I was a busy man working a lot of hours in a week, and I had three small children at home. Life can get tiring even for somebody who believed he was a genius.

I don't know how long I slept while the hoses gushed their gallons. All I know is that I woke up drenched and with enough water on that ground to have staged an Olympic diving event from the top board!

You probably know the story but this one's worth re-telling because it involved the establishment – Sir Stanley Rous, President of FIFA, no less. Apart from ticking me off for my

Sam Longson
introduces me and
Peter Taylor to the
Derby County squad
on our arrival in
June 1967.

COLORSPORT

Shaking hands with
Dave Mackay after
winning the second
division title in 1969.
I never did a better
piece of business in
my entire career than
when I signed him.

EMPICS

Three years later
and Peter Taylor
and I had our hands
on yet another trophy.
This time it was
the big one –
the Championship.

The first our chairman knew of the fact that we'd signed Colin Todd for a huge fee of £175,000 was when I sent him a telegram to let him know. It was a lot of money but he was worth it.

Simon and Nigel get a helping hand from me and Peter Taylor.

Walking out on Derby in October 1973 was probably the biggest mistake I ever made. Although the support of the fans was very gratifying, I feel sure I could have taken Derby even further.

Leading out the Leeds United side for the Charity Shield in 1974.
After all the criticism I'd made of the side, it was always going to be
a tough job there, especially without Peter Taylor.

Alongside Joe Jordan in the Leeds dug-out. My reign of just
44 days may not have been a record, but the players were never
going to accept me.

It was an extraordinary decision to get rid of Sir Alf Ramsey as England manager. But, as I found out when I went to Lancaster Gate for my interview for the England manager's job in 1977, those in charge seemed not to have a clue about who was the best man for the job.

Leading the Nottingham Forest side onto the plane ahead of our European Cup final in 1979. Trevor Francis, the first million-pound signing, follows close behind with John McGovern and Fred Reacher also in attendance.

The Clough and Taylor magic really worked that night in Munich when a Trevor Francis goal secured the 1979 European Cup title for Nottingham Forest.

POPPERFOTO

John McGovern lifts the European Cup after Forest beat SV Hamburg 1–0 in the final in 1980.

Polishing the silverware at the City Ground. As you can see, during my time it became pretty much a full-time occupation.

POPPERFOTO

The FA Cup – the one that got away. Being introduced to Prince Charles ahead of the 1991 final.

Being escorted off the ground in May 1993 after a season at Forest where I made too many bad decisions. I still can't forgive myself for leading the club to relegation in my last year.

EMPICS

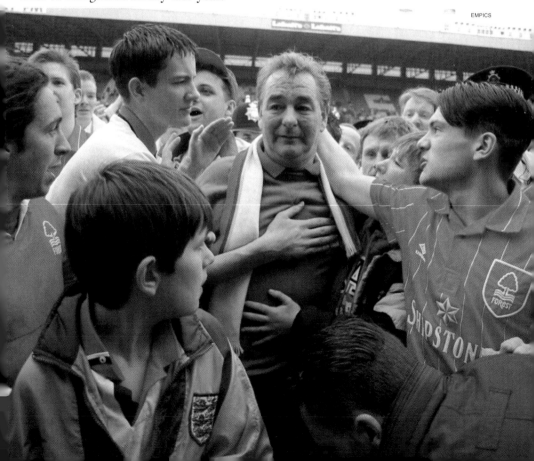

Here I am with Wilf Mannion and his wife Bernadette. Wilf was one of my great heroes at Middlesbrough.

At ease in the countryside.

shouting during the match, he had taken one look at the pitch and wondered how it could have been inches deep in mud when there had been no rain whatsoever at his hotel just up the road. I explained that the weather could be like that in Derby. We often had torrential downpours at the Baseball Ground when they didn't get a drop half a mile away in town. It was one of the wonders of mother nature.

It did the trick, I know that. Benfica couldn't live with us or the pitch, the crowd, the atmosphere and particularly the football we played. In the second leg, despite their refusal to let us have the ball in the early stages, we didn't need a hosepipe to douse their optimism. We just got a grip, defended the way you're supposed to defend in Europe and clung to a goalless draw. We'd beaten one of the big names of continental football, one of the magical names. We'd held our own in the Stadium of Light, one of the legendary venues of Europe. We'd survived and prospered partly because of what I'd done in the dark. Don't ever try telling me there is nothing to be gained by falling asleep on the job.

Chairmen change. Sam Longson changed very quickly from the friendly, generous old man who regarded me as the son he'd never had, who bought us gifts and often lent Barbara and me his gleaming Mercedes, to a vulnerable individual who put his own interests, image and reputation before those of the club. He'd often tell me to calm down when my name hit the papers under some controversial, provocative headline, which it did on a regular basis. He'd occasionally suggest I gave it more thought before I opened my mouth. But I was popular with the media. I was doing the TV panels with the likes of Jimmy Hill, Jack Charlton, Malcolm Allison and Bill Shankly. It was like a football *Who's Who* on the box at that time, and I was usually the one who said something that was seized on by the press. I never did see the point of going on television, expected to voice an honest opinion, and then saying next to nothing or being cautious and particularly careful just to avoid upsetting some-body. There are too many supposed pundits who do exactly that now. What a life! Get yourself on TV, get paid a small fortune, smile a lot and say next to nowt. Now that is nice work if you can get it.

I don't know whether it was jealousy, a wee bit of envy, but Sam Longson's attitude cooled towards Taylor and me. I was forever in the papers or on TV, spouting about every footballing subject under the sun, and some people might have gained the impression that I was in charge of everything at Derby. I was told that Longson started to go around insisting in that gravel voice of his, 'I'm the one who runs Derby County – not Brian Clough.' That was what started the rot, that and the arrival of a director called Jack Kirkland.

Pete Taylor had already told me to beware of the club secretary, the dapper little Stuart Webb. Taylor was brilliant at detecting those we should be wary of – directors or any club employee. We needed to be able to trust everybody – from the chairman to the secretary to the bloke who drove the team bus and the ladies who made the tea or did the laundry.

Taylor was suspicious of Kirkland from the outset, an inquisitive so-and-so poking his nose into this and that. So we had the secretary trying to do a balancing act as a friend of the management and the boardroom, we had the chairman realising that I had too big a profile for his liking and we had a nosey old bugger as a new director, who seemed determined to find out exactly how this successful club was being run.

We feared nobody as a team – we were that good. Not even the prospect of playing Manchester United at Old Trafford worried us in the slightest. We had respect for them because we had respect for all opponents but we had so much faith in the collective ability at Derby – mine, Taylor's, coach Jimmy Gordon's and particularly the team's – that we honestly believed we could beat anybody anywhere, unless there was a

German referee, that is! Yet Kirkland wanted to stick his nose into it all.

One October afternoon when we'd gone to Old Trafford and beaten United, Taylor and I accepted their chairman Louis Edwards' invitation to the boardroom, which wasn't our usual style. Get the match over, get on the coach as quickly as possible and get home – that was our familiar routine. Who knows, if we had followed our usual pattern that day, we might not have made what I consider to have been the worst decision of our lives.

It was the beginning of the end when Taylor revealed on the journey back to Derby that Kirkland had called him over and said he had to meet him on the Monday to explain the details and the precise nature of his duties. We had won a league championship, we had carried that club from nowhere to the top of the tree, we had been cheated out of the European Cup at the semi-final stage, and this interfering bugger wanted to know what Taylor did for his living. I could have told him what he did – he had helped build a football club that had enough appeal and popularity for Jack Kirkland to want to join its board of directors.

Taylor kept the meeting and was convinced that the directors, or a section of them, were attempting to unsettle me by getting at him. He had been humiliated by a man who was not entitled to question anything unless he'd been asking Peter for the time of day. They talk about the end of a beautiful friendship – well this was the end of a fantastic relationship between a club and the management team who had transformed it. It was a relationship that I cherished.

I had been interviewed for the job of Barcelona manager along the way. You don't turn down the chance of at least talking to a club of that magnitude if you've any sense. But I think I blew my chances when I was asked how I would respond to a situation in which more than 100,000 fans were waving white handkerchiefs in my direction.

'I'd have learned enough Spanish to be able to tell them all to piss off,' I said, or something as equally silly as that. The same bloke was reassured by Taylor – 'Don't worry, he'll be able to look after anything the crowd can send his way. In any case, he'll have 100,000 of them waving flags and dancing the Flamenco by the time he's finished. They'll be celebrating and you'll be holding trophies and we'll have taken all the worries off your shoulders.' It was a very persuasive attitude and it often made people feel a million dollars, but it didn't work on that occasion.

Neither did my attempts to steer Peter away from his conclusion that we were not fully appreciated at Derby, that the board were after our blood, that what Kirkland had done had sent out the clear message that we should quit and be on our way. He wouldn't budge and it was me who did the quitting with no fuss, no looking over my shoulder. It was straight into the boardroom and straight out with it – 'I want you to accept our resignations.' I seem to remember one voice, maybe two, quietly asking me to reconsider but Longson's wasn't among them. I didn't wait for a yes or a no. I went to tell Taylor that we had quit. There was no money, no compensation, we were out but we knew we'd have no problem getting another job.

What we didn't know was that there would be so many people involved in that extraordinary campaign to get us reinstated. No football club had witnessed scenes like those ever before and, to my knowledge, nothing like them has been seen since. There were public marches through the town with protest banners everywhere and protest meetings. The ground was besieged by supporters and the media for days on end. The players, my players, led the protests and even threatened a sit-down strike. It was brilliantly organised and well executed, which is not that surprising because I was behind most of it. Having resigned, you might wonder why I took so much trouble involving myself with the revolution that swept the town. Feelings really were running that high, believe me. It was revolution and in my heart I thought those directors would invite us back. Never underestimate the toughness of a man who earns his living from stone quarries. Sam Longson didn't flinch and neither did his fellow directors apart from the late Mike Keeling who had become a good friend and who quit the board when Taylor and I stormed out.

The scenes at Derby were astounding – club officials locked themselves in the boardroom and, too scared to come out, had to relieve themselves in a champagne bucket. My appearance at the home game the following Saturday set off a crowd reaction as loud as the one that had accompanied the defeat of Benfica, and I went on the Michael Parkinson show that very night. Then the appointment of Dave Mackay as my successor was announced despite captain Roy McFarland's phone call warning him not to take the job because they were trying to get Taylor and me reinstated. The warning failed, Mackay came striding in as only a man of his courage and reputation could and, as I mentioned, was eventually to win Derby another championship.

That achievement was further proof of the mistake Taylor and I made. It was the biggest professional mistake of my career. We should have stayed, ridden the storm and seen it out on the strength of the talent that had turned Derby County into the football club with the greatest potential in the country. I'm prepared to go as far as to say that if we'd stayed at Derby, they would have been the Manchester United of the present day, certainly in terms of success on the field. What a thing to be saying in the very year they've just lost their status in the top division of the English game.

When we left, Derby had the youngest side up there and it was a team of outstanding quality. We had Roy McFarland who was undoubtedly the best centre-half in the country, and Colin

Todd can't have been too bad seeing that he gained twenty-seven England caps in his time. We had John McGovern, everybody's idea of the perfect midfield player. He played for Scotland and was to become the Nottingham Forest captain who was presented with the European Cup two years in succession. We had John O'Hare, another Scottish international, at centre-forward with Kevin Hector alongside him, and he was good enough to play for England. We had Alan Hinton on the left-wing and I'm telling you that if England could call on anybody nearly as effective as him in that position today, we wouldn't have been talking about a weakness on the left flank before the team left to play in the 2002 World Cup. So we had enough – more than enough. Other teams would have progressed but we'd have kept pace and gone ahead of them. Having some of the best players already, we'd have kept winning and the better players from other clubs would have wanted to join us. Success really does breed success.

Had Taylor and I been in our right minds and stayed at Derby, no team would have been allowed to run away with things, to dominate the game in the way Manchester United have done in recent years. Inevitably, the bigger clubs would have joined the picture – Arsenal, Liverpool and of course Manchester United among them – but little Derby would have established themselves among the élite and grown until they were as big as any of them.

I wish I had tried to prolong my playing career after the injury at Sunderland. I know I should have prolonged my managerial career at the Baseball Ground. Resigning when we did was crazy – I can see that even more clearly now than I did ten years ago. Anger impaired my vision. For a moment or two I lost sight of what I had created and threw it all away. If I'd stayed at Derby, I wouldn't have won one thing for two years or five years – I'd have won everything for ten years at least. Nobody could have touched us. Don't forget when it came to signing players, we were the best in the business; and I was undoubtedly the best at getting maximum performance from those at our disposal. As for running the club, we ran it from A to Z. We had the formula for lasting success. One man discovered penicillin and we had discovered the equivalent in the footballing world.

No, time hasn't healed the wound I inflicted on myself by quitting the job for what amounted to selfish reasons of pride and ego – my conceit again although it was Taylor's idea originally. Boiling it all down, we left for childish reasons.

In those days we believed everything we did was right. We made decisions instantly. Taylor wasn't a wilting flower as an assistant manager. Don't forget he had been a pal of mine for years. He was a strong personality and could be persuasive. When he said he was packing in, I took it for granted that he *was* packing in. If I'd been slightly more mature, a few years older, I wouldn't have gone along with him. I'd have called round to see him on that Saturday night or the Sunday morning and said, 'Hey, come on. Look at what we've built together, look at what we've got, look at how far we could go with this club. Let's sit down and give it some serious thought.' Peter influenced me almost 100 per cent. We had nothing else in the pipeline but quitting is made easier when you know alternative offers will not be in terribly short supply. We made a huge mistake by sticking to our guns.

If Taylor was obsessed with anything beyond building football teams and winning matches, it was money. It wasn't long before he came to me and announced, 'I've got us a deal. I've got us fifteen grand between us. We can take over at Brighton.'

I should have seen it coming. He always wanted to finish his working life and end up retired at the seaside.

CHAPTER 13

IN NEED OF A FRIEND

Whenever people recall that I managed Brighton for thirty-two matches – and won only twelve, incidentally – they still believe it was just a convenience, a temporary easy-picking to tide me over until a bigger job came along. They were wrong to think it at the time and they are still wrong to believe it today. I was sincere in my agreement to join Mike Bamber, the pleasantest and finest chairman who ever employed me.

It is twenty-nine years since I made that huge mistake at Derby and dropped two divisions to pick up my career in the third, travelling from Derby to the south coast. Despite the luxury of life in a posh hotel, it was still a chore to be away from Barbara and the children for several days on end. The kids' schooling meant that Barbara had to spend the majority of the time in the East Midlands. To begin with, Taylor was not around a lot, either. But I knew all this when we accepted Bamber's offer. I was not a man to go for a stop-gap post, never was and never could be. If I went in for something, it was with both eyes open and fully intent on committing myself totally to the task.

Bamber was the owner of a local nightclub so it was

159

inevitable that I brushed shoulders occasionally with showbiz people, including the lovely Dora Bryan who told us we could stay at her house in Brighton, Bruce Forsyth and the late Les Dawson. He left a telling impression on me when we were introduced by limiting our conversation to, 'Sorry, but I'm bloody well working.' And so he was. He was perfectly entitled to avoid pointless niceties at a time like that. Maybe I learned it from him; throughout the rest of my career in management, I had no time for polite chat when I was working.

It was by no means the only lesson I learned at Brighton. A 4–0 defeat by Walton and Hersham in the first round of the FA Cup was the first time any such thing had happened to me. My system had to get used to shocks. The scoreline of a home game against Bristol Rovers is etched in my mind as deeply as the two European Cup finals I was to win years later. We lost 8–2, and I'll tell you why we lost 8–2. It was not just because we had a terrible team with players who couldn't play. It was because they were petrified of me.

There is still a wrong impression about Brian Clough in English football. Too many idiots, some of them respected observers of the game, still argue that fear was my biggest weapon as a manager, a weapon and a means of motivation. That's another chip on my shoulder that has grown bigger in retirement. Of all the things said about me, of all the attempts to explain my success, that one is the biggest load of crap I have ever heard in my life. My teams, my Derby and Nottingham Forest teams, could not have played the kind of football they produced if they'd been frightened. There was not an ounce of fear in their game – they played with a kind of freedom and sheer joy that you rarely see from teams today.

I tried to avoid instilling fear rather than imposing it but that day at Brighton when we conceded eight goals, I knew they were frightened because they were all inferior players who had never known success and never encountered anybody like me. If I'd told them to cut their wrists I believe every single one of them would have done it right there in the dressing room and that was before the match! They were rigid, virtually frozen to the spot by fear and out on the pitch there was so much apprehension that they couldn't lift their legs, let alone raise a gallop.

Offers of alternative employment came along. I could have been an MP after receiving a second invitation from the Labour party to contest Manchester's Moss Side against young Winston Churchill; and I was offered the national team manager's job in Iran. This was in the days of the Shah. There was much for me to admire in that country, not least his Thoroughbred horses, but the life was not for me; nor for that matter was my life in Brighton. I was too often away from Barbara and the bairns, and for the first time, I sensed that Peter Taylor was not quite as full of himself as usual, or particularly happy in his work.

As luck would have it, the big offer came along. Don Revie was leaving Leeds to be manager of England and they wanted me to take over. I jumped at it but Taylor didn't. I've thought a lot about his reasons for saying 'we'll be fine' at Brighton, urging me to give it another season and insisting he would 'stay put' when I demanded a clear answer. I've thought about it long and hard in retirement. I discovered Mike Bamber had offered him more money to stay and I always knew Pete fancied a crack at management in his own right. He never did learn about that, did he? He had another crack at solo management at Derby after retiring from Forest, and it was never going to work out for him there, either. So, just as it was his initial instinct for us to walk away from all we had created at Derby, it was Pete who broke up our partnership. I went; he stayed down south.

Money would have got Pete to Leeds. It might have cost their chairman Manny Cussins a few grand but money could have lured him to Elland Road. I think one reason he wanted to stay on the south coast was because I had just helped get his daughter a job on the local paper. She was happy, Pete had everybody together in his apartment in Brighton and, as I was well aware, he'd always wanted to be beside the seaside. Even in our early days together, whenever conversation drifted towards eventual retirement Pete would say, 'I'm going to keep heading south every year. In the end after landing a job on the coast, that's where I'll retire. That's my ambition. And if Scarborough was in the south, I'd pack in and go and live there right now.' Maybe it was because Pete hailed from Nottingham. Can you get further away from the seaside than that? Strange that he would later abandon his intended 'retirement home' in Brighton and return to his roots, joining up with me again and going on to achieve our greatest moments together with Forest.

At least I had a chance of getting a look at the European Cup with Leeds. Pete had no chance of cracking management on his own, however appealing life in Brighton might have been. He had no chance whatsoever.

As it turned out, I had no chance either, not the way I went about taking over from Don Revie. I don't know whether my sacking after forty-four days was a record but it was no real surprise in view of the way I tackled the job, trying to do in minutes what should have taken months, maybe even years. I went at it like a bull at a fence. I rushed it. Now I realise that I blew it. I've said before that they disliked me at Elland Road, the majority of the players that is, but I reckon they actually hated my guts. Reflection tells me that the biggest mistake of all was my eagerness to accept the job in the first place. Leeds weren't for me and I wasn't for them.

You don't need reminding of too much of the detail or the way I had criticised that Leeds side, one of the most cynical and dirtiest as well as talented I had ever seen. I was a big admirer of Revie's but I had serious reservations about the way the 'family', as he called it, sometimes went about their business. Leeds, with Billy Bremner, Johnny Giles, Norman Hunter, big Jack Charlton and Allan Clarke up front, had players in every position to make other managers envious. They were a wonderful side who set a wonderful example for the most part. In fact, I had the impression that Leeds could have been more dazzling still had Revie been less systematic and allowed them off that tight rein of his.

They paid a price for their cynicism, their intimidation of referees and the over-physical element of their game. It undermined public respect for what they achieved. They became notorious and are still remembered for being 'dirty Leeds' rather than for the terrific football they played. That's a shame, but it is also a kind of justice.

My criticism of them meant I was confronted by a seething, resentful, spiteful dressing room when I arrived on my first morning, fresh from holiday in Cala Millor, with my boys Simon and Nigel for company. It makes me flinch just a little to this day, remembering that scene. It was like walking straight into an ambush. You could have cut the atmosphere with a knife. Revie might have left but his presence and influence was everywhere. I was daft enough to believe that a bit of tongue-in-cheek banter might ease the situation – a word about Hunter and Giles clattering people, a wisecrack to point out that if a racehorse had had as many injuries as Scottish winger Eddie Gray he'd have been put down months ago. Nobody was laughing. It's a well-known saying of mine that football management can be a lonely job. It was never lonelier than at Elland Road where I was made to feel like the arch enemy. I felt something worse than misery – I was desolate.

The extent of my misery possibly impaired my better judgement because I ignored the sound advice of scout Tony Collins who urged me to take my time with the changes I had in mind. He warned me not to be too hasty, that Leeds didn't take kindly to anybody who appeared to be rocking their boat. I just ploughed on through the waves and was determined that one or two were going overboard. Despite his international caps for Scotland, I believed we needed a better goalkeeper than David Harvey. I wanted Giles out of the place too. I certainly knew he had been Revie's recommendation for the manager's job and he was extremely influential. The other players had enormous respect for the little Irishman and with good reason. My plan to flog him to Tottenham backfired when Giles turned down the chance to go to White Hart Lane, spurning an opportunity to be schooled as the likely successor to Bill Nicholson.

Never has a man given me less time to get him to know and to like me, or dislike me for that matter. I'm sure it wasn't anything personal; it was just that he thought he was going to get the Leeds job and knew that the rest of the players were in favour of him getting it. Instead, the club brought me in – not just an outsider, gate-crashing the happy family, but an enemy, a man who was against almost everything that Leeds stood for. If Bremner had disliked me – and I don't think he did – he would have let me know straight out. Having begun to wonder why Leeds had appointed me at all, I asked Manny Cussins. He said, 'When a group of players is prepared to go on strike for a manager, that manager has got to be good' – a reference to Derby of course. He could also have said that any manager who walked out on a team as good as that one at Derby couldn't have been much of a judge.

I never did get to know John Giles, still don't. In view of all the circumstances, I talked less at Leeds than in any job I ever had. I think I must have been waiting for their fabled professionalism to show itself. What I did know about Giles was the extent of his talent in midfield. He could grab hold of a match, tuck it in his back pocket and carry it around with him. He didn't need to find space; it was as if space found him. It was always available to him – a tribute to his perception, footballing brain and the wonderful natural instinct that separates great players from the rest. He could play a pass of the most delicate nature and perfect precision. He had the reputation of being one who could deliver immediate justice on the pitch.

Most little players were aggressive players, probably making up for their limited physique. Bremner had his nasty side, too. Bobby Collins, Giles's predecessor as the fulcrum of the team, was another and I had two similar types in Willie Carlin and Archie Gemmill. For all that aspect of his game, I respected Giles because of his tremendous ability. His knowledge of the game was proved in his short time in management at West Brom and I wish now that things could have been different at Leeds and we could have got our heads and our talents together over a longish period of time. Who knows, Giles could have become my Peter Taylor. He'd certainly have needed to get that close if he was going to have any input into the management of Leeds United while I was there. Who knows what might have happened if we'd got together.

I know one thing – had Taylor not opted to remain at Brighton he would have twigged the situation, possibly within minutes. He could sniff them out because he was what I called a sitter-back. He'd take a look at the situation from a quiet corner or in a crowded dressing room. He'd look for telltale signs that indicated whether someone was with us or against us. It didn't take him long and he was rarely wrong.

I wasn't exactly a mug in the game. After all, I'd won the championship at Derby in such a short time and was still under forty years of age. I hadn't broken any eggs at Brighton but that didn't really matter because, football-wise, nobody knew where Brighton was. But I felt hostility from just about every quarter at Leeds apart from Allan Clarke, 'Sniffer' as they affectionately called the England international striker.

I suppose there were others who didn't necessarily dislike me

– Bremner, for a start. What a player! What a tragedy that he was to die so suddenly and so young. Bill Shankly always rated Billy among the greats and I go along with that. But Clarkey was the one who offered me some warmth and comfort. He was the one who showed genuine friendship, and friendship was in extremely short supply.

Those people who believe I instilled fear at the clubs I worked for should have seen me during those forty-four days. I couldn't have imposed fear at Leeds if I'd tried. They had endured and overcome all the fear, apprehension and uncertainty that go through the minds of successful players during the winning of championships, cups and European tournaments. Leeds had done it all; they were the kings of English football. They weren't threatened, any of them, because they felt they were bigger than me. When I went to Derby and Brighton, everybody looked up to me. When I went to Leeds, the boot was on the other foot. I was the one looking up because they were the stars – internationals wherever you cared to look, on the teamsheet and off it.

For all that, I knew I was inheriting a side on its last legs. They were getting old together. Revie had left several contracts still to be negotiated and players around the thirty mark worry about their futures. But nobody at Leeds was more worried than I was. I didn't feel the remotest connection with the team. Just before the Charity Shield match at Wembley, the game between the champions and FA Cup winners that traditionally kicks off the season, I telephoned Revie and told him to lead them out because Leeds was his team not mine, even though I knew I would be passing up the chance to march out alongside Bill Shankly and his beloved Liverpool. Revie, of course, declined my invitation. Invitation? I suppose I was thinking more of myself than of him at the time. It was all part of that feeling of detachment from the club who had hired me as the best man for their job.

If I felt sorry for myself that day, I was to feel even sorrier for Kevin Keegan. You'll remember the famous picture of him, flinging down his shirt as he was sent off. Now for Keegan to throw down the cherished shirt of Liverpool the circumstances had to be extreme and they were. For once, I fully understood the reaction of a player who had taken too much intimidation and physical bruising. Bremner, my captain, had whacked him uphill and down dale. With little or no protection from the referee, Keegan snapped. He could take no more. He retaliated and got himself sent off alongside Bremner. Oh, what a lovely day that turned out to be!

You never need friends more than when you're lonely. Take my time? I couldn't get friendly faces into Elland Road quickly enough. I signed John McGovern and John O'Hare from Derby and Duncan McKenzie, that flamboyant striker – eccentric may be a better description – from Forest.

McGovern's talents were not as obvious as those of the other two – his immense physical and moral courage, his willingness to put in his lot whatever the circumstances, his total trustworthiness and reliability, his ability to play a pass. They humiliated him at Leeds, players and crowd alike. John was to have the last laugh in years to come as the player who twice accepted the European Cup as the winning captain. But at the time of his Leeds experience, it was difficult if not impossible to imagine that anything could compensate for what that lot put him through, and it had been my fault because I was the one who put him in what became an intolerable situation.

I was still determined to steer the boat through the stormy waters even if it meant rocking the bloody thing from side to side in the process. I was convinced we needed a better goalkeeper and that's what sank my boat altogether. Typical me, I informed Harvey that I wanted to sign Peter Shilton. The balloon went up, the boat went down – forty-four days, over and out.

Thank heavens for Colin Lawrence. It was my dear friend Colin who helped me come to terms with the fact that I had been sacked. In denting my ego and showing me the door, Leeds United did me the biggest favour of my professional life.

Realising that the situation was reaching a head, I had Colin with me at Elland Road the day I was bombed out. I had no time for the legal profession in those days. I treated lawyers with contempt, believing that all they were good at was sending bills. Fortunately for me, Colin knew a solicitor called Charles Dodsworth, from York I believe. Colin asked him to come to the ground and it was because of his presence and the legal document he helped to draw up that Leeds finished up paying off the contract and all the tax.

I had signed a four-year contract and told Manny Cussins, 'You'll have to square it up.'

'Right,' Cussins replied, but I bet he didn't realise what he'd let himself in for; 'grossing-up' I think it was called, or something like that. Whatever the term, what I do know is that Leeds signed an agreement that committed them to paying all my tax for the following three years. Instead of costing them £25,000 as a pay-off, it finally worked out at £98,000. I came out of Elland Road a little crestfallen professionally, but quite rich. I was financially secure for the first time in my life and I knew that whatever job came my way, I would be able to do it with complete peace of mind.

Colin Lawrence was a dear, dear friend – a loyal pal who stuck with me through thick and thin and whose sudden death in July 2001 not only shook me to the core but left a gap in my life that can never ever be filled. I had known Colin since my Derby days. He wasn't a hanger-on as some people turned out to be; he wasn't friendly simply because I was what he would call famous as the manager of the local football club. A rotund, jolly figure with a smile as wide as his ample frame, Colin's genuineness was as big as the man himself. He never missed coming to see me, especially in my retirement. He drove me wherever I wanted to go, providing it wasn't the off-licence. He was as keen as anybody to get me off the dreaded drink, and he wasn't afraid to tell me. That's what true friends are prepared to do – raise the subject you might want to talk about least of all.

Thankfully, when I think of Colin I can smile. We hadn't been in Derby very long when he arrived on our doorstep one day out of the blue. I was at work but Colin explained to Barbara that he lived nearby and had a friend visiting him that weekend – Gordon Turner, the former Luton footballer who was, sadly, suffering from motor neurone disease. He wondered whether it would be possible for Gordon to meet me. Typically, Colin Lawrence was being kind and thinking of others.

Next day he popped round with a pair of nylons for Barbara and we all sat and chatted as he told us about his job as a sales rep. I met poor Gordon Turner that weekend and Colin was such a thoroughly nice man that he was immediately welcomed into my family and the close friendship developed, for which I will be eternally grateful.

Colin, like me, bought an apartment in Cala Millor where, along with his wife Wendy, Barbara and I spent so many idyllic times. He moved on to owning some post-office/newsagent's shops, which remain in the family. He loved his retirement, and relished the thought of taking me to television studios and radio stations, meeting the famous – the good and even the bad and the ugly.

Ironically, Barbara and I had just arrived in Cala Millor when we got a phone call from our Simon back in England saying that Colin had died. He hadn't been home long, having spent three weeks with Wendy at his apartment in Majorca. He and Wendy had had a wonderful time. He'd returned a few pounds heavier but happy.

'Colin Lawrence has died.' I'll never forget hearing those

words. I still don't want to believe them although I know they're true. Sometimes, even now, at around half past ten in the morning I expect Colin to come breezing in with that big round happy face, casting a lovely ray of sunshine into my life on the dullest, rainiest days. In all honesty, I don't have that many people I can regard as genuine close friends and I miss him. He was part of my world, a near and extremely dear part, and that world will never be quite the same again.

CHAPTER 14

I SHOULD HAVE
TRIED TO UNDERSTAND

The feeling of independence and security that Leeds gave me together with the sack was a big factor in winning so much during my eighteen years as manager of Nottingham Forest, not least the league championship and two European Cups. It meant I could approach the job without a financial care in the world. I could follow my instincts and hunches and gut feelings and to hell with the consequences should it all go wrong.

Not much did go wrong, of course. It was success virtually all the way once I'd settled in, sorted things out and freshened up a decaying club that was dying on its feet when I breezed into the place in January 1975. They were struggling too close to the wrong end of the second division, with not enough players in the dressing room who could kick a ball properly or head a ball adequately, let alone with the ability to play the game. Isn't it odd to look back to that time with the reminder that when I arrived at the City Ground, Martin O'Neill and John Robertson were among the players who were up for sale. Look at them now, doing great things together in charge of Celtic. How times do change.

The Leeds experience, for all the benefit it did my bank

account and peace of mind, also savaged my ego. The sack does hurt, no matter how substantial the compensation money, which goes some way towards cushioning the fall. So it was some time before I was able to walk on water even though my very first game in charge was an FA Cup replay at Tottenham that we won against the odds. We followed it up with another victory at Fulham on the Saturday, but if the people of Nottingham, the Forest supporters, believed the miracle was happening immediately, they were in for a rude awakening. By the end of that initial season, we'd won just three out of seventeen matches, including that Cup-tie at White Hart Lane. We were bloody fortunate not to get relegated to the third division.

A sorting-out process was necessary, with bodies in as well as out. You don't change a stagnant pool by staring at the water; you have to disturb it – eliminate the pollution and introduce the elements that can make it fresh again. Well, I turfed out the crap and added some players who could actually play football to operate alongside the likes of Tony Woodcock, Ian Bowyer, O'Neill and Robertson, and the right-back, Viv Anderson.

Little things, the odd moment or two from the past, give you a glow of satisfaction on rainy days in retirement when there is little else to do but sit and ponder. Going back to Leeds to re-sign John O'Hare and John McGovern is a memory that still manages to keep me warm when the central heating's gone off. Leeds' directors didn't know what they had in their possession with those two. That's why I was able to buy them back for less than I'd forked out on Leeds' behalf in the first place. They were familiar faces, and had undoubted ability. A manager cannot surround himself with too many people of genuine calibre, which was why Jimmy Gordon, sacked by Leeds when they kicked me out, was recruited to the ranks at the City Ground. Trainer? Coach? The job title didn't matter to me. Coach, if you like. Whatever the handle, Jimmy was brought in because he was as honest as the day is long, knew the game inside out and was good with players. I'd seen all that in him during my younger days at Middlesbrough where Jimmy was among the leading professionals.

I suppose eighth place wasn't too bad for my first complete season in the job but there was still an important element missing. Peter Taylor had staked everything on promotion at Brighton and had just failed. Almost as much for his ability to make me laugh as for his ability as a talent spotter, for whatever reason, for all reasons, Taylor's contribution to the revolution that took place at Nottingham Forest cannot be overestimated. The flight to Majorca to see him at his villa was possibly the most productive flight I ever made. His coyness was just a front. Despite that ambition of his to retire by the seaside, I knew he would leap at the chance to help manage Nottingham Forest, his home-town club, no matter how far it happened to be from the nearest beach. Once again, I wasn't wrong.

The memories from the City Ground are many and marvellous apart from that awful, avoidable last season of mine. It is easy to confine your thoughts to the good times, the success, the uplifting feeling you get as a manager at the moment of triumph. But it is dishonest to ignore times you would rather forget – the occasions when you would do things differently if you could do them all over again, when you look back and think to yourself, 'I wish I hadn't dealt with the situation in that way.'

I'm thinking of Justin Fashanu. I've thought about Justin Fashanu quite a lot over the past four years or so. I used to think about him with anger. I was angry that I allowed Pete Taylor to persuade me into believing the lad was worth £1 million of Nottingham Forest's money – paid in the belief that he could be part of another fine side to follow the one that won those two European Cups. We were wrong, not for the first time or the last. We were wrong to believe that the striker who made his name with the 'Match of the Day' Goal of the Season against Liverpool could be part of any team we had in mind. He turned out to be absolutely hopeless but by the time it all came to a head, Taylor had gone. He had asked me to negotiate his retirement and walked away from the game with more than £25,000 as a golden handshake – only to bloody well walk back again that summer of '82 as manager of Derby of all places, that special club of ours, the very club that had made several unsuccessful attempts to lure the pair of us back on previous occasions.

Pete left me with one or two of his dodgier protégés but Fashanu was the worst case. He couldn't get us a goal of any shape or form let alone one that was regarded as the best of the season. Not only did he disappoint me, he infuriated me, time and again – for missing chances, for chucking his boots into the crowd, for getting himself sent off on a number of occasions, for leaving his Jeep in prohibited areas so many times and getting so many parking tickets that I think the local authority were considering appointing his own personal traffic-warden.

You probably know the story of the day he came to me and confided, 'I've found God,' and I told him, 'Good – you should get him to sign your cheques.' He was a confused young man who probably thought that joining the born-again Christians would help him sort out his life. I was certainly no help, not when he was failing to do the job I wanted him to do after investing so much of the club's money, and not when he seemed to be reeling from one avoidable problem to another, insisting he was genuine yet telling lie after lie.

It didn't help his cause when I began to hear he was a regular visitor at a club notorious for the gathering of homosexuals. It wasn't the fact that Fashanu was gay that concerned me; his sexuality alone was not the issue. I was brutally frank with him, though – too frank on one occasion. I asked him where he'd go for a loaf of bread or a joint of meat and when he gave the obvious replies I hit him with, 'So why is it that you are regularly seen in that poofs club in Nottingham?' His shrug of the shoulders was no answer and he continued to irritate me with his employment of a religious instructor and his own personal masseur.

A former boxer, Fash was an extremely articulate boy with a pleasant demeanour and likeable personality. If only he could have told the truth more often and faced facts about himself and his life. He seemed to carry so much baggage; nothing was ever straightforward or simple, certainly not when it came to sticking the ball in the net. I believe I'm right in saying he managed three goals in thirty-one league games – some return for a player who cost me a million quid.

So he had no chance the day he appeared at our training ground with one of his mates, the religious bloke or the masseur. He had to go. He had to go from my training ground and he had to go from my club. It's one of football's well-known training stories that I phoned the police and asked them to come and nick my own centre-forward. Actually, I just wanted him escorted away from the place and two coppers got the job done. I'm not sure Forest's loss was much of a gain for our neighbours Notts County but they took him. He didn't stay there long, either. But we'd seen him through the door, which was all that mattered to me. He didn't depart quite as spectacularly as he did one night in Spain. He was sharing a room with Viv Anderson and, waking up in the middle of a nightmare, he hurled himself like a missile through the wooden door, leaving it like one of those you see in a Tom and Jerry cartoon. But this wasn't make-believe, this happened for real.

None of it – the unorthodox lifestyle, the unfulfilled talent, if there was real talent there at all, or the sexuality that he tried to hide for so long – prepared me for the headlines in the summer of 1998 that recorded Justin Fashanu's terrible, lonely death. He was found hanged in a lock-up garage in London's East End. That shook me, stunned me. When you hear of a lad taking his own life in squalid circumstances like that, a lad you once worked with and were responsible for, you have to look back and wonder if you could have done things differently. I know now that I should have dealt with Fashanu differently, certainly with a little more compassion and understanding.

I didn't show much of that the day I had him removed from the training ground by two of the tiniest police officers in the Nottingham force. They were so small I'm surprised they qualified for a uniform. When Fashanu at first refused to leave, I resorted to a tactic that had been used against me countless times as a player. I kicked him in the calf. Now when you get kicked in the calf it makes you bend the leg slightly.

'If you don't get off this training pitch,' I yelled at him, 'I'm going to kick you in the other one and reduce you to the same size as these two policemen.'

Typical me at the time, but I'd had more than enough of an individual who had denied the truth about himself to such an extent that he once announced he was going to get married. He even brought the girl down from London. She was stunning.

'I'd like you to meet my girlfriend,' he said to me, and added, 'I'm engaged.'

I went to meet her because that was part and parcel of my job as a manager – I used to encourage ladies into the ground and into relationships because I never found anything more beneficial to a footballer than a good and stable home life. I promoted it and encouraged young players to get married to settle down, and advised, 'Don't leave it too late before you have children.'

Fashanu's supposed fiancée was petite with high cheekbones, and absolutely beautiful. She made Elizabeth Taylor in her prime look like Dracula. I realised it was all a con, a charade, or at least that's what I believed and still do. It was Fashanu's way of trying to convince me he wasn't gay. That's how big a fraud I believed him to be.

Unless people come to terms with what they are they must suffer very, very long periods of loneliness and frustration. They daren't destroy the public perception of themselves, the image they promote. They are two people. They are what they are within themselves but when they open the door of the house and step outside they become what they want others to believe of them.

On reflection I don't believe I was wrong to confront him about his sexuality but I should have done it more privately. I did it in front of the other players and in front of almost anybody I talked to. I was extremely unkind to him. Barbara took me to task over it, pointing out that if he was that way inclined, that was his business, his life. He was entitled to be who and what he was. Barbara would not accept that I could make his private life a public matter.

Perhaps I should have employed one of the golden rules of my style of management – keeping things in-house. Nobody looks after his private life more than I do. Yes, I dropped a clanger with Fashanu. When Notts County took him for £25,000, I warned them he'd get their manager the sack. I had twigged him after a few weeks but I also helped destroy him as a player because I exposed him for what he was – a playboy rather than a footballer. He tried to portray the macho image but he wasn't macho, he was flamboyant.

For all that, I didn't treat him with the respect he deserved or give him the help that I gave to a lot of players who were better than him. I should have recognised his problems quicker and not broken ranks. I shouldn't have told people.

It was no surprise to me that he went to the United States eventually. I can't say I was particularly surprised to see his name linked with the alleged molesting of a seventeen-year-old boy, either. I don't know whether he was wanted by the American police but I do know Justin could have faced a long time behind bars if he'd been found guilty of sexual assault

177

charges there. Apparently, his suicide note included denials of the assault. We'll never know the truth of it – only that he returned to this country in a hurry and took his own life.

He had gone out of my life years earlier, of course. He had gone from my memory, too, because I had carried on trying to run a football club and that's enough for any man to think about. But to take his own life – that must have been through desperation or fear or loneliness, or a combination of all three. Whatever it was, he couldn't live with it. Perhaps he wasn't quite brave enough. Perhaps he should have declared himself a long time ago, 'come out' as they say these days – easy for me to say but it would have been hellishly difficult for him to do, especially as a professional footballer at the time.

When I am chastised by my dear wife about my treatment of Justin Fashanu, I agree with most of it, but I do feel I had a wee bit of justification, if only because he had tried to fool me and I saw through his make-believe. After his death, my sadness stemmed from the fact that I could have understood better than I did at the time he was with me at Forest, and possibly helped him. I had a responsibility towards him because he was under my jurisdiction as the manager of the club, and I gave him nothing.

C H A P T E R   1 5

OLD HABITS DIE HARD – AND LIVE ON AT CELTIC

Players didn't fall off trees to land at Nottingham Forest. We had to search for them, high and low. You name it, Taylor and I did it. There were long car journeys, sometimes to non-league matches, defying the elements on a piss-it-down Tuesday night somewhere. Often we also defied the majority opinion of others watching the man we had targeted.

If there was a magic formula to our style of management, we were the ones who invented it. We dragged the new recruits from all corners, nooks and crannies and the occasional dog track in our time. Frank Clark, a left-back, that rarest of breeds, came on a free transfer from Newcastle at the age of thirty-two – the bargain of all bargains. Larry Lloyd came from Coventry where he seemed to have disappeared after managing to earn himself an England cap or two at Liverpool. Kenny Burns came from Birmingham after Taylor had him shadowed to his favourite greyhound stadium and reported that the Scot with a harsh reputation for violence, drink and gambling was not that type of lad at all. I still talk to him from time to time to this day. Garry Birtles was signed from Long Eaton for about two grand, and Archie Gemmill was nicked

179

from Derby for twenty-five grand. Oh yes, and there was the small matter of £270,000 for Peter Shilton from Stoke. We were 'mad' in many people's eyes to spend a record fee on him but Taylor and I knew our history in advance. History now tells us that Shilton was worth twice the price. We weren't mad at all; we were magic.

You will notice from that handful of names, and there are too many others to mention, that there was a familiar, tried-and-trusted formula – a goalkeeper, two centre-halves in this instance, and a centre-forward. There they are. There's part of the secret, that's the framework, the backbone, those are the key components in the skeleton of any side.

Our conceit and fanaticism were vital as well. We needed the belief that we could do no wrong. Taylor may have been different from me but he was still a conceited man. It didn't come across publicly because he rarely opened his mouth but if ever he'd been offered a part in a film he'd have been the one with the gun. I'd have been the unfortunate so-and-so who was seen loading it and then handing it to the police, saying, 'This is the weapon I used to shoot the fella.'

That was the difference between us and it was a combination that worked brilliantly. I was totally blind to pitfalls and criticism; Peter was the shrewdy, slightly in the background if not the shadows. I've lost count of the number of occasions when he put up an idea and I followed it through in my inimitable, sod-the-lot-of-'em kind of way.

'Do you know what you're doing?' Pete would say.

'Of course I know what I'm bloody well doing.'

'Well, you'll never get away with that.'

One example, back in our Derby days, was the signing of David Nish, Leicester's left-back, another of those rarities, whom we turned into an international player. I actually gate-crashed a board meeting at Leicester – breezed straight in, large as life, and told them I'd come to sign Nish. Well, I had.

I wasn't in Leicester for a night out so I didn't see the point of beating about the bush. Whether those directors were so gobsmacked, so taken aback at the sudden arrival of this loud-mouthed impostor, I didn't know and I didn't give a toss. All that mattered was that we signed David Nish, just as we signed so many from right under other people's noses. I got away with it.

To be honest, I did ride the wind as a manager and at times too close to it. It didn't worry me because I didn't think I was doing anything wrong. I would never claim to be an angel but if I did offend people in the process of my work, I just wallowed in my conceit, believing nobody had been harmed. I certainly didn't harm anyone intentionally.

My manner and our success meant I made enemies and Taylor would say, 'You do know they don't like you, don't you?' He was talking about various people, other managers, directors, the authorities. 'They don't like you because they're jealous of you.' I didn't recognise that but Peter did. If I made enemies, it was because of our success, not because I'd done them out of ten quid or fiddled them at cards.

The point I'm coming to is that the Clough–Taylor managerial partnership was unique. It remains unique to this day, partly because we could not be copied and partly because if anybody had attempted it, they would have fallen flat on their faces. However, there is a partnership in British football management that bears a striking resemblance. Martin O'Neill and John Robertson might not be carbon copies of Clough and Taylor but they look like turning out to be pretty similar and the next best thing. What an impact they have had in two years at Parkhead with back-to-back league championships. Celtic have not dominated Scottish football in such a way for twenty years.

As I said, they were already at Forest when I bowled into the place, on the transfer list, fed up with the feeling of decline around the City Ground. They stayed because they had talent, and that talent was to help them win medals they can never have imagined they'd win in their weirdest dreams.

I've said often enough that I wasn't sure why I persevered with Robertson. At first sight he could have been the bloody groundsman rather than the outside-left who was going to make one of the goals and score the other that won the club those two European Cups in consecutive seasons. He was out of condition, overweight, ate too many chips, smoked too many fags, and the unshaven chin made him look as scruffy as the clothes he wore. If there was a player in the entire League who was slower than this lad and looked less like a professional footballer, I never saw him. Yet if you think David Beckham is fairly handy with his right foot, you should have seen the way Robbo eventually crossed a ball with his left – or his right if need be!

There was some indefinable quality about this Scottish scruff that persuaded me to think he might just be worth a chance. It certainly wasn't his initial attitude, which sometimes made me want to cry, but it might have had something to do with the fact that he could make you laugh.

So let's look at O'Neill and Robertson, let's see where the managerial expertise comes from. The easy answer is to say that they couldn't have worked with Taylor and me for so long without some of the magic rubbing off. I sure hope it did. One thing's for certain, they'd have had to be as thick as planks not to have learned something, picked up the odd tip or home truth here and there, and neither of them is thick.

O'Neill's intelligence was clear to me the moment I was confronted by him at Forest. He was bright, highly charged-up even on the field, hyper-active almost. If there was one player I clashed with more than any other during my time in management, it was Martin O'Neill. I think management has given him the platform on which he can display his intelligence.

He had an opinion on almost anything and was never slow to express it, not unlike the young Clough, I suppose, in the dressing room and on the training field at Middlesbrough all those years ago. He definitely had an inflated value of his own playing ability and I was constantly having to put him straight about that. No, he wasn't Stanley Matthews and Tom Finney rolled into one – he just thought he was. Whenever he was left out of the side at Forest his frustration used to boil over and pour out of him; he couldn't control it.

He had the ability to communicate better than most. He had been clever enough to go to university and gain qualifications and he repeatedly hung this over me like the sword of Damocles. That made me furious on two counts – a) I wasn't on his level, academically, and b) I didn't want it ramming down my throat every time he didn't appear on the teamsheet. He had to learn that I ran the show – it was as simple as that.

Of course he will have learned along the way. His intelligence, his knowledge of football and the way players behave and react, his ability and his willingness to display it for the manager he hardly regarded as his best friend – all of it would have been part of the learning process. He took his first steps into management with Grantham, and then, with so much success, Wycombe. He was briefly at Norwich and spectacularly at Leicester. That intelligence of his convinced him that he shouldn't replace me when I retired at the City Ground and that the Celtic job was the perfect calling after he'd taken Leicester just about as far as they are likely to go.

He'll have learned one of his sharpest lessons on 12 August 1978, not the Glorious Twelfth for Martin as things turned out although he did score two of the five goals we put past Ipswich in the Charity Shield at Wembley. I hauled him off. If he'd thought I was against him before that day, he must have been absolutely certain when I made my decision to substitute him.

Two goals to his name and he wanted to be a bigger hero still. He wanted a bloody hat-trick.

'Gerrim off,' I snapped at Jimmy Gordon alongside me on the Wembley bench.

'You can't do it.'

'Can't I? If you don't get O'Neill off that pitch right now, I'll sack you.'

It was unusual to talk to Jimmy like that. Given our background at Middlesbrough – him among the senior professionals and me still wearing L plates – I regarded and treated him like my elder brother. I paid him as much respect as anybody ever paid any coach. Anyway, he did as I asked, or demanded, and O'Neill came off. He didn't say a word until after the match and then I knew it was coming.

'Why did you bring me off?'

'To save money for the FA,' I told him. 'The way the match was developing they'd have needed to chuck on an extra ball – one for everybody else as well as the one you were keeping to yourself.'

'Well,' he protested, 'I had got two goals.'

'I know – but you weren't going to get a third by playing on your own. That was a certainty and that's why you had to come off.'

Of course he didn't like it. Players never do like decisions that go against them, decisions that let them know the truth. But they do remember them and for any player contemplating a career in management, those are the decisions most worth remembering. O'Neill just wouldn't give the ball to anybody. He was after his third goal but in looking for it he had stopped playing for the team. We were playing Ipswich off the pitch. I don't know what the biggest score ever was for a Charity Shield but we were threatening to break all records. Nevertheless, even though victory was assured against a very accomplished side, O'Neill's selfishness still had to be eliminated in the wider interests of the team. It took him weeks and weeks to get over it.

There were many times when I clashed with him, usually when I left him out of the side, and I was forever hearing him moan, 'I might as well pack my bags and go back to university.' I heard it once too often and pulled him in front of all the other players.

'Martin,' I said, 'I've done you a big favour.'

'What's that, Boss?' It was a growl or a sulk more than the civilised tone I was entitled to from an educated young man.

'I've arranged that flight for you back to Ireland and I've organised a place at university. Get on it.'

He never mentioned university again. Eventually, despite our clashes, he did become an integral part of the side but, for somebody so bright, it surprised me that I had to teach him the game. He didn't know it at first, not properly. He finished up as second-highest goalscorer one season and he might have been our top scorer but he didn't know where those goals were coming from. He hadn't twigged, until I pointed it out, that most of those goals could be traced to the feet of John Robertson.

'Your goals are coming from the left. You're standing there on your own when that ball comes to you because the opposition have been drawn to the magnet on our left-wing. That's why you're getting so many chances.'

I had to explain things like that to him. It took him a couple of years into his managerial career before he asked John Robertson, 'What was all that the gaffer used to shout at me – "Get the ball"? He used to shout it at me all the time and always after we'd scored.'

'If we had the ball, the other side hadn't got it,' Robbo replied. 'Simple as that.' Robbo had known what I meant.

Martin began to twig daft little things like that, familiar phrases and sayings he had heard from me almost on a day-to-day basis. It took him years to cotton on to the jargon and the importance of possession. A team can't play if it doesn't have the ball. He was puzzled by another regular cry from me in the dug-out. 'Stop that bloody ball going in the box,' I'd shout time after time. Robbo, I gather, had to explain, 'Where's the goal? In the penalty area. Well, if our team make sure the ball doesn't go into our box, there's a good chance it won't go in our net.'

It will all have become second nature to Martin by now. He will say things, do things, almost without thinking.

I'm certain he will still reflect from time to time on the day I denied him his place in the 1979 European Cup final. It was in Munich against Malmo, the Swedish champions. I'm sure Archie Gemmill still resents that big decision of mine because I left him out as well. Everybody wants to play in a match like that. Players who are not fit will say they are, so, yet again, it all comes down to the judgement of the man in charge.

No decision was necessary as far as Frank Clark was concerned – he had been ruled out already – but O'Neill and Gemmill had been trying to work off their injuries and insisted they were fine. Not in my book, they weren't. They were doing what I would have done as a player in the same circumstances. I would have insisted I was fit even if I couldn't walk, let alone run. They were borderline but my hunch was not to risk either of them so I told them they were out. Hard decisions have to be taken. They're the ones that separate good managers from rotten managers.

We were sitting on the grass that day, me squatting on a football with all the players in front of me. I made sure none of them had the chance to sneak up behind me and kick the ball away because that had happened to me before and it bloody well hurts your backside. Archie insisted he was 'absolutely perfect' and, if I remember correctly, Martin answered my inquiry about his fitness by saying, 'I'm as right as rain, Gaffer.'

'Oh,' I said, 'I'm absolutely delighted. So everybody's fit. Smashing. But you two are not playing.'

They thought I was kidding. They both had hamstring problems and ought to have known what was coming – those rules again. If somebody had a hamstring problem and said he was fit, I invariably ordered two more weeks' rest. I'd have a word with the physio on a Thursday and if he said the lad was fit, I would still order another couple of weeks. It meant missing one more match but two weeks was invaluable for anybody recovering from an injury.

Archie's response was typical of the miserable little bugger – little, perhaps, but big enough to take the disappointment. He said something like, 'Fuck you, then. If you're not playing me, you're not playing me.' I know what Martin said – nothing. Again, it took him weeks to get over it. He avoided me at every opportunity but once our victory celebrations were over back home, it was the close season and he was away playing for Northern Ireland – not a lot, mind, because he broke down with, you've guessed it, a hamstring problem.

He got his resentment out of his system during the summer. He needed to because he had enough to worry about, trying to convince me he was worth a place in my team the following season. He managed it twenty-eight times in the League but scored just three goals, the same number, would you believe, as Larry Lloyd – the lumbering centre-half. We surrounded Lloyd with people who could play and got so much out of him that he finished up in the England team again only to make a balls of it and not get selected again.

Martin was fit enough, and had obviously done enough, for me to pick him for that second European Cup final in Madrid against Kevin Keegan's lot, Hamburg. It was before that game that he and the rest of them learned an unorthodox but effective way of preparing a football team for a big event. There are times, particularly at the end of a long, hard season, when players have had enough of training. What they want most is a break, time to relax and put their feet up. I'll bet Martin remembers well enough what we did in the week prior to beating Hamburg at the Bernabeu Stadium. I'm sure he learned the value of that lovely little break in Cala Millor, busy doing nothing. They were given no orders other than to relax completely and behave like responsible professionals. There was to be no training, no deadlines, no booze restrictions, providing they had a good lie-in to sleep off any hangover and didn't bother me with their bad heads.

You can spot the players who've done their bit in a full season just by looking at their faces – pale, hollow-cheeked and with eyes deep in their sockets. A beer is a better proposition than a ball for them at a time like that. I know one thing, my team welcomed the return of a ball to their feet that night in the Spanish capital. Despite injuries that cost us the services of Trevor Francis, whose header had won us the trophy a year earlier, we saw off Keegan and his new mates. We overcame the suffocating heat and we retained European football's most prestigious trophy thanks to the only goal of an ordinary game – from John Robertson's right foot.

There was a controversial aftermath and O'Neill and Robertson were in the middle of it. They were among the bunch who defied my refusal to let them leave the team hotel and travel miles into Madrid to join the wives and girlfriends and club staff who were staying in the city. I wasn't having Forest's sense of togetherness broken by anybody, especially on an occasion like that. My decision to take their winners' medals away from them couldn't have stuck but I was very close to doing it anyway. You can't have players defying your instructions, not even when they've just conquered Europe, so they had to be fined.

It was all part of the learning process that some absorb and others don't. I knew that O'Neill would stay in football because he was absorbing everything and it was clear to me that he would have too much to offer for the game to let him go. This was not an individual who would hang up his boots and disappear, not after living with me for a few years and all the tips he must have picked up. I also knew those who wouldn't make it if ever they tried their hand at management. Frank Clark was one, despite him making an impression at Leyton Orient, and taking over from me at Forest and putting them back in the Premiership for a spell. Once he took his boots off he reverted back to being Frank, strumming his guitar and smiling. We loved him – everybody loved Frank Clark – but management, certainly team management, just wasn't in him as far as I could see. He is far better suited to the administrative side to the business.

Trevor Francis was another. I've often described him as being too nice a bloke to be a manager. Also, if he was good at one thing apart from playing, it was crossing the 't's and dotting the 'i's on contracts. He always seemed to get a longer contract than anybody else.

There's nothing worse than a great performer losing some of his public appeal when he puts on a different hat. Francis in management was like watching Frank Sinatra attempting to become a juggler and dropping the balls all over the stage. Trevor didn't need to think all that much as a player because he could run like the wind, cross a ball at full pace and get his fair share of goals. He wasn't injured all that much because he was so quick and so nimble. But none of those attributes were of any use to him in management. Where's he been? He was at Queens Park Rangers, then spent four years at Sheffield Wednesday where he didn't do too badly, especially in Cup competitions. After that he was at Birmingham for nearly six years without managing to pull off promotion to the top division, and now he's at Crystal Palace. So he's had a few years, here and there, and I think we're still waiting for him to prove he can be a top-notch manager.

Martin O'Neill was a man of the world in a young man's clothes. He had an awareness of life beyond his years; his awareness of football couldn't fail to develop while he worked with me and once he put his own interpretation of management into practice. He started at Grantham out of necessity. He was hardly likely to have the big clubs clamouring because he wasn't exactly the biggest name in the game. Without being derogatory or rude, Northern Irish international caps are not the be-all and end-all. Martin had sixty-four of them by the time we'd finished with him and he'd ended his playing days via Norwich, Manchester City and Notts County. Gaining an Irish cap is not quite like climbing Everest. The scarcity of players meant the good ones tended to be capped a great deal. Apart from his caps and the bit of glory he gained with Forest, he wasn't that well known within the game.

It wasn't planned, the Grantham job. It wasn't a case of 'I'll start at the bottom and work my way up'. There's another comparison with me – I didn't plan going into management at Hartlepools, either. It's a bit like a drowning man. If you can't swim, you grab anything. I grabbed Hartlepools, Martin clutched Grantham and we both survived – eventually to look back and be glad that we learned our trade at the foot of the ladder. He has also reached the top because that's what happens with talent.

His ability began to show itself at Wycombe, the little club he led into the Football League and swept to promotion. It was inevitable that Forest would want him as my successor but I understood perfectly when he rejected the chance. He would have weighed up the pros and cons. Not many people would have wanted to follow me, anyway, particularly at Forest who were never what you would call a big club. To think that as a player I was watched by 30,000 people at Notts County but I couldn't get 30,000 to come to watch Forest even in a semi-final of the European Cup.

Martin would have weighed everything up, knowing that it would be one long battle at the City Ground, and finished up going to another East Midlands club after an extremely short spell at Norwich. He went to Leicester – a similar club to Forest only worse. They have never struck me as the most ambitious of clubs either, but Martin did what all promising managers do. He held his own. Then he took them to the Premiership and into Europe having won the Worthington Cup twice – the one they used to call the League Cup, the trophy we won so many times at Forest that we regarded it as much our property as the tea-urn in the guest room.

He'd had John Robertson alongside him all the way from Grantham. They were always mates as players. When I arrived at Forest they had something else in common apart from being on the transfer list – neither of them was in the team. Some people raised their eyebrows when they paired-up in non-league management in Maggie Thatcher's home town. I didn't. When you enter an unknown world, which management was to Martin O'Neill, irrespective of the club or the level, you take someone you know. You take a pal. Just like I took Peter Taylor, Martin O'Neill took his best mate.

If you ever need someone to relax with – and there are countless times in football management when the need for relaxation is vital – I can think of few better companions than Robertson. Sometimes a manager needs to switch off, even if it's only for five minutes over a cup of coffee, and you need to feel safe because there are too many occasions when you are consumed by panic. If you have never experienced real panic, I can tell you it is not a pleasant feeling at all.

Football management can be a torment, even to those who are deservedly regarded as the best. All it takes is a difficult spell, a poor run of results, a lousy season and sometimes you don't know which door to walk through, who to shout at or clout, which pen to pick up, which bell to push, which player to pick, which telephone to answer. Panic. Then John Robertson walks in. Panic over. He can evaporate it like a magician. He would have made a good street performer. He'd just amble up with a fag in his mouth and change the atmosphere, the entire environment, almost without knowing it. He could dry tears, make sad people happy and complaining people realise how lucky they really were. He would make you smile, relax you completely and it wouldn't take longer than five minutes. He is one of that rare breed of men who can cheer you up without trying. Honest, you couldn't fall out with John Robertson if he was knocking off your wife!

Pete Taylor was another who could change your mood from depression to delight, lethargy to laughter, in a trice. Taylor was more of a hardened professional than Robertson but as relaxation therapists, if that's an appropriate term for somebody who spreads laughter, they are exactly the same. It's another oddity of life that Taylor and I should fall out over Robbo when Pete nicked him and took him to Derby. It was a stupid reason for not talking until it was too late but there it is, another reason for regret. When we were still on speaking terms, Pete had said to me on several occasions, 'Bye, but it's a bloody lonely job, in't it?' I'll tell you this, with all his success at Celtic, winning the Scottish title two years on the trot, there would have been times when O'Neill felt lonely. He'll have felt far less lonely thanks to Robbo being around. It's helped him seize the big chance.

Martin did have one thing going for him when he arrived up there in Glasgow – he didn't need to work too hard to get fans to come to the ground. All he had to do was tell them it's a Saturday! What a luxury, massive home crowds virtually guaranteed. The crowds are absolutely guaranteed these days because O'Neill and Robertson have done their stuff, and in a way not dissimilar to the way they did it at Leicester. They spot talent others seem to be unaware of; they know what the team needs and how and where to buy replacements without always having to pay a fortune; and they get the best out of the squad they've assembled. That's management. That's what Peter Taylor and I did as a partnership – not always with the approval of our employers or the establishment but always knowing exactly why we were doing it.

The example of John Robertson is an important one in all this. As I've said, he didn't look anything like a professional athlete when I first clapped eyes on him. In fact, there were times when he barely resembled a member of the human race. He's the only man I've ever known who insisted on wearing suede shoes even when there was no suede visible to the naked eye. They were so old, shabby little bits of leather that used to be suede shoes, but he wore them week in week out. They became a household joke at the City Ground. Taylor used to hold them up in the dressing room. It was all he needed to do to have everybody laughing. Robbo's trousers never fitted him either. He had trousers with flared bottoms before they were invented, and he had big legs for such a short lad. But we're talking about one of the most talented footballers I ever saw.

What God gave him was the same dimensions all the way down from his neck. His neck, his chest, his stomach, his thighs and his calves were all the same size! If you'd melted him down and he lost weight from everywhere – a bit from his calves, a bit from his thighs, a bit from his middle – he would have been three stone lighter but exactly the same shape.

You should have seen him get on the coach. He didn't jump on or spring on with the air and surefootedness of an athlete; he waddled up to it, put his left foot first on the bottom step and was the only player to use the handrails to help himself through the door. Oh yeah, and you'd occasionally see him squash his fag under his other foot. He used to think I hadn't seen him smoking. I didn't have to see him – I could smell him from the other end of the car park. To think this was the player who won two European Cups – the first with that left-footed cross for Trevor Francis's header and the second with his own right-footed winner.

Robbo and O'Neill roomed together with Forest whenever possible. Sometimes I split everybody up as part of the blending process. It served two purposes. It helped the sense of togetherness – after all, we relied on each other on matchdays so it was as well that everybody got on. Secondly, it helped me assert my authority. Once they realised they had to do what I told them, it solved a million possible problems.

So there you have them, Martin O'Neill and John Robertson, the academic and the scruff, the Irishman and the Scotsman, chalk and cheese just like Peter Taylor and me. Right now they look like being the best managerial twosome in the British game, odds-on to take over at Manchester United eventually, I'd say. They've a bit to do yet, especially in Europe, because providing you beat Rangers a few times, the Scottish title is not the most difficult thing in the world to win. I know they won't have tried to copy Pete and me because neither of them is that barmy. They're not the new Clough and Taylor because nobody can be and they wouldn't want to be. What I do hope is that Pete and I contributed something towards the success they are enjoying and I'm sure will continue to enjoy. I hope we gave them some idea. I like to think we helped. We must have done. Just a little bit.

C H A P T E R   1 6

BOTTLES AND BUFFOONS

I had to smile when Manchester United were eliminated from the European Cup at the end of April 2002, not because they'd lost but because of the way it happened, having drawn the home leg of their semi-final with Bayer Leverkusen. They'd conceded two goals at Old Trafford and the 1–1 they managed in Germany put paid to their hopes.

It put paid to Alex Ferguson's big night in Glasgow as well. Having announced his retirement and then done a U-turn, oh how he must have set his heart on winning the European Cup in his home town. Had he done it, Glasgow really would have belonged to him!

I smiled when I kept hearing what a tough prospect United had set themselves for that second leg, how the damage had been done at home, serious damage so it was reckoned, and they would need one of their greatest-ever performances abroad if they were to pull it off. Bullshit. Aye, they'd made things difficult for themselves but they had ninety minutes in which to retrieve the situation against a team who, while having considerable talent, were hardly regarded among the all-time giants of Continental football.

I was entitled to smile because Nottingham Forest left themselves a daunting proposition at the same stage of the tournament in 1979. Just for the record, that was the year we retained the Charity Shield, retained the League Cup, completed that incredible run of forty-two league games without defeat – the equivalent of an entire season in those days – and we won the European Cup.

Manchester United thought they had problems having drawn 2–2 at home to Leverkusen. We conceded three goals at home to FC Cologne in the drawn first leg of our semi-final and the general consensus of the so-called experts, the sportswriters and the television pundits, was that we were out of the competition already. If I'd listened to that lot I wouldn't have bothered taking the team to Germany for the return game. When there are still ninety minutes available and you're level, it's just a match to be won. It doesn't matter where it's to be played, it's your team against the other bloke's. It's up to you and the players you have assembled – simple as that.

I gave short shrift to anybody who dared write off our chances. My attitude was, 'So Cologne have three away goals – so what? My team is still capable of scoring more than them next time we meet. See you over there.' By the time we reached Cologne, our players, even without Archie Gemmill, were convinced they were a better side than the Germans. No doubt Martin O'Neill and John Robertson, who were both in the side, remember the way we prepared for that second leg – not dwelling on the fact that we'd conceded three at our place but convincing ourselves that it was just a match to be won in Cologne. A score of 1–0 would do and 1–0 it turned out to be, thanks to Ian Bowyer. No, Manchester United weren't knocked out of the European Cup because they conceded two goals at home. That might be the mathematics of it but they were knocked out because they weren't good enough to win the second leg. A victory in Leverkusen should have been well within the scope of a team as good as they believe themselves to be.

At Nottingham Forest, we rarely did things like anybody else. They used to say I was never at the ground and never at the training ground. Where do people pick up garbage like that? One of my proudest achievements in management was that sequence of forty-two matches. We were undefeated from November 1978 when we lost 1–0 at Leeds through to December 1979 when we lost 2–0 at Liverpool. A run like that from a team that was to end the season with three trophies, including the one Fergie didn't win in Glasgow, would surely be worth a knighthood these days, at the very least. The format has changed now with fewer matches in the Premiership than we had to play in the old first division, but it will be an awfully long time before anybody gets close to equalling that extraordinary record of ours.

It wasn't done on the strength of filling players' minds with technical and tactical jargon or coaching gobbledygook. It was done by keeping everything as simple as possible, by keeping minds neat and tidy and free from clutter. It was done by making sure that whatever the situation, however daunting the next match might look, Nottingham Forest would be represented by good players who were relaxed. Fear? If I ruled my club with anything, it was relaxation!

That's why we had beer on the coach during the journey to Munich's Olympic stadium for that 1979 final against Malmo. OK, so it turned out to be a fairly crappy encounter apart from the Robertson cross that set up Trevor Francis's winning header, but Forest's footballers weren't uptight footballers when they took the field. What's wrong with a beer or two *en route* to the ground? It was better than sitting there bored to a stupor watching a bloody video of opponents who weren't as good as us even though we were one or two players short of our best side.

Forest did a lot of smiling in those days. As you may know,

the following season we took them to the red-light district in Amsterdam before the semi-final with Ajax. Pete Taylor's attempts to organise a discount for twenty-odd players and officials didn't quite work but the effect did. I don't think anybody seriously wanted to watch one of those notorious live shows but the laughter that followed Taylor's attempted negotiations was more valuable to my side than anything they could have taught us at Lilleshall.

We were unconventional to say the least but boredom was something we wanted to avoid at all costs even though, on occasions, the unorthodox approach had its price. Like one pre-season trip to Holland where I took the players to a kind of fitness club with swimming pool, saunas, all that kind of stuff. It was just a knock-about session, something to break the daily routine, something to do rather than train. It all seemed a very good idea at the time until a member of the coaching staff reported that one player had damaged his ankle and another had all but broken his wrist. Both had slipped, clambering out of the jacuzzi! A slight hitch to the pre-session planning although we didn't let it bother us too much.

They were together; I think it's called 'bonding' in modern parlance. Whatever it was, we won all three games on that tour.

On another occasion, before one of our League Cup finals, I had half-a-dozen bottles of champagne put into ice-buckets as I joined a card school with some of the players. You can get carried away playing cards. When Jimmy Gordon marched in and announced, 'Do you lot realise it's ten o'clock?' I said, 'It feels as if we've only just arrived.' Jimmy wasn't slow or afraid to express his opinion and said, 'We've been here since six. Surely you're not starting with bridge schools at this time. The players certainly aren't staying up all night.'

'Get the champagne open,' was my response.

'No, it's too late for that as well.'

'How come?' I argued. 'Have all the staff gone to bed? You

get hold of the manager – he can open it.'

'It's not that, but Archie Gemmill's already gone to bed.'

'Well go and get him up, then.'

'He's asleep,' Jimmy said. 'I can't do that.'

But he did. It was an instruction from the gaffer but it was the usual grumpy Gemmill who reluctantly joined us, refused a drink and complained, 'This is ridiculous. Getting us out of bed when we're preparing for a League Cup final.'

Now he had a point, of course, but he was isolating himself and his mood offended me.

'It's going to be a long night,' I told him, 'because everybody is staying right here until you drink that glass of champagne.'

He sat me out until gone half past eleven. The lads had had maybe a glass and a half each. I think it was Kenny Burns who said, 'I'm ready for bed, Gaffer,' and then turning to Gemmill, said, 'If you don't drink that bloody champagne, I'm going to choke you with it.'

Archie swigged it down in one and everybody was in bed within five minutes. For better, for worse, those were the kind of things we used to do; and, nearly always, it was for the better. I couldn't understand the song and dance that was made about England players playing cards and watching horse racing at the 2000 European Championship. For a start, I don't believe some of the figures that were bandied about – tens of thousands of pounds on the table.

However, I played cards with the players both at Derby and at Forest, and for money. There was nothing sinister or serious about it and I'm not aware that it ever caused the slightest ripple of a problem among the players. But it's not valid to compare what England did and what I used to do as a manager because players' wages haven't just increased, they have gone through the roof. The highest-paid player at Derby was probably on about forty quid a week and at Forest on £200 to £250. The married players looked after their cash, and the single players – well, they had more money to play with. As for me, I was earning £22,000 a year at Derby, the highest salary of all. I had a rule that nobody got more money than me because I was the manager.

It wasn't the players' card schools and televised horse racing that was the problem for Keegan at Euro 2000. It was what happened on the field, not off it. Too little happened on the field if truth be known, and he didn't seem to know what to do about it. How the memories came flooding back when Keegan resigned from the very job that I had wanted more than any other – manager of England. Who was better qualified in 1977 after Don Revie turned his back and fled to Dubai, lured by the money? The offer from the United Arab Emirates had been made with perfect timing because England's results were not turning out as Revie had hoped they would. I was not only ready for the job, I was perfect for it because I would have been good at it.

Time has done nothing to change my view that, had Revie's successor been selected on the strength of the interviews carried out in London, the job would have been mine – mine and Peter Taylor's because I would certainly have insisted that he was appointed as well.

I didn't have a challenger apart from Bobby Robson who never did win the league championship at Ipswich but was always likely to become national manager somewhere along the line – and did when he was better equipped for the job. Lawrie McMenemy's main claim to fame had been winning the FA Cup with Southampton and keeping them in the first division. No disrespect to Lawrie but anybody can win a Cup with a bit of luck – it's only six ties for a club from the top division.

Lawrie was to wear that cherished FA blazer with the three lions on the breast pocket as Graham Taylor's assistant after the Robson regime. Dear Lawrie, a fellow Northeasterner – I don't think he kicked a ball as a professional footballer. He completed his apprenticeship as a manager at Doncaster and Grimsby and, funnily enough, worked as a coach for my old mentor Alan Brown at Sheffield Wednesday. He finished up getting a lot closer to the England manager's job than I did, even though the other contenders on the short list I think shouldn't have been contenders at all – director of coaching Allen Wade and Charlie Hughes.

When I sit at home, busy doing not a great deal at all, and think back again to that day I bowled into Lancaster Gate as if I already owned the place, I remain unshakeable in my belief that the whole interviewing process was a charade. It wouldn't have made the slightest difference one way or the other because the England job was already earmarked for a man who wasn't even on the list of those to be interviewed. Ron Greenwood had been standing in since Revie quit. It was done and dusted, decided near as damn it before the FA lot got down to talking to Bobby, Lawrie and the candidate who was best qualified of all – me.

Greenwood had a good name in the game as manager of the West Ham side that included Bobby Moore, Martin Peters and Geoff Hurst, three of the Boys of '66. He was generally described as one of the most knowledgeable and respected of all coaches and I'm sure he was although I remain baffled by the fact that he couldn't decide who was the better goalkeeper – Peter Shilton from our place or Ray Clemence from Liverpool. They were both the same according to Greenwood, so he alternated, picking first one then the other. They might call it rotation today but as far as I was concerned it was indecision way back then, an instance of a manager who couldn't make a positive choice – clear evidence of uncertainty and a lack of emphatic judgement.

I wasn't comfortable with most of the company at that interview. Many of them are now dead, of course. The panel included Professor Sir Harold Thompson who hadn't a clue about my business; Bert Millichip, since knighted, who couldn't have been my biggest fan after some of the things I'd said about the way they did things at his club, West Brom; Peter Swales who promised me his vote; and Dick Wragg from Sheffield who promised everybody he'd buy them lunch the next time they happened to be in his town. I had nothing in common with any of them so you can imagine how grateful I was to see Sir Matt Busby sitting there. He knew my business; he knew what made a manager. He must have known I was the best man for the job and maybe his vote was the only one I received. It didn't come from Swales, the bloke who said I could bank on his support. See what I mean? Football directors!

They could have saved us all a lot of time and bother because Greenwood seemed merely to be rubber-stamped. He was given the job and most of those silly committee men would have gone home and boasted to their wives and friends, in-laws and golf-club cronies, that they had appointed that nice Ron Greenwood, a first-class diplomat as well as a fine coach, and they had given the bum's rush to that objectionable braggart from Nottingham Forest.

What they didn't know and couldn't have told their cronies at that stage was that the braggart from Nottingham was about to embark on a period of his career that would lead Nottingham Forest to the league championship, two League Cup triumphs, two European Cups and the European Super Cup – oh, and that little matter of forty-two league games unbeaten, in the process – all in less than three years. Who could object to that? I think England's supporters might just have welcomed having a braggart in charge of the team.

The way England managers are appointed still puzzles me and sometimes keeps me awake at night. It frustrates and annoys me – I become vitriolic, furious. When I think of the power they have, I shudder. It's not the power of an American president, perhaps, the man with his finger on the nuclear button. What they don't tell you is that the button was disconnected some time ago in case daft buggers like Ronald Reagan or Bill Clinton pressed it at the wrong time.

The selection process seems to lack plenty in the way of professional knowledge and expertise. It's changed to some extent in that one or two professionals have been consulted, but I gather the appointment of Sven-Goran Eriksson, the first foreign coach in charge of the England team, was mainly down to the FA's chief executive Adam Crozier. Isn't this the man from the world of advertising or some such? And isn't he a Scotsman? Now I'm not being racist or prejudiced in any way. Eriksson might turn out to be the best manager England ever had. It's just that I would have preferred it if an Englishman rather than a Scotsman had been appointing the England manager, and preferably an Englishman steeped in the game – a former player and manager together with other former players and managers or people with sound experience and judgement that could not be questioned.

How could those, apart from Sir Matt Busby, who pretended to interview me seriously for their job ignore such credentials and public support? I'll tell you. It's the reason why Len Shackleton left a blank page in his autobiography to illustrate how much such people know about the game.

I wanted the England job because I knew I'd be good at it. But I shouldn't have been walking into what felt like an alien environment. I should have been walking in there like a vicar entering his church to meet the bishops. He wouldn't have felt out of place because he was joining people of the same persuasion and way of life; he'd have felt comfortable. Instead, despite my confidence, despite telling them England had enough good players to win trophies, I was still made to feel like an outsider.

C H A P T E R   1 7

WAS KEEGAN
RUNNING SCARED?

Even if Ron Greenwood hadn't been favourite, I think that conceit of mine would have cost me the England job – the way I walked into the interview room giving the impression that I felt superior to everybody else there. Apart from Matt Busby, I was of course, but you'd be amazed at the reaction of some people in those circumstances. I'm sure one or two of them were saying to themselves, 'Who the hell does this man think he is, walking in here like that?' When you are conceited, when you are full of yourself and oozing confidence, you are completely unaware of the effect it has on others.

That interview has occupied my thoughts a lot since I finished with football and I'm convinced I made one serious mistake that gave the committee the ideal opportunity to push me to one side. Me and my big mouth! Sir Matt asked if I was serious when I told them I would take anything they cared to offer, any job they might have in mind. They seized the opportunity to chuck me the booby prize. They gave me the chance to get involved with the England youth team and, as you might imagine, Taylor and I jumped in with both feet. Not content simply to observe during a tournament in Las Palmas, as was expected of us, we took over. I couldn't stand the sight of the coach, a man by the name of Ken Burton, running the show like an amateur. It was as if reaching the final was enough for the FA bods who had travelled out there. The Russian side was expected to win the tournament anyway. When that team of ours walked out of the dressing room there was no feeling of inferiority, I can tell you. Whatever else I did on that little trip, I made sure that the England lads knew they had every right to be contesting that final against the youngsters from Russia. The only goal of the match gave that youth side their first tournament victory since God knows when – satisfying, for all that our involvement had been fairly limited. Taylor and I had made our point, but it was not a job for us long term. It was no compensation for missing out on the big one so we jacked it in after a year or so and concentrated all our efforts on making history with Nottingham Forest.

I've been asked a million times, and asked myself on a few occasions, why I would have made a good England manager. Time to dwell has only increased my certainty that I would have been successful. I already had a bond with the players. Those people who might question whether my style of management would have worked at international level are entitled to their opinion. I don't mind them having an opinion just as long as they realise that mine is better informed than theirs.

Those players knew I had been one of them for a longish period of my life. Even the dim ones will have known that I used to be a centre-forward, and a bloody good 'un, so the respect would have been immediate. Centre-forward, or striker in today's language, remains the most difficult position on the field. Has there ever been a single football match in the entire history of the game after which somebody hasn't said 'he should have put that one away' or 'we could have won the game if he hadn't missed that sitter'? There's always a scoring chance made in a football match and it's nearly always the bloke up front who carries the burden. So my record as a player would have helped me, and for those who weren't aware of it I'd have probably plastered it on the dressing-room wall at Wembley.

Also, I knew most of the better players in the country. I'd worked with some of them. They would have enjoyed my verbal approach to the job. I'm not being flippant but if I told one of them to 'piss off' he'd recognise the language and, after a period of time, would know that I meant it. They would have understood all my terminology, on and off the training ground.

I would have known who were the good players and who were the ones who didn't have a prayer of getting a place in my England team. You would be staggered by the number of managers who don't know their best team. Even the worst manager might get nine names right but it's the other two who can make the difference between a poor team and a winning one. I keep going back to Ron Greenwood and the problem he had in deciding between the merits of Peter Shilton and Ray Clemence – and he was the man who landed the job I went for!

I had established that the goalkeeper is as important as anyone else on the field, if not more important than some. Goalkeepers used to be regarded as a bit of a joke. Anybody could get a goalkeeper. They didn't attract big money. I paid £270,000 to Stoke for Shilton because I knew that with him behind that team at Forest there were no limits on the scope of their potential. I decided what Ron Greenwood couldn't decide to save his life. I decided Peter Shilton was the best keeper in England. No disrespect to Clemence whatsoever but, in my judgement, Shilton was just that little bit better.

So, being on the right wavelength and starting with the best keeper of all as the first name on my teamsheet, I would have been a tenth of the way there. Hey, I'd have had the finest footballers in the country available to me. We'd have had a lot of fun together. It would have been the most relaxed England set-up of all time. We would have had a colourful team, playing the type of football the public wants to see, and it would have been winning football as well. Oh, I might have had to tone down the language on occasions when the FA were within earshot but I'm a players' man and the England lads would have known it. As for missing the day-to-day involvement of club football, I would have relished the prospect of working with the best in the land once every three months or so. We would have been as fresh as daisies every time we got together. So don't tell me I would have failed as England manager. I'll never believe it for a second. Me? Working with the best of the very best? I couldn't have failed.

The sense of leadership was in my blood and, from somewhere, I had the knack of making players feel good about themselves. There was no fear in my dressing room, unless it was among the juniors on the staff who still had so many things to learn. Fear would have created the very opposite of what I was trying to build. Fear makes you tighten up, your face goes rigid and you freeze. I never froze a player in my life. I sent them out thinking they were the best since Tom Finney, Stanley Matthews and Billy Wright.

It's hard to pay yourself compliments but, deep down, I'm proud. I'd argue with a policeman in the same way that I used to argue with the bus conductress at Middlesbrough when she left people standing on the pavement with six seats available upstairs. Peter Taylor used to say, 'I've never known anybody fight lost causes the way you do.' It's just the way I was brought up, the way I am. And in my book, the England football team was a lost cause. It's been a lost cause for years. It has rarely given an accurate reflection of the talent that has been available in this country since Alf Ramsey won the World Cup all those years ago.

One thing's for sure – I'd have done a better job than Kevin Keegan. When he trudged off the Wembley pitch in the pouring rain after the defeat by Germany in October 2000, I saw a man who was not only saturated but who seemed scared. I've heard a theory that if it had been a pleasant evening rather than a wet and miserable one, he might not have quit, but I don't buy that. That night, possibly for the first time in his life, he found himself exposed and isolated, not knowing where to turn for a solution to his crisis.

That defeat, coming after ropey performances at the European Championship a few months earlier, left England's World Cup qualification in serious doubt. He didn't seem to know what to do. He couldn't whip them into the frenzy he created with such spectacular effect at Newcastle and to a lesser extent with Fulham. He looked at his wits' end. The future seemed to hold nothing but fear. A man gets frightened when he knows he can't cope and I think Kevin Keegan couldn't cope. A big match had been lost, the heavens had opened and a section of the crowd had booed him. Now that wasn't a situation Keegan was familiar with at all.

There was a certain courage and honesty in the way he came clean and immediately announced his resignation, confessing that he didn't have what was needed to get the best out of those England players. But I sensed there was desperation in what he did, too.

It had been so different for him on Tyneside where he made his start as a manager after living in Spain for years. The fervour was there already – he just tapped into it. There is no region quite like the Northeast for its intensity, its fanaticism, where football is concerned. Keegan had enjoyed great success and popularity with the St James' Park fans as a player. Goodwill was guaranteed if he could get results, get promotion and re-establish the club in the top division. But he couldn't feel much goodwill from the crowd at the last match England would ever play at the old Wembley. He couldn't feel anybody patting him on his back – only a crushing weight on his shoulders.

He stayed on too long. He should have gone at the end of

Euro 2000. England were knocked out in the early stages and he must have questioned himself, but he lingered for some reason. There was nothing in the way England had played to suggest that he was getting it right. I think he faced Germany with more hope than expectation. He hoped something would change for the better, something would come out of the blue, something would enable him to carry on for a bit longer – certainly long enough to complete the match against Finland a few days later. But when things don't go right, many have commented on how he walks away. I respected him for the way he went and the words he expressed at Wembley, but I wasn't surprised in the slightest.

He wasn't as good a manager as he was a player but when he took the England job, he knew the calibre of the players available. He knew what Wembley was like. He knew he couldn't call on the talents of Frenchmen, Argentinians, Brazilians. I would have advised him not to take the job in the first place. But here was a man who'd enjoyed everything the game had to offer, thanks to the opportunities that came his way because of his talent. From small beginnings at Scunthorpe, he moved on to hero-worship at Liverpool and being voted European Player of the Year at Hamburg. He'd made lots of money from his various interests by the time he agreed to have a crack at management. More success on Tyneside followed. He had a lovely family around him, and racehorses that actually won. Then he walked away from Newcastle because somebody or something upset him. It was something to do with Newcastle becoming a plc, so they tell me. Then he walked away from Fulham, having been success-ful there over a short period and dabbled with the England job at the same time.

When he took over as England manager I had the impression he wouldn't be leaving Fulham until he'd seen out his contract. When he did leave and took on the England job full time, I remember seeing a middle-aged Fulham supporter on television, downhearted and angry saying something to the effect that, 'Keegan told us he was committed to Fulham and wouldn't be leaving. Well, now he's gone.'

It strikes me there's a bit of a flaw with Keegan. He seemed perfect in every way, never really failed at anything he touched in football until he became England manager, apart from not winning the European Cup with Hamburg because my Forest team beat them. He was perfect, or as near as you can be, on the field because he worked for his team, did justice to his talent and scored goals. He was perfect in harnessing his own destiny with the timing of his departure from Liverpool to meet the new challenge of football on the Continent. He was perfect in the way he exploited the fanaticism at Newcastle whose fans will still tell you, 'Kevin Keegan gave us everything apart from his life.' Actually, he didn't give them a league title despite leading the table by a mile at one stage.

He's fine when everything is running in his favour but not when he's facing adversity, when, in his opinion, his job is being made more difficult than it should be. He's on top of his world again at Manchester City. It's familiar ground in the sense that he knows club management. It must be a bit like Newcastle – a passionate crowd filling Maine Road week-in week-out, and high expectations at a club desperate to return to the top level. And there's a few bob to spend in the process.

Promotion at the first attempt is a major achievement. It was like turning back the pages, flitting back in time, tapping in to what he'd done before. Keegan's managerial record at club level meant that City fans were not just hoping for a quick return to the Premiership – they were expecting it. And so was I. His philosophy worked with club sides. He tried to get his teams to play the way he played – with pride in the badge and his heart on his sleeve. He played the same way at Scunthorpe, Liverpool and Hamburg. He just got older and better and played alongside better-class team-mates as he went along. He was a cavalier player who, as a manager, wanted his teams to play cavalier football. It was exciting and compelling, and it made for terrific entertainment, not least on television. It made Newcastle the second-favourite team of just about every football fan in England. No, it didn't win a championship but then it was hardly likely to because Keegan seemed to have so much trouble finding and signing a goalkeeper to lay the first foundation stone of his defence. He gave the people of Tyneside what they had longed for over so many years but that didn't mean his approach to the job was going to work at a different level.

There was always a question mark about Keegan the manager as far as I was concerned. I wondered whether he could adapt his managerial approach to meet the needs of international football. It's one thing to beat the drum, point to the three little lions on the shirt and tell them to think of England. It's quite another to pick the right team even when you are blessed with the finest talent the nation has to offer. Keegan clearly couldn't transmit that undoubted pride and passion of his into an England team performance. I don't remember England ever looking like a Keegan team. They looked uninterested rather than inspired, confused rather than cavalier. His life as a player and as a manager was something of a fairytale until he took the England job, but there was nothing magical about the way it all turned out. They couldn't play the way he had Newcastle and Fulham playing, partly because they were meeting a better calibre of opposition.

If truth be known, Keegan remained a player at heart, thinking like a player, determined that his teams would perform the way he performed as a player. That was his big mistake.

He was brave as a player, I know that. You have to be brave to play where he did, at the sharp end against defenders only too ready to kick you uphill and down dale and stick you on your arse. Then again, there are different types of bravery. With Keegan I have the feeling that in a critical situation he would look after himself first. He has enjoyed the privilege of choice, been able to do most things to suit himself and his family, and there's nothing wrong with that apart from giving the impression that self-interest dominates all others.

He's had to endure a lot of criticism and reservations about his tactical knowledge. With the number of goals his teams conceded – and continue to concede, looking at Manchester City – it's easy to accuse him of knowing nothing about the art of defending. He can't have known much about it because with the lead they had at Newcastle, he should have won the title with a bit to spare. All he had to do was lock the door. Tactically, he was found wanting, and he didn't believe it could happen to him. Wasn't that the season he lost his rag and blew his top on television because Alex Ferguson had said something to upset him? Fergie won the League.

Keegan was a popular choice as England manager, though, stemming from the entertaining stuff his teams dished up, particularly Newcastle. But it wasn't the kind of football that could succeed with England and anybody who thought it could shouldn't have been given the job to begin with. Something devastated him on that bloody awful night at Wembley, something dawned. It's odd how most men change when they become the England manager. It's fear that does it, the fear of not being able to do the job. How on earth can you cope if you don't know what to do? Keegan walked with fear that night. They tell me that he made up his mind in the time it takes to stride from the bench to the dressing room. If that's true, he demeaned the job because it deserves more than 100 yards and one man's personal disappointment.

I made my biggest career error by walking out on Derby – and we were a cracking good side. I felt a touch sorry for

Kevin Keegan that night but I felt bloody angry as well. This was another bloke who'd had the job that was denied to me, another one on his bike with not too much to show for his efforts. I wouldn't have left it like that, couldn't have done it. For a start, I wouldn't have just lost at home, not to a team from Germany. I took great delight in beating the Germans at every opportunity.

POPPERFOTO

Nowadays I feel football has prostituted itself to television. But it wasn't always that way. Here I am with Brian Moore, the best of his generation, and Johan Cruyff.

Kenneth Wolstenholme's understated commentary can hardly be improved upon, I feel. But today, people like Andy Gray (*below right*) seem close to hysteria at the smallest event.

EMPICS

EMPICS

In my opinion, Glenn Hoddle's achievements as a manager no way qualified him for the England job. While Keegan (*below*) admitted that he didn't have what was needed to get the best out of the England players. Here he leaves Wembley after losing to Germany in the World Cup qualifiers.

Peter Taylor's friends in the media seemed to me to have talked up his abilities beyond what the results would show.

I'm amazed to see that David Platt is still involved in the England set-up after what happened during his time at Nottingham Forest.
Even now I feel I could do a better job as England manager than he will ever be able to do.

Sir Robert Robson still shows his passion for the game even at his age. It makes me feel much younger seeing him in action.

Terry Venables was one of the better England coaches of recent times and I certainly respect his ability.

Paul Gascoigne is in agony after damaging his cruciate ligaments during the 1991 FA Cup final, when he should probably have been sent off for two reckless challenges. After that I feel he never quite gave his clubs full value for money and it was sad to see such talent fail to fulfil its potential.

Above: My old mate Colin Lawrence, sadly no longer with us, joins me meeting up with Martin O'Neill and John Robertson at Leicester City.

Right: One of my biggest regrets when I look back on my career is how I humiliated Justin Fashanu. After his tragic suicide, I wonder if I could have helped him more earlier in his career.

Below: Alex Ferguson with new acquisition Roy Keane in pre-season training in 1993. I am sure that Sir Alex looking back on his career will feel that this was one of his best signings.

Geoffrey Boycott caught and bowled Brian Clough at Lord's. It's not often you saw Boycott with a smile on his face after he was out.

Politics has always been important to me. Here I am supporting the redundant miners in Nottingham in 1992.

EMPICS

Meeting Roy Hattersley and former Minister for Sport Denis Howell at the Labour Party Conference.

EMPICS

Right: I was very pleased to be awarded an MA by the University of Nottingham in July 1990.

Left: My eldest grandson Stephen joins me at the unveiling of a bust at the City Ground.

POPPERFOTO

In the presence of Ali I was nobody. And I can tell you there's not many that would make Old Big 'ead say that.

In retirement some of the greatest pleasure I get comes from watching Nigel's team Burton Albion in action. This is the way to enjoy football.

EMPICS

CHAPTER 18

GAZZAMATAZZ AND HODDLEDYGOOK

England had a chance of fulfilling their potential when Terry Venables had the job. There were real signs of progress under a man who knew what he was doing but they blew it again, those in charge of the set-up. Venables wanted assurances about the future, which seemed reasonable enough to me. Too much was made of his business dealings and problems that had nothing to do with his ability to manage a team. When he left, a big opportunity was lost.

I was never a Venables fanatic exactly, but I did recognise and respect his ability as a manager. I think he preferred to call himself a coach but he was a manager, believe me. He knew how to cope with players, how to buy the right ones for the most part, and how to get on with them and develop them as a collective unit. He had a bit of luck during Euro '96, his only tournament in charge, because we were beaten by Spain with a perfectly legitimate goal that was called offside. But the football we played in hammering the Dutch was, I'd say, some of the best ever seen from an England side in a competitive match at Wembley. It could be said that his luck turned the other way when we were eliminated by the Germans in another of those bloody penalty shoot-outs.

But Venables had proved his point. He could cope with the job and deal with its demands. He was popular with the press, which I'm certain is a vital element in the job. Mind you, if he couldn't be popular with the sports journalists, nobody could. For a start, most of the influential ones work on his patch and from what I hear most of them enjoyed a drink at his London restaurant. His bond with the journalists was as close as his bond with the players by the sound of it!

Terry Venables, a bit of a cockney Jack-the-lad, had done his homework and learned his trade. It helped being capped by England at every level. He served his apprenticeship in management at various places, not least at Tottenham and with Barcelona where he won the Spanish title but couldn't win the European Cup. I regarded him as a likeable rogue. Nobody in football doubted his managerial ability until those business difficulties arose. It was daft that anybody should connect the two. His behaviour in business shouldn't have had the slightest influence on what he was allowed to do as a football manager.

Part of his managerial reputation was built on the strength of his Tottenham side beating my lot from Nottingham in the 1991 FA Cup final. That was the one in which the referee, Roger Milford, should have sent off Paul Gascoigne not once but twice, if that's possible. He should have sent him off for ramming his boot into Garry Parker's chest, and he should have sent him off for clattering into Gary Charles despite Gascoigne being carried off with his knee busted by his own reckless stupidity. We'll never know, of course, but had the referee done his job in the first place and waved a red card at Gascoigne at the first opportunity, history might have turned out differently. The lad might have enjoyed a more productive career. He was blessed with enormous talent, but he lost his way off the field. I'm sure that knee injury, which took so long to heal, had a detrimental effect on his career. In my eyes, his talent was never properly fulfilled.

Somebody told me recently that Roger Milford has become a referees' assessor. He's in the stand on a Saturday afternoon, sitting in judgement on the man in the middle. Milford, the bloke who didn't do his job in that FA Cup final, marking the performance of the modern referee? I don't have to believe that and I'm not going to. This was the man who didn't even show a yellow card to the player who should have been shown the red. This was the man who took years before he actually admitted he'd made a mistake.

Nobody knows what would have happened if Milford had sent Gascoigne packing in the opening minutes of the match but I know one thing. If we'd been playing against ten men instead of eleven it wouldn't have done our chances any harm. As it was, we led at half-time only to lose with a Des Walker own-goal in extra time. A Cup final produces a lot of memories but, for my retirement, Gascoigne's behaviour dominates the recollections of that disappointing day. When he was carried past me flat on his back on a stretcher, I turned to our coaches and said, 'He's finished as a player if he's got what I think he's got.' That forecast wasn't far wrong. He'd knackered a cruciate ligament and despite his efforts he's rarely had a long run at full fitness since then. He might have been bought for a lot of money by the Italians and by Glasgow Rangers, and he might have rejoined manager Walter Smith at Everton, but he was pretty much a spent force. In fact, he never fulfilled his potential for one reason and another, the main one being the knee he wrecked at Wembley.

For all Gazza's stupidity and excesses in life, he was still a big part of England's challenge for the European Championship of '96. Venables, knowing him well from their days together at White Hart Lane, brought out the best of what was left. It's amazing how, despite adversity – or, more likely, because of it –

Gascoigne has remained something of a household name, even before his attempts to sort out his personal life, and he's to be admired and congratulated for that. But I grew sick of turning on the telly and finding that he was news whether he was picked or left out. It was news if he was among the substitutes, it was news if he wasn't even on the bench. How can a player still be news if he's not good enough to be in the club's best sixteen?

To my mind, Gascoigne has cheated himself. He's also let down some of those who paid big transfer fees for his services, and those who paid for their season tickets in the belief that they would see him play.

The subject of Paul Gascoigne annoys and upsets me and always will because he's wasted the gifts he was blessed with and doesn't have an excuse. It upsets me because I had to finish as a player at twenty-nine years of age, and I was good. I wasn't the best centre-forward who has ever played and I certainly wasn't better than some who will come along in the next five years. I was just me and I thought I was good – unfortunate, too, when I remember that season at Middlesbrough when I scored forty-three goals in forty-two league games and we didn't get promotion because the centre-half was letting them in and eventually finished up in Pentonville. What a game, in't it!

It was ironic that Gascoigne lasted longer than Terry Venables in the England set-up. He was still playing after Terry had left, and was there in Rome the night of the team's best performance under their new manager, Glenn Hoddle – a goalless draw with Italy that took them to the World Cup finals in France in 1998 – which brings me nicely to Hoddle. Dear me, that's the man who, in my book, had the least right of anybody to be appointed as the manager of England. I have a bit of a problem with Hoddle because I see him as part of the coaching fraternity. He talks about 'technical players' and when he was in charge of England I grew tired of reading about tactics, formations and systems. When I read of what Hoddle had been saying, I didn't know whether to reach for a dictionary or a calculator.

In case anybody is inclined to believe I might be a wee bit prejudiced against him, let me say right here that I was one of Hoddle's greatest fans when he was a player. Had I managed to land the England job, he would have been a certainty – one of the first names on the teamsheet. Why so many people remained unconvinced about his talent I'll never know. Couldn't they see he could play passes that were beyond the scope of anybody else in the country? Couldn't they see he could play them with perfect distance and pace and angle? Couldn't they recognise a football brain of the highest quality? For God's sake, all I seemed to hear about him was that he didn't tackle and he didn't get back and defend enough. There you have one of the main reasons why so many people fail in football management. They don't have the first clue.

In my opinion, Hoddle didn't have enough of a clue to be appointed England manager. Where had he been as a manager? He'd had a bit of success with Swindon, taking them into the top division, and three years at Chelsea where he spent quite a lot of money and left them exactly where he found them, in the middle of the Premiership. That was no apprenticeship to qualify him for the top job in the country.

Then there was Eileen! It's hard for me not to laugh when I think of Hoddle and Eileen Drewery – his friend and his faith healer who apparently did so much to get him over some of the injuries he had as a player. Is it right that he said his biggest mistake was that he didn't take her as part of the England set-up for the start of those World Cup finals? And that she'd have given the team an extra 10 per cent? The only extra 10 per cent I can think she could have given them would have been in discount!

He says he didn't inflict the lady on his players but that, if they felt the need of help, she was there for them. Well, I don't care whether he inflicted her on them or not, he talked about her so often in public and clearly believed in her so implicitly that we came to accept that she was part of the set-up, part of the regime. The first thing to say is that it didn't do England's results much good. It didn't prevent young Beckham from flicking his heel at that Argentinian and getting himself sent off in the match England might otherwise have won. Perhaps Beckham hadn't consulted her.

For Hoddle to associate her as closely with the game as he did was out of order. It was ridiculous, an insult to the intelligence. If I had been a player in his squad, I would have said to his face, 'Who are you trying to kid?' and walked out there and then. It takes me back to one of my pet subjects – the people who hire England managers. Didn't they do their homework? Didn't somebody mark their card? Just as we never fathomed Baldrick's 'cunning plan' in 'Blackadder', we never got to know Hoddle's cunning plan with the Drewery woman at France '98. But if Eileen was capable of giving the team 10 per cent extra, he should have sacked his assistant John Gorman and appointed her as his number two. On second thoughts, if Hoddle seriously believed that her influence would have been that strong, the FA should have sacked Gorman and installed her in his place because they could have argued it was a change made in the national interest.

There were times when Hoddle spoke utter garbage. Having had a few years to reflect, I think he would have to confess that he made a mistake or two or didn't know what he was saying or was under so much pressure that he felt run-down. I'm trying to be kind, as far as possible.

But he talked of his one mistake, or main mistake, in France and he didn't talk about the goalkeeper or picking the wrong striker or maybe even the wrong team. He wasn't referring to anything to do with the normal football environment as we knew it. He was blaming the absence of a faith healer. Some people carry a rabbit's foot for luck. I think Eileen Drewery was Hoddle's rabbit's foot. He can believe in her if he wants to. He can hold whatever beliefs he wishes. But when he mentions those beliefs publicly, when he employs them and pontificates about them, that's when he runs a big and unnecessary risk. I'm trying hard to treat this as something of a joke because I honestly can't believe he was serious. When he started going on about people in this life paying for mistakes or sins in a previous life, I'm telling you I thought he was ready for the funny-farm. When he mentioned karma, I thought he'd arranged a friendly against a club side in Sri Lanka.

Then there was the issue of his World Cup diaries, his account of the build-up to the tournament and England's involvement in the finals, for the short time it lasted. Two things baffle me about that – how Hoddle could have been misguided enough to do it, and how David Davies has kept his job at the FA having ghosted the thing on Hoddle's behalf. Only Hoddle can explain the first. The book was as big a mistake as Hoddle's appointment had been to start with. He wasn't sufficiently competent or experienced enough for the task. If his short career in club management had been the subject of a school report, it would have said something like, 'Disappointing after a promising start. Room for a great deal of improvement.' If promotion with Swindon and keeping Chelsea in eleventh place qualifies a man to lead England on a campaign against the Germans and the Argentinians and the French, a bloke who can make a paper aeroplane is qualified to pilot a jumbo jet.

Hoddle wasn't exactly flying with Chelsea when England took him on but by the time he'd been in the job for a little while some of us were beginning to believe they'd found him on Mars. He could take to the job only what he had. He couldn't suddenly develop something new, something extra overnight that would make him better qualified for it, and what he had was nowhere near enough. I'm no philosopher or psychiatrist but it's my hunch that Hoddle should have taken Eileen Drewery to bed with him the way a child takes its favourite teddy bear – no, not for any other reason – something to cuddle, something for comfort, something to ease the mind. Eileen was possibly his main source of comfort, a kind of fallback if all else went wrong. I'm sure he talked to her about many topics but I do hope they never discussed the merits of Argentina's central defenders. Seriously, they couldn't have ever talked about football, could they?

He might have been well advised to discuss the book before he and Davies put it together. It didn't take a faith healer to know that Hoddle's exposure of some things that should have remained 'in-house' would cost him the goodwill of some extremely important people; and no one can be more important to a manager than his players.

I suspect that England's players had already twigged that Hoddle had little or no idea, but if he was a nice lad – you can have no idea but still be a nice lad – they would still have liked him and respected him for that. He alienated some of them with that book. A manager must have control – it is an essential part of the job – but that control has to be accompanied by fairness and decent values. If you demand loyalty of the players, they in turn are entitled to expect loyalty from you. That's the damage Hoddle's silly little book did. It betrayed the very people on whom he depended most in his professional life. It betrayed his players, it destroyed their trust, and there wasn't much that Eileen could do to save him once the deed had been done.

I gather he was a bit unfortunate with the actual straw that broke the camel's back. They tell me he believed his conversation with a journalist about people in wheelchairs being punished for what they'd done in a previous existence was private (forgive me if I've not fully understood what he was on about). It became front-page news and it cost him his job. Mind you, I expect a few England players were a bit surprised to discover one or two matters they thought were private appearing in Hoddle's book. You can't have the best of both worlds, either in this one or any other that his friend Eileen might have told him about.

In so much of what I've heard and read about Hoddle the manager, whether the subject was football or life after death, he came across as the deep thinking, bit mixed up analyst. I think he was looking for reasons out of desperation.

CHAPTER 19

REASONS TO BE THANKFUL

Glenn Hoddle gave me the impression that he had a theory about football and how a team should play, and that he was on some kind of personal crusade to prove that his theory worked. Whenever his teams were under discussion – his club teams or the international side – it was never long before the subject of formation cropped up. I'm not sure how important the formation is. What I do know is that players need to feel comfortable with the job you're asking them to carry out and the manager needs to be able to recognise talent the moment he sees it.

Maybe Hoddle expressed doubts about some players because of the fact that so many people had reservations about him, even when he was at his peak. Madness ruled in our country for a while because many people seemed obsessed by the fact that this lad didn't do enough defensively. They allowed negative thought to cloud their judgement when Hoddle's talent shone like a beacon and should have been obvious to everybody with the slightest knowledge about the game. But then, as the England manager, Hoddle expressed uncertainties. He didn't think Michael Owen was a natural goalscorer and was reluctant to stick him in the side at the start of the 1998 World Cup finals. He was wrong. There was nothing wrong with Owen's goalscoring ability, as he proved when Hoddle eventually gave him the chance. There was nothing wrong with young Owen's temperament, either. The World Cup was never likely to worry him because he had an old head on those teenaged shoulders and that plus his ability should have been a godsend for his manager.

While Hoddle was concerning himself with formations and systems and doubting whether somebody could score goals at the highest level, his team got off to a poor start. It might have been just my impression but England began like a team with doubts rather than the belief that they were as good if not better than the opposition.

That hadn't applied under Terry Venables during Euro '96. The players reflected their manager. They were full of themselves, self-assured to the point of cockiness. They played with a spring in their step and a glint in their eye. They looked like a team who knew what they were doing and who were enjoying every second of it even though they didn't start all that brilliantly.

Didn't you find it strange that in May 2002 Steve McManaman picked up his second European Cup winners' medal with Real Madrid yet couldn't land a place in Sven-Goran Eriksson's squad for the World Cup? I found it staggering, especially as England were crying out for some-body who could do a bit from the left flank. Venables recognised that McManaman could play a valuable part for the national side, never mind that the lad had a reputation for failing to produce his Liverpool form in an international shirt. Venables recognised the undeniable fact that McManaman can play. It is the job of the manager to use that player in a position or a role where he can do justice to himself. That's not theory, that's simplicity. Venables didn't tie McManaman to the left touchline but allowed him to wander and pick up the ball where he could do most damage. Most of his better work was carried out cutting in from the right. When he did that, he frightened defenders to death.

It wasn't coaching that got Teddy Sheringham into that side, either. It was Venables' knowledge of the game. He followed his belief that Sheringham's style was perfect for pairing with Alan Shearer. That's simple, straightforward selection, and it was so successful that it helped Sheringham land a place in the squad that flew off to Japan in summer 2002. Oh, I know he won medals with Manchester United, including that European Cup victory that came from nowhere in the Nou Camp, and I know he's kept things ticking over, having returned to Tottenham. But I'm certain that his exploits at Wembley in 1996 stamped his pedigree and proved him to be a player who could be perfectly at home on the big stage providing he had a role that suited him and team-mates who could respond.

Some people still claim that the biggest clanger I dropped at Nottingham Forest was when I sold Sheringham to Tottenham after three matches of my last, ill-fated season in football management. They're wrong. I could have made a better job of replacing him if I'd been in better nick but selling him was the right decision. It was right then and it would still be right, in the same circumstances, today. He wanted to leave. His heart was obviously not with Forest and in a situation like that there is only one decision for a manager to make – you get rid! He'd been with us barely a year but, separated from his girlfriend and able to see his little boy just at weekends, he was unsettled. Once he knew he could get a move to Tottenham his enthusiasm and commitment to Nottingham Forest were bound to be affected.

If I have explained the details of Sheringham's transfer to White Hart Lane once, I've repeated it a thousand times. The only reason I've needed to explain it in print and to an FA inquiry was because of Tottenham chairman Alan Sugar's mention in the High Court that Venables had said Brian Clough 'liked a bung'. Venables denied saying it but the damage was done. That word 'bung' seemed to be linked with my name every time it was mentioned for ages afterwards, with no good, legitimate reason whatsoever.

I'll repeat it yet again for the benefit of those who missed it, or who are too stubborn to have got the message the first time. The court case was a Tottenham affair, part of the saga that developed around the differences between Sugar and Venables. Suddenly, out of the blue, my name was mentioned and I felt as if I had been dragged into something that was not of my making and none of my business. We had paid £2 million to Millwall for Sheringham and I was determined Forest should get their money back once I eventually agreed on the timing of his departure. Seeing that the player was entitled to a £100,000 signing-on fee for each of the three years of his contract, I decided Tottenham could have him for £2.1 million. That meant everybody was financially looked after. Forest had their money back, Sheringham had his signing-on fee and Tottenham had their man. It was simple, straightforward and all done within the rules, and then Alan Sugar talked about a bung.

A figure of £50,000 was also mentioned in that courtroom and, for the record, I'll repeat what I've said about that. As I understand it, that was the fee paid to agents Frank McLintock and Graham Smith for the work they did on Tottenham's behalf. It certainly wasn't paid to me, not in any shape or form. That was my position then and it was what I told the official FA inquiry. It remains my position to this day for one good reason – that's what happened, that's how the Sheringham deal was done. End of story.

I'm sick of the mention of bungs. I'm delighted the FA chose not to hold a disciplinary hearing. As far as I was concerned, there were complete answers for any questions they might have wanted to ask about other transfer deals – in the later stages of my time at Forest I had next to nothing to do with most transfers anyway. My delight and gratitude stemmed not from having anything to hide but from the fact that if enough mud is thrown, some of it sticks. I don't like my name being linked with that tiresome word Alan Sugar came out with in court. When I'm gone I want to be remembered as somebody who contributed good things to the English game – not least the winning of trophies with teams that played football with good manners, according to the rules imposed by referees, and with style and a bit of a swagger. Let them remember me as a bigheaded so-and-so, a conceited bugger who believed he was always right and sometimes said things he shouldn't. But don't remember Cloughie for any of the negatives of life – apart from having one drink too many too often.

All that stuff became part of an unhappy departure from Nottingham Forest when so much was achieved in my time there. Controversy walked hand-in-hand with me during my entire managerial career but there was too much of it towards the end and it has left a nasty taste in my mouth. It has also left a real sense of sadness. I should be able to walk into the City Ground for any match I choose, feeling a sense of warmth, pride and satisfaction. But I don't. In fact, I've been back on a handful of occasions only because I still resent the way I was treated after taking the club from the virtual wilderness and turning them into the champions of Europe. The Chris Wootton episode, chairman Fred Reacher's premature announcement of my intention to retire at the end of that final, awful season, the reappointment of Wootton to the board first chance they had . . . it all festered within me, and the resentment still rages inside. I don't suppose it will ever go away.

It was nice that they named a stand in my honour – although, after what I did, they could have named the entire stadium after me – and they've erected a bust of me in the main entrance.

In December 2001 the press reported that my old club, the one that won and retained the European Cup some twenty years earlier, were facing bankruptcy. Trading in the clubs shares had been suspended – something about the accounts not being presented on time. The club was said to be losing more than £100,000 a week and to be in debt to the tune of £12 million. I should have felt sorry for them, but all I felt was anger and a certain amount of contempt. How could they have been daft enough to spend so many millions on players who weren't worth a fraction of what they cost? How, for instance, could they borrow £5 million to buy David Johnson from Ipswich? As far as I was concerned, the Forest directors had brought it on themselves by appointing the wrong managers and then going along with the wrong judgements.

If there is any sympathy to be offered, mine goes to their latest manager Paul Hart. He is the one who has to pick up the pieces, make-do-and-mend, try to build a winning team when he knows he has to sell any youngster with outstanding talent who bursts on the scene. That's no way to set out in management but if he comes through it, he'll be able to look forward to a big career.

It's all a far cry from those good days when we conquered Europe, when the only thing we had to complain about was the lack of credit we were given by the media, especially when we won that big Cup, first time around. OK so it was hardly a classic against Malmo but we were under-strength in the first place and then I took the decision to leave out Martin O'Neill and Archie Gemmill. But we won it all the same. In all the circumstances, it was a hell of a triumph despite being a dull encounter. If Manchester United, Arsenal or Liverpool did something similar today, we'd never hear the last of it and rightly so.

Despite my reluctance to go to watch my old club, I refuse to let the bad taste spoil the good memories. Of course, there are bad memories as well. One is Peter Taylor's eagerness to retire and the unresolved row that developed between us when he took over at Derby and took Robertson with him. Another is that final season when I was not myself and failed to do enough about the threat of relegation that became a constant, intimidating companion. I built another fine team after Pete packed in at the City Ground – at least I can look back on reaching the semi-finals of the UEFA Cup, winning two League Cups and reaching the FA Cup final, to name but a few.

Watching Roy Keane captaining Manchester United makes me think of that day in 1990 when he arrived from Ireland, a shy young man snapped up for £20,000 from a club called Cobh Ramblers by Ron Fenton with a little help from coach Liam O'Kane. What is he worth today as one of the best midfield dictators in the world? I know what he cost Manchester United after I packed in – £3.75 million, and he picked up £650,000 as a loyalty bonus. It still makes my blood boil when I recall how my son Nigel left soon after my retirement but, unlike Keane, received nothing from Forest simply because he hadn't signed a contract while he waited to see what the future held for me.

I don't blame Keano. If that's what he was owed as part of his deal, he was entitled to every penny. I don't look back with anger at anything else the Irishman was involved in at Forest apart from that little incident at a hotel during a pre-season trip to Jersey. He soon discovered from my reaction the way I ran things at Forest although he didn't believe me at first when I told him to get on the next plane home. He hung around but only long enough for me to discover he thought I'd been pulling his leg. Reality dawned on him when I made sure he went to the airport and boarded the first available plane.

In Keane's early days at the City Ground we thought about bringing in an interpreter. His Irish brogue was so pronounced and rich that, for a second or two, I thought we'd been landed with somebody from the Continent. Shy off the field, on the pitch the boy was a revelation. One or two rough edges needed smoothing, but he was so self-assured that I once played him at centre-half despite him being just a kid. I knew midfield was his position but we were struggling for central defenders at the time and I remember asking my staff, 'Who's the best header of a ball in this club?' The answer was unanimous – 'Roy Keane.'

'So that's who we'll play at centre-half,' I said. I had no qualms, no reservations or hesitation. His ability, even at such a young age, solved my immediate problem. I suppose some would refer to it as another example of my managerial simplicity. I regarded it as straightforward common sense.

Keane got better as we knew he would. He improved quickly after that nice, comfortable debut I gave him – against Liverpool at Anfield! Well, they all have to start somewhere. Keane had that aggressive streak that is so important to players in his position providing they can control it. We made sure he could control it but I'm not so certain he found himself quite as restricted once he moved to Old Trafford. I got fed-up seeing him sent off on television or reading about it in the papers. I became incensed at those close-ups of him ranting and raving at the referee or a linesman, or leading a pack of United players pursuing a match official who had made a decision that had upset them. He wouldn't have got away with any of that when he worked for me and he knows it.

But I'll let that pass because Roy Keane is – and was for me – the genuine article. I never remember him giving an ounce less than his utmost, his absolute maximum, in a Forest shirt. The best example of it has painful memories for me because it goes back to that final season of mine when Nottingham Forest fell out of the Premiership.

I took exception to Stuart Pearce's attitude. He was injured for a long time, but I believed that as club captain he could have popped his head in the dressing room more often on match-days, done more to try to lift spirits and morale. There had been a problem with an improved contract and we just had the feeling that 'Psycho', as he was affectionately known, wasn't quite as enthusiastic or as committed to the cause as he always had been. Aggravating a groin injury at an England training session where he was supposed to take it easy didn't help endear him to me at the time. But time and a lot of thought has softened my view of it all. Maybe Stuart just felt things at Forest weren't as they should be, and the standards of old weren't being retained. Maybe he was affected as much as anyone by the depression that descended on the place.

A lot of the players were affected in their different ways. Some weren't scoring the goals we had come to expect, including Nigel, hard as he tried. Some couldn't get the ball the way they used to. Some gave it away when they'd not done that before. Some just weren't up to it and that was my fault for having them in the side in the first place.

Roy Keane shone like a beacon through all the gloom of that desolate season. I knew other clubs had taken note of his outstanding talent – they'd have been blind not to see it. If Fergie needed any confirmation about his ability and attitude, the joy he gained from just playing football, he got it during that final season of mine. Keane played forty league games for me that season. He even scored six goals although, the way we performed, he had to spend most of his time defending. If Keane could perform like that, in a team like that and in circumstances like those, how good could he become with a team like Manchester United? It didn't take a genius to work that out. Alex Ferguson had known it for ages. I'm not sure whom he regards as his best-ever signing at Old Trafford but there can't have been one better than Keano.

During those later seasons at Forest, Stuart Pearce would often tell me I was too hard on Nigel. I was reminded of that when I went to see his Burton Albion side pick up the Unibond League championship trophy in April, having comfortably won promotion to the Conference. Now, as you know, I've had my hands on a lot of silverware in my time, but none of those trophies gave me the depth of pleasure I felt when I picked up the one they gave to Burton that day. It was the family connection, the fact that our Nige was the manager – or player-manager. I know he was proud but he couldn't have felt prouder than his old man even though we had won other cups together with me as the gaffer and him in the team.

It was a lovely day at Burton. There was a good crowd to celebrate a rare event, goodwill all round the place. And Barbara was there. My wife stopped going to football matches a long time ago, partly because she doesn't particularly like football but mostly because of the way I am on matchdays. I've never before experienced the sensation I felt as our Nige led his triumphant team on their lap of honour. I think he might just have taken to the managerial side of the business. I think he might have a chance. I must have a quiet word with him one of these days to try to find out what he intends to do with his future. I'm pretty certain he'll do what I have always recommended to any player who has bothered to ask – he'll keep playing for as long as his legs keep offering him the chance.

I had a special relationship with Nigel. Not many sons can work with their fathers. He worked for me as an amateur at first, playing for local side AC Hunters on a Sunday morning having played for Forest against Liverpool, say, the afternoon before. He was playing for nothing, for both of them.

When he'd passed his A levels, I remember him coming to me and saying, 'Dad, don't you think I should get some money now. All the others are getting paid.'

'You're getting nowt,' I said. 'You get enough.'

It was my way of making sure I was never seen to favour my son ahead of any player at the club. I know now that I went too far the other way. I'd be quick to criticise him on the training ground or in the dressing-room. I was quick to fine him on the slightest pretext. In fact, I treated him worse than I treated the other players. Garry Birtles, the centre-forward who went to Manchester United, has since told me as well that I was too hard on our Nige.

Ron Fenton pushed his case to be paid. He pushed it hard and often and insisted I was being unfair. In the end I relented and told Ron to deal with the contract. Forest did quite nicely out of him when you think about it. He hadn't cost a cup of tea to sign and they sold him to Liverpool for £2 million. Keane got £650,000 to help him on his way; our Nige got not a penny. He has every right to be a little bit bitter towards Nottingham Forest, but he's not. I think he has his mother's nature rather than mine. Barbara likes everybody as well.

It would have given Alex Ferguson a lot of pleasure and pride if his boy, Darren, had made it at top level. If he'd come to work with me at Forest he might have made it, who knows? It gives you comfort, working with your bairn because a father always worries about what his sons are going to do. You can push them at school for a time but, like anything else, if you push too hard they reject it.

A famous manager's son can tend to believe he doesn't have to do too much at school because he gets a few more perks than other kids get. If you're not careful, he can go the other way – that's why so many bairns with famous fathers land in trouble. Even the Prime Minister's son was found in the street pissed!

So I was secretly chuffed that our Nige signed with Forest, but I was still always conscious that I mustn't display the merest sign of favouritism. I never thought he should ever put a ball wrong, put a pass astray. I talked as if he should never miss the target with a shot or a header and would ask him, 'Can't you play a ball, for God's sake? Can't you head a ball, either?' I was always looking for that bit more and, worst of all, I was critical of him in front of the other players. He was extremely popular with them because they knew he didn't blab. He never said a word to me about any of the goings on within the squad and they loved him for that.

I referred to him as the No. 9 at work and he referred to me as Boss. That might sound a bit cold on my part, but that's the way it was. I felt I needed to be hard on him so that the rest of the players knew that's the way it was. There could be no family loyalty in those circumstances.

Our Nige was a bloody good player who could pass a ball as well as anybody at the time and who scored more than his fair share of goals. When Graham Taylor was England manager he loved my lad, as a player and a man, but I'm not sure he ever employed a formation or picked the right blend to get the best out of him at international level. Still, Nigel got fourteen caps in all, which is a dozen more than his old man, and if he'd managed a goal or two here and there I think he'd have got a lot more.

I constructed the Forest team around him to get the best out of him and it worked, not only for the team but for individuals within it. For instance, Stuart Pearce said to me on one of those occasions when he was accusing me of being too hard on the lad, 'I wouldn't be half the player I am without your Nige in the side – and I play left-back.' Even Teddy Sheringham, with whom I didn't get on that well, told me after that one full season of his, 'I've scored twenty-odd goals this year but without your Nige in the side I wouldn't have got ten.' Oh yes, the players knew he had talent.

He wasn't that quick but it didn't matter that much; it never does. I've worked with players who could do 100 yards in ten seconds or a bit more but on the pitch it would take them ten seconds to do ten yards once the penalty box was in sight. Real pace is only an asset to players who are prepared to use it when it matters most.

I'm glad I worked with my son for a few years and I'm sorry that I was too hard on him. I hope he keeps playing for as long as he can because then I'll know he's still taking notice of the advice I gave him: 'The day you stop playing is the day you're nothing. Never mind that you're a manager, once you are no longer a player, something goes out of your life that is irreplaceable.'

When you think about it, there are not many things in life that can't be replaced. You can replace a knee – I should have replaced one of mine years ago. You can replace a heart, a kidney; you can even replace a wife. But you can't turn back the clock and start playing football at the age of sixty-seven. I wish I could.

I have many reasons to be thankful. Many people, especially players, are entitled to my gratitude. I'm most thankful for being able to do my little bit to improve the game that has been my life, and through that improve the lives of others.

CHAPTER 20

FERGIE'S FOLLY

It wasn't a very good year for King Rat in 2002. In fact, by his and Manchester United's standards it wasn't good at all. Third place in the Premiership might be regarded as a great finish by the majority of clubs but it won't have gone down too well at Old Trafford where it was their worst finish in more than a decade and left them needing to pre-qualify for the Champions League. Sir Alex Ferguson might have been better advised to stick to his retirement plan after all instead of volunteering himself to be shot at for another year or two.

I call Alex 'King Rat' not as an insult but because of the example he has set with Manchester United, the lead he has given with the dynasty that has been created and the financial empire built around the success of the teams he has assembled. It has become a rat race with all other clubs trying to emulate Manchester United although most have not the slightest hope of achieving it and many seem to be risking bankruptcy in their chase after the impossible dream. Apart from anything else, Manchester United's success has increased the demands and pressures put on his fellow managers, if that's possible. It's always been a hazardous profession with a high casualty rate but now they're getting fired in September and October!

Chairmen panic. With so much money at stake these days – and don't forget it's the appeal of covering the so-called glamour clubs such as Manchester United that has tempted the television industry to pay so much – those who run the clubs are petrified of losing their place around the honey-pot. It's like an epidemic, a plague has swept the game and, as far as I can see, it started with the huge transformation that turned United into the richest club in the world – thanks almost entirely to Ferguson's ability to create a winning team. Believe me, without his contribution there would not have been a Manchester United on the scale that we see and admire today, nothing like it. Every aspect of that club, the expansion of Old Trafford into one of the finest arenas in the world, the value of the club on the stock market, the sales of replica kits throughout the world, all of it is traceable to the success of the team on the field. Not quite as many fans would be walking about with David Beckham's or Roy Keane's name across their red shirts if Manchester United were finishing their season at the arse-end of the table.

But the best of men, the greatest of managers, can make mistakes and I think Fergie made a big mistake when he announced he would retire at the end of the 2001–02 season and then changed his mind. He should have stuck to that first instinct, the gut feeling that the time had arrived for him to hand over the reins. You can always come up with a reason for changing your mind. You can always claim to have rediscovered the enthusiasm to carry on but, usually, the original decision is the right one. I'll bet that crossed his mind when the season ended with nothing to show for it.

As I said, third place would suit most clubs, most of the bigger clubs for that matter, but United have been used to winning the Premiership title. They made it virtually their own property until Arsene Wenger came along, produced a better side at Arsenal and made off with not only the Premiership trophy but the FA Cup for good measure. How it must have stung Fergie that night when Arsenal clinched the title by beating United on their own patch. If he was hurting already, the United manager must have been in agony at the sight of Arsenal rubbing United's noses in it in front of more than 60,000 of their own supporters at Old Trafford. What should have been such a memorable year, a glorious and incomparable year for the Scotsman, turned out to be the worst one he'd had for some time, no matter how hard he tried to convince everybody that they had played some wonderful football and had been unfortunate.

They had played some wonderful football on occasions but Arsenal, for all their rotten disciplinary record earlier in the season, played football that was just as wonderful and for longer. They produced it on a regular basis, scoring in every Premiership match, and remained unbeaten away from home – that should leave nobody in the slightest doubt that Arsenal were the outstanding team of the season by some distance. And what a year to do it!

It had been billed as United's year, Alex Ferguson's year, the year the European Cup final would be played in Fergie's home town, Glasgow. To listen to some people you'd have thought the entire season and the venue for that European final had been laid out like a red carpet on Manchester United's behalf. Before Alex's U-turn on his retirement plan it had seemed like the perfect finale to his distinguished career – winning the European Cup at Hampden.

United's hierarchy and fans were certainly entitled to antici-pate at least one trophy from the season, something to show for what Ferguson had done in his latest efforts to turn a bloody good side into an even better one. With the European Cup final scheduled for Glasgow you can bet that was at the top of his list of priorities. He had set his stall out to win it, set his sights and his heart on it. I reckon he tried to reconstruct the United team with that night in Glasgow very much in mind. He reshaped it, tinkered with it here and there in an effort to create a team with an even greater chance of winning Europe's biggest prize.

There wasn't much wrong with United domestically. There couldn't have been because they'd won the Premiership for the previous few years and won it at a canter the previous season. But he went out and spent close on £50 million on two players – Ruud Van Nistelrooy and Juan Sebastian Veron. That's a striker and a midfield player. It could have been argued that United's defence was in more need of improvement than the attack. Still, that was Alex's decision, his judgement, his prerogative; and nobody could dispute that Van Nistelrooy contributed brilliantly with his thirty-odd goals. Aye, he went a long way towards justifying the £19 million he cost, if ever that kind of money can be justified in one season. So Fergie spent all that money adding to a squad that had skated the league championship the year before and he ended up winning nowt. Fergie had fallen on his own trap!

He was accused of buying Veron simply because he was available. Here was an outstanding footballer, widely accepted as being genuinely world-class, and United were in the business of recruiting the best. With hindsight, people said Fergie had bought him without much thought for where he would play him. Some argued he'd been bought for that precious European campaign to help bring about the manager's night of nights in Glasgow. Whatever Alex's intentions and plans were the day Veron put pen to paper, the signing had awkward repercussions, not only for the Argentinian but also for the manager. He had to muck about with the side and the players who had won him the previous season's championship with plenty to spare. We had the barmy spectacle of David Beckham sitting on the bench – the England skipper rested while one of our main World Cup opponents was selected ahead of him. We had little

Paul Scholes, the perfect professional as far as I could see, so brassed off about having to take on an unfamiliar role that he refused to play in an under-strength line-up for a Cup-tie against Arsenal. We had United changing systems, often with five men in midfield and only Van Nistelrooy up front.

Only Ferguson knows the truth of it, of course. Only he knows whether he had genuine doubts about the chances of his Premiership winners taking him to another triumph in Europe or whether he felt they needed a different approach if Glasgow was to be the ultimate destination. Whatever was behind it, he left himself open to criticism. I never want to see Sir Alex Ferguson held up for criticism or ridicule because the man doesn't deserve it. Someone with his incredible managerial record, at his age, his time of life, doesn't deserve it, and certainly not in the very year that he intended to be his last in charge at Old Trafford.

Although we were never particularly close, I did have a good deal of affection for Alex because I saw a lot of myself in him. I was a better player than he was but we both came from working-class backgrounds and never lost sight or track of our roots. Like me, he was and presumably still is a staunch Labour man. I never hid my support, backing the unions on their marches and picket lines and once almost running for Parliament against Winston Churchill's grandson. That was the way I was – subtlety was never my strong point in any aspect of life and I suppose that's how I made a lot of enemies. Alex hid his socialism at first but there were times when he was among the militants of football management.

He started at a smaller club, and when he was sacked by St Mirren he took them to court. Like me, he told directors they knew nothing about football and we were both dead right on that. He saw the job as I saw it – to give yourself the best chance of succeeding, you need to be able to run your club virtually from top to bottom. You also need to instil a strict code of discipline which, when you think about it, is basic common sense although others might regard it as ruling by fear.

In other words, we were pretty much two of a kind apart from the face we presented to the outside world. Mine was conceited, arrogant, full of bravado. Alex's was dour and sometimes almost downright miserable. In his early days, he never looked comfortable in front of a television camera and microphone. He's happier doing it now because he's used to it. He's won so much, he's forever in demand although there are times when I get the impression that he'd love to control the media the way he's able to control his dressing-room!

Even now he can come across sounding a wee bit abrupt. When he had a poor start to the season in 2001–02, especially after losing at home to West Ham and slipping to somewhere around halfway in the table, he looked drawn and distraught. He looked like a manager who was worried that his team might be coming apart at the seams although the chances of that were less than unlikely with the class of player he was able to call on. In the end, it didn't quite come right. United contested the championship almost to the last day and reached the semi-finals of the European Cup but that was only coming half right. After winning the previous season's championship and spending vast sums on two players, few would have forecast that third place in the Premiership and not a trophy on the sideboard. I'm telling you, there were times towards the end of the season when he looked uncomfortable again on TV. In fact, the biggest smile I saw from him had nothing to do with football at all. It was when his racehorse was winning – especially when it landed him one of the Classics. That was when the man's response was natural, spontaneous and warm.

Despite our many similarities, there were differences as well. I'm sure Fergie adored winning trophies, particularly in his early days as a manager when he won them at home and in

Europe with Aberdeen, much to the irritation of Scotland's Old Firm, Rangers and Celtic. But I wonder whether he felt the same deep, intimate joy that I experienced when I won my first League Cup with Nottingham Forest in 1978. I sometimes gaze at the television set today and still see it – not on the screen but on the top where I stuck the trophy on our return from beating Liverpool in the replayed final with a penalty from John Robertson. I wonder if Fergie ever did something like that – arrive home with the Cup and stand it on the telly while you sit and eat fish and chips and gaze at it. I gazed at it for most of the night and then gazed at it again next morning, wanting to clutch it tight and show the kids and everybody else in town and the neighbourhood and never let it go. That's the way I felt about that first trophy I won with Forest.

I know how Fergie was feeling when I took my Forest side to Old Trafford in his earlier days. He was on his knees, not because of anything that happened that day or any particular result but because he was having a hard time of it, trying to succeed as the latest United manager to follow Sir Matt Busby. Others had attempted it and failed, and Fergie looked about at the end of his tether.

I gathered that his wife, Cathy, had been unwell and felt the need to go back home to Scotland. I think the pressure of the United job on Alex had been getting her down as well. I can just imagine how he was feeling. Going back to an empty house, for a start, is the worst thing I could wish on anybody. Having a bad time in whatever job you do and then returning home to nobody – that's a killer, especially if you love the person who used to be always there. Even if it's 90 degrees outside, you feel the chill the moment you open the front door – no noise, no kids, no wife, no smell of cooking, nothing. You've probably had a hard day, drawn or maybe lost a match, and you know the result was a fair one. So what are you going to do? Sit down and drink alone? Go out for a drink? Go out and find another woman? Forget the last one – I've been married for forty-three years and never felt the need to go that far. I'm sure Alex hasn't, either, but there must have been times when he felt totally desolate. You leave behind a packed arena and find yourself surrounded by emptiness. You leave the circus and find yourself in solitary. Even your own front room looks darker than it should be; the trees outside look the wrong colour. You don't feel like tackling the little bits and bobs that need doing around the house, the flowers that might have wilted or the water in the vase that could do with changing.

I knew that Alex was in the depths of despair that day at Old Trafford. I wanted to say, 'Come on, get on our coach and I'll take you home with me.' It was as if he wanted to talk but couldn't quite bring himself to say what he was really feeling inside. It was at the time when the media were speculating about his future. Some so-called experts said he was close to getting the sack – thankfully, we'll never know. But I did feel concerned that day. I remember shaking his hand, telling him I had to go and saying, 'You make sure you look after yourself. Take care, pal.' That was it – short words, inadequate words for a man who was clearly in trouble. He knew he could ring me at any time if he felt the need but I couldn't pick his team for him or win him a match. He did mention something that day that I'll never forget. Apart from briefly admitting that he was having a bad time, he told me he would like his son Darren to come and play for Nottingham Forest.

'Smashing,' I said. 'I'll look after him like I look after my own son.' And I meant it. The chances are I might have looked after him slightly better than I looked after our Nige on occasions. But it was not to be. Darren never did play for me and I've never really known why it fell through. It's dangerous to respond to rumours but I did hear that somebody at Old Trafford said something to the effect that, 'If he's good enough to play for Cloughie, he's good enough to stay at Manchester

United.' That was common sense and fair enough, even though it came from a director. But Fergie wanted the lad to spread his wings somewhere else, with a first-team place that he couldn't guarantee him. The fact that he was prepared to entrust me with the welfare of his bairn I took as a very big compliment indeed.

Maybe I did help Fergie inadvertently at a time when I had not the slightest intention of helping him at all. It was 7 January 1990 in the third round of the FA Cup at the City Ground. The rumour-mongers had been at it for a while and speculation was rife. This was the big crunch for Alex Ferguson, the match that would decide his fate. If he lost, he'd lose his job at Manchester United. At least, that was the theory and the build-up. I think that if we had knocked United out of the Cup there would have been two alternatives – he'd either have got the sack or said 'enough is enough' and walked away. If that was the make-or-break match for Fergie, he is entitled to be grateful to one player in particular for the rest of his days. Young Mark Robins was hardly a regular in the United side but he did have a bit of a reputation as a goalscorer. He was still scoring them for Rotherham, the last time I checked. He scored the only goal in that Cup-tie and the United team didn't give my Forest side a kick. I remember that United battled and battled with the intensity of a team who seemed to know there was something a bit more than the next round at stake.

We had a reputation for overwhelming the opposition at home, for getting the ball and keeping it. That was our golden rule. United were struggling, we were riding high. We were on our way to finishing ninth in the table and winning the League Cup again. But in front of probably our biggest crowd of the season, United pissed on us. It was they who kept the ball; it was Forest who couldn't get it. They adopted our golden rule and beat us with it. Perhaps that *was* the result that kept Fergie in the job at Old Trafford. From then on, he hardly looked back. Times change, all right.

An instance springs to mind of taking Forest to Old Trafford and winning. That was the day Manchester United were consumed by fear. I'm not sure of the precise occasion but I remember walking into our dressing room before the game and saying to the players, 'This lot are here to be done. We've just entered a ground that is shaking with fear.' I could feel it, smell it. The whole place was tense and apprehensive, even the gatemen weren't their usual cheery selves.

After we'd won, I told our lot, 'They were so frightened it spread everywhere – to the chairman, the gatemen, the spectators and eventually right through to the players. They were frightened of me and they were frightened of you. More important, they were frightened of themselves. They were frightened of losing and there is nothing worse than that for a team.'

It sounds daft, relating memories like that today after United have won so much and established themselves among the genuine major powers of world football thanks to Fergie's ability to build a team. Yet I still allow myself a little smile from time to time and a feeling of satisfaction, knowing that Fergie still hasn't won two European Cups in successive seasons and led a team through forty-two league games without defeat like I have!

Idiots keep repeating those age-old phrases 'it's tough at the top' and 'nothing goes for you when you're at the bottom'. Well, I don't know when it isn't hard for a manager and I've been at the top and the bottom. I'll tell you what – if you've got a choice between two guns, one that fires a single shot and one that just keeps on firing, I'll take the machine gun. The same goes with football. I'd rather be with the strongest than the weakest. I admire Alex Ferguson for his strength and his staying power as well as for his talent. He has the big advantage of managing one of the biggest clubs in Europe but even so, a manager has to prove himself. Success decides his stature and place in the pecking order of all time greats, and if Fergie is not the best club manager of all time, he can't be far off. He's shrewder than many people think and he's as hard as nails – a quality that will have been valuable in a season in which he spent a fortune and ended up winning bugger all!

I hang on to the fact that however good he is, and he is good; however talented he is and he is talented; however shrewd he is, and shrewdness is his middle name – he's still only won the European Cup once, and he was bloody lucky to win that one. However long he intends to delay his retirement date, he's going to have to be quick to win it and retain it as I did.

His first intention, to retire and remain with United as some kind of ambassador, struck me as odd, to say the least. I always thought Sir Bobby Charlton was Old Trafford's ambassador. What was it supposed to mean? What was Fergie going to do with his time? I thought he should have made a complete break in 2002 – no ambassador's job, no staying on as manager. I packed it in at the bottom of the table and didn't have horse racing as an interest to occupy me away from football. Fergie appears to be steeped in racing, to love every second of his involvement and he'd love it even more if he hadn't volunteered to continue worrying about football, morning, afternoon and night.

He might win another league championship. He might win another European Cup but he's been there, done that. There are no more mountains to climb because he's already scaled the heights and achieved the happy memories to keep him warm in retirement. Whatever he might win in the future, I still believe he should have stuck to his decision to retire and made a clean break from the game. Managers who have won all there is to be won shouldn't stick around longer than necessary. It would be heartbreaking to see him being held to account, abused and shot at from all angles should things not go according to his plans at Manchester United. But that is the risk he is taking by staying in the trenches.

What he's achieved with Manchester United entitles him to the admiration of all of us but he has also created a great deal of worry for those other clubs I was talking about. I think he has changed the structure of football in England more than any manager in history. Together with that wonderful crop of youngsters he developed, he has built a team of stars that has become the envy of all of us and only a few, a very few, are able to compete. For those who are not able to compete, envy becomes extremely dangerous, even to the extent where, if the chairmen continue to spend recklessly, it can threaten the very existence of a club. Standards have been changed by Ferguson. He has the money to spend and others have had to try to keep up. Consequently we have a frantic scramble for money and success that has greed as the basic element. That includes players and agents as well as managers who are being given less and less time in which to establish themselves.

What I've never understood about Fergie is the way in which he severely criticised two men he'd worked with for long periods of his professional life. He hammered his former number two Brian Kidd and former player Gordon Strachan in his autobiography. I can't understand what reason he could have had. I have had a dig or two about my old mate Peter Taylor from time to time but most of it was said with a twinkle in the eye or tongue in cheek – for fun, more than anything, but never with a malicious or grudging thought in my head.

I sometimes wonder what more Sir Alex Ferguson wants from life. He has won all there is to be won in football. He's had a salary in seven figures, they say his book made him a million and the nation has rewarded him with the ultimate honour – a knighthood. What else can the man want?

He certainly has no right whatsoever to complain about the

pressures and the weariness of the job. Give anybody in Europe the chance to manage a football club, bearing in mind there are stresses and strains involved, and which club would be first choice? I know which one I'd go to – Manchester United. I'd go there without a second thought. They've got a team of internationals and another team of internationals to call on if necessary, a crowd of 67,000 for every home game, the biggest turnover in merchandise of any club you care to mention and they are the richest club in the country. Stress? I had more stress at Hartlepools – and I'm not kidding. If I hadn't been successful, relatively successful, in my first year as a manager, Hartlepools would have been kicked out of the League.

I had the impression that Fergie was trying to solicit sympathy for the bad start to the 2001–02 season. Well, he's been an unpopular manager in some quarters despite all his success. He made a bit of a reputation for being awkward but that could be his nature so we'll forgive him for it. The public certainly didn't fall for the sympathy stuff. Those who don't support Manchester United or hang on his every word just recalled all the championships he'd won and the European Cup and the £50 million he spent on two players on behalf of the biggest club in Europe, and maybe some of them smiled rather than sympathised when the man who'd done it all suddenly found himself struggling to win a match.

The casualty rate in management now is absurd. If you're looking from the outside it is a pleasant job where everything in the garden comes up roses, but there are some extremely dangerous thorns that penetrate the skin and the ego, and they hurt. If you are the sensitive type and go home and worry, it's a rotten job on occasions. But if, like Ferguson, you have the ultimate job, you also have the choice. You can stay in it or you can get out. I hope he never regrets his decision not to get out.

Men stay for various reasons. They think they can still do it, they can do nothing else, or it is a matter of pride or money. Maybe Fergie was fooled by his own team. Maybe, when they won a whole string of matches and went to the top of the table again after that poor start, he believed they were capable of winning the lot and dominating the game in this country for a few years to come.

He must have wondered about the wisdom of altering his retirement plan. He must have wondered just a little bit when his big night in Glasgow was taken away from him by Bayer Leverkusen. I'm absolutely convinced he'll have wondered whether he made the right choice the night Arsenal went to Old Trafford and made off with what Manchester United regarded as the family silver.

I hope nobody laughed out loud at Sir Alex Ferguson's misfortune that evening but I wouldn't count on it. What is it they say? The bigger you are, the harder you fall? I'll swear I heard a big thud when that Arsenal winner went in. It must have been the sound of King Rat coming down to earth.

C H A P T E R   2 1

WHAT HAVE THEY DONE TO MY GAME?

I didn't know the depths to which I would miss football when I retired at the age of fifty-eight. If I'd sat down with my family and held council, not been so pig-headed and dogmatic – and not been drinking quite as much – I think I would have eased off, taken a break and gone back into management.

In one of the last public speeches I made, in front of 350 people at some gathering or another, I told them that if I could find one particular bloke, I was prepared to kill him. I don't know who he is or where he is, in fact I don't know whether it was a man or a woman, but somebody was first to say, 'life begins at forty'. They should have been shot the moment they said it. There is nothing I can do now, in my sixties, better than I could do it at forty. They say that experience makes up for it – what a load of old cobblers. Take the most basic subject of all, sex. What's the good of all the experience in the world if you can't manage it!

I could run faster, eat more, drink more and sleep better at forty. I could swim better, went on more holidays, had a bigger house. I didn't have as many memories but I have trouble recalling the extra ones anyway. When you get to my age, you don't want to remember too many of the details because each one reminds you that you're past it. I haven't had a sauna for six or seven years, I haven't played squash for ten years and I used to love them both.

So retiring is one of my regrets, having had these past few years in which to do a lot of thinking – despite the agonies of that final season, despite the knowledge that I was not myself and despite relegation, which will remain as a stigma for the rest of my days. I'm a bit more brutal with myself nowadays. I used to think I was the best in the business and it never entered my head to have any kind of inferiority complex. Honestly, I really did believe I was the best thing since sliced bread. So many people told me that I actually believed it. But I was quite good at my job, for all that.

It is inevitable that you mellow with the years. I miss football management, yes. I miss it a lot. I miss the involvement. I miss the quality, wonderful quality that I see on occasions these days, and I miss the opportunity to do something about the lack of quality – and I see just as much of that.

I know that when I was in my pomp, other managers worried about me, were wary of me. I wasn't conscious of it until Peter Taylor marked my card one day.

'You do realise that you're gonna get a lot of stick, don't you?' he said.

'Me? Stick? I can't get any stick. I don't do anybody any harm.'

'Oh but you do,' Peter said. 'You beat them and they're jealous. They go home to their families and they meet their friends and their golf partners and they'll be all too quick to say they can't stand you.'

It baffled me because I was only doing the job as I saw it. I was doing it my way. When they employed me as a pundit on television alongside Don Revie, Malcolm Allison, Bill Shankly and Jack Charlton, I believed people wanted opinion. If I was asked a question, I'd answer it. If I believed one player was better than another, I'd say so and give the reasons why. If I thought somebody had dropped a clanger, I'd say that as well. None of it was malicious or personal. It was simply my opinion. Apparently you're not supposed to express your opinion quite as openly and bluntly as I did, but I'm sure it interested the viewers more than some of the bland drivel some pundits have been spouting for donkey's years.

Taylor once advised me to 'put yourself about a bit'. I didn't know what he meant, seeing that I was working seven days a week already.

'Come with me, racing,' he said.

'No chance. I don't like racing.'

'Well, you've got to do something,' Peter urged. 'You've got to get in among more football people. You don't even have a drink with them after a match.' I had a simple answer to that one.

'I've got no desire to sit and swap pleasantries with the manager from the other team. What are you supposed to talk about when you've just pissed on them?'

I had no time and no wish for false camaraderie. I regard it as bullshit and always did. One of the most difficult tasks I had on matchdays was shaking hands with the opposing manager if I'd lost. You see them putting their arms around one another and smiling. Whenever I lost on a Saturday, I couldn't smile at all before Monday. So I didn't invite my opposite number for a drink on too many occasions. I'd point to the door leading to my office at the City Ground and instruct the commissionaire, 'You make sure nobody comes through there.' That's just the way I was, but I eased off a wee bit in the last couple of years or so.

I have a close-knit circle of friends these days. Archie Gemmill comes to see me every week and other former players call from time to time. Most of those I worked with say they're my friends but they have their own lives to live and, anyway, my new house isn't big enough to accommodate them in the front room!

I suppose I've become a bit of a loner since parting from the game but that's because I feel as if I'm in a goldfish bowl whenever I go out. It's as if everybody is looking at me, wanting this signed and that signed, wanting to shake hands and ask about the past as well as the present. I know how much respect there is for me out there and how much warmth and goodwill, but I'm not one to wallow in all that. I do the occasional newspaper and magazine column, I've done a fair bit of TV and I enjoy a local phone-in programme fronted by my old centre-forward Garry Birtles on local radio in Nottingham. I could do a lot more. People tell me I could still make a fortune as a television pundit but it doesn't interest me. I couldn't be bothered with the travel and the hassle and, in any case, I have more than enough money to get by.

I have one particular advantage over some of the more prominent managers of my era. I've outlived them, somehow. Fergie's still thriving, of course, and what about dear Robert Robson – still soldiering on and winning matches, charming everybody in his seventieth year and leading Newcastle into the Champions League. What a lovely, lovely man he is! Sir Bobby now, and rightly so. He makes no bones about it, he's survived serious illness and still takes training every day because of football. He can't do without it and that's nothing to be ashamed of – not when you're as successful at it as he is and when you're still enjoying every single second of every day, as I'm sure Bobby Robson does. He loves not only the game but most of the people in it. I never felt the need to surround myself with football people – not beyond the club I worked for anyway.

I was more obsessed with my family, Barbara and the children. I still regard myself as a loner because I always sense that people want something from me, even though it may only be a word here and there. They want to know what I'm doing in retirement but I'm not the slightest bit interested in what they do. I don't even ask but they don't seem to understand.

Boredom can be a problem, especially in the months when I can't get out and do a bit around the garden. On days when the sun doesn't shine, I sometimes sit and dwell, and I keep getting a recurring reminder that my children own better houses than mine. I'm proud to say that, but it's another reminder that life doesn't begin or get more glamorous at forty.

I suppose you could say that I live the retired life. I don't know how many pensioners there are in this country but if it's 15 million, I'm one in 15 million. I've a bit more money than some of them, I have my bairns around me because they still live nearby, and I have the best grandchildren imaginable. They just happen to like me. And for some reason, thank God, Barbara is still sticking by me after forty-three years. That's one of the genuine wonders of the world. Hey, I'm happy with my lot. Some would say I'm wasting my last years because I could be doing more with my time but if it's extraordinary to turn down countless opportunities to lead a high-profile life, then call me extraordinary. I'm used to it.

There is a routine to being retired. It's like being used to travelling on luxury jet aircraft and then swapping to a single-engined job. You drop your speed, and your mind and body adjusts accordingly. I've discovered how to be patient at long last. I can even stay fairly quiet while Barbara watches 'Countdown' although some of the drivel Richard Whiteley comes out with gives me the chance to be angry out loud. Racing on television has become a source of entertainment although I'm not a gambling man. If there's nothing of particular interest on the box, old John Wayne westerns, Clint Eastwood films and musicals provide a standby; otherwise I'll stick on a tape, usually Sinatra or the Ink Spots.

I'm able to do the little things my job didn't allow me to do because I was involved, one way or another, the whole time. I can still find something to occupy me if boredom threatens but that doesn't happen very often.

As the days, months and years go by, I miss the involvement a little less. But I still do miss the routine most of all – the routine of getting up in the morning and getting off to work for a certain time, and having the privilege of being the worst time-keeper in the business with the power to bollock anyone who was late. I miss getting my gear off and scrambling into what I called my 'working clothes'. I miss having my own peg in the dressing room. I didn't need any other therapy when I was in my prime as a manager. I didn't need drugs, cigarettes, alcohol. I wanted a little bit of grass with a few trees on the side, a group of footballers, a ball and a little bit of noise. That was my idea of heaven and I could be in heaven five days a week.

I look at the leading players today with their fat salaries, fabulous houses and expensive cars, and I wonder if they can possibly get any more pleasure from the game than we enjoyed at Forest. We used to walk to and from training and somebody would always ask, 'Which way back then, Gaffer?' 'Under the bridge today, lads,' was one of my replies, and we'd stroll back along the banks of the River Trent. A bloke with a kiosk eventually took my advice and started selling pasties and Bovril. He probably quadrupled his turnover just from what he sold to my players on our walks back to the City Ground.

Knowing you're respected is some compensation for the retired life, however happy you might be. I still get reminders of that. One letter from the bagful I receive every week brought a little lump to my throat early in 2002. It was from a seventy-five-year-old lady in Wales. The envelope included a card and a little note explaining that she was sending it to herself and wanted me to sign it and address the other envelope she had provided, stamp attached. She wanted a card from me so she bought it and sent it on for me to sign, insisting, 'I've always wanted to meet you and I'm going to before I die.' Life might not begin at forty but another old saying certainly does apply – little things mean a hell of a lot.

I must admit that I don't watch anywhere near as much football as I used to. If I want to see a live game, I'd much rather go to Burton Albion than Nottingham Forest. Televised games have started to drive me round the bend. The game as I knew it and as the ordinary working men and women knew it has changed almost beyond recognition. I used to regard it as the rape of football, but after more thought I prefer to call it the prostitution of football, the game 'on the game' since the television people set it awash with money. Rupert Murdoch's Sky TV revolutionised the business almost from top to bottom, certainly at the top.

If there are any people involved in football who are deserving of sympathy, it has to be the fans. They still love it but it's costing them a fortune – not only to watch matches live but often when they watch it from the comfort of their own home. The money being paid for players in transfer fees and in wages has reached a stage where it is beyond all reason. I keep reading that the transfer record has been broken again, another fee of tens of millions has been handed over. I read of David Beckham getting £100,000 a week or some such. Young Beckham is among the most talented of footballers and I don't begrudge him one penny of his salary because he helps to pack Old Trafford every time Manchester United play there, and that helps to swell their coffers off the field, but I'm telling you it can't go on. Rising transfer fees, rising wages – there has to be a point where the upward trend stops. If it doesn't, some clubs are bound to go bust. That's not opinion from an expert, financial brain – it is downright common sense.

I don't blame Beckham or any of the others for wanting as much as they can get from what will always be a short professional career. It's not the players' fault that clubs are prepared to fork out more and more – partly out of fear that if they don't pay up, several other clubs, in England or abroad, will be only too ready to satisfy the demands of the wanted men and their agents. It's the chairmen, the people who run the clubs, who are to blame. They just seem to keep running towards the cliff like lemmings and one of these days one or two of them are going to disappear headfirst over the edge. The collapse of the television channel ITV Digital is a symptom of the madness that seems to have overtaken those who believed football was a passion and a fashion on which you could safely hang your hat. It is as if the commercial world thought they had struck gold, believing that football provided a guaranteed link to success and untold riches. Well ITV caught a cold. Somebody got carried away and paid far too much for the chance to show football outside the Premiership. Unfortunately, the consequences don't only involve the television companies. Without that money, many of the smaller clubs are left to worry not just about their position in the league table but about their existence. It's all got out of hand as a result of the interest television has shown in the game, escalating out of all proportion over the last few years.

Of course things change, they have to and change is good providing it doesn't go too far. I'm not an old fuddy-duddy but I honestly believe football does not give as much pleasure now as it used to – and don't try telling me that it does simply by quoting increased crowd figures.

I don't enjoy it like I did unless I go to watch our Nige's team. And do you know why I don't watch it on television quite so much these days? It's because television keeps ramming it down my throat that football is so good, so exciting that I can't fail to love every second of it. It's the hype that drives me barmy. Andy Gray's tone of voice, for instance, makes the award of a corner kick sound as dramatic and historic as the moment somebody won the FA Cup, European Cup or the bloody World Cup for that matter. Andy's a nice lad, good at his job, and he's not the only offender when it comes to overstating football's appeal. They don't give the viewer much of a chance to make up his or her mind – they tell them how wonderful and fantastic it all is. They replay the slightest moment of simple skill, they glorify it all – and in the middle of it they'll be telling you how exciting their next live game is going to be.

The truth is, of course, that sometimes the football is brilliant, sometimes it is absolute garbage and most of the time it is somewhere in between. When it's good, I know it's good, and when it's garbage, I know that too. I don't want anybody trying to tell me that it's any better than I can recognise with my own eyes.

This is how football is exploited. Television pays a fortune for the privilege and football allows them to dictate. On Sundays, there's football at midday, football in the afternoon or at a silly time in the evening. I forget when they make the FA Cup draw but I do know one thing – it was far better, everybody looked forward to it more, when it was done on the radio at lunchtime on a Monday.

The modern game with all its money has laid bare the greed of the human being. There is greed in every one of us; it's an instinct within us all. Players and their intrusive agents wanted a bigger slice of the cake and so did the managers. The importance and promotion of the Premiership became paramount. Television was welcomed with open arms so we should not be too surprised that they're telling us what we're watching, even though a lot of the time I'm watching something that's nowhere near as good as they want me to believe.

It's reached a stage where some of the interviewers don't interview a manager or a player, they tell them what's happened – 'What a wonderful goal that was, needing a perfect first touch with one foot before he struck it into the top corner with the other, Sir Alex.' Or 'You must have been delighted with that free-kick, up and over the wall, wrong-footing the keeper in the process . . .'

Commentators and journalists are talking like coaches, using coaching terminology, droning on about systems, formations, diagonal runs and spinning off the shoulder of the last defender. What the hell they're on about is often beyond me. It's a foreign language and I suspect it's all part of the brainwashing process intended to convince the viewer that everybody involved is an expert. It doesn't convince me, it doesn't entertain me and if it's supposed to make sure I tune in to the next match, I've got news for them. They've failed. I pick and choose the matches I watch nowadays. There are too many matches on television anyway – seven days a week if you've enough channels and enough resilience. I put the box on when there's a match I fancy but don't bother half the time, and it's my belief that there are an awful lot more people who are beginning to do the same. Television is not just trying to brainwash the public about the appeal of football, it's drowning us.

So, no, from my point of view, football hasn't changed for the better in all aspects, even though young Beckham might disagree and argue that I'm living in the past. Don't try telling me that the introduction of so many foreign players has done nothing but good for our game. It's done a lot of good because the better ones have brought great talent that inevitably rubs off on our lot. But I think there are now too many of them, too many ordinary players who are restricting opportunities for our own youngsters, and we've gone right over the top in copying not only the good points but the things we used to detest.

I'm talking about cheating. Remember how we used to watch World Cups and European Championships, even club matches against teams from abroad, and how we used to hate the way the foreigners cheated at every opportunity – diving all over the place, rolling about and screaming in mock agony if they were breathed on too heavily, never mind tackled? We quite rightly objected to it as a matter of principle. It was the British stiff upper lip, insistence on fair play and all that. It was only a few years ago, but not any more. I see our players cheating with the best of the foreigners. In my day, we didn't cheat; these days we are learning how to cheat better than ever. You can't expect me to enjoy watching any of that.

That and the hype turn me off. Television is spoiling the game for me. Hang on to your pride and your sanity because, if you don't, some of the modern commentators will make you feel like a backward five-year-old. I'm sure it stems from the people who control the programmes, the producers and directors who insist, 'You've got to make sure you keep everybody on the edge of their seats while they're watching the game.' Well they're wrong. People want to be excited by good, pure, honest football – not by somebody screeching hysterically from the commentary box.

I've already mentioned some good friends I've lost recently. Another is Brian Moore with whom I worked on many occasions and whom I regarded as the best of his generation. He didn't overstate anything, he didn't insist on doing a radio-style commentary because he appreciated the fact that the viewer was watching what he was watching so he didn't have to bombard the audience with unnecessary words. He knew that silence could sometimes be as important as a whole string of sentences.

Kenneth Wolstenholme was known for understating his commentary rather than overdoing it, and for that spontaneous, off-the-cuff string of eight simple words that immortalised England's World Cup victory in 1966 as Geoff Hurst thumped in the final goal – 'They think it's all over – it is now.' That wasn't hysteria even though Wolstenholme was caught up in the excitement of England's finest hour. It would do some of the current breed of commentators a lot of good to listen to recordings of Wolstenholme at work. They might just discover the difference between excited response and hysterical gibberish. John Motson is the nearest to it of the modern crowd. He's a veteran now, and I suppose you only last that long if you're good at what you do, particularly if you work for the BBC.

All I ask from television is that they are genuine about the game that is so important to their business, and that they employ people to explain what is happening when explanation is necessary – and if it's rubbish to say it's rubbish. Don't employ people who are there to make a name for themselves and scream at such a pitch that I have to grab the remote and turn the sound down.

If television isn't careful it will turn people off football, make them sick of it. For a start, it must be causing more trouble in families than if the man of the house is knocking off a bird. The fanatic can watch football every night of the week. I wonder how many fathers put their kids in the bath nowadays. When our children were little, my 'happy hour' was not in a pub for half-price drinks, it was putting the kids in the bath, going to the park or reading nursery rhymes. I appreciate times have to change, but not as much as they have. Not to the extent where somebody feels the need to scream in my ear that the football I'm paying to watch is fantastic from beginning to end. Times don't have to change that much, surely.

Times shouldn't change so much that England have to go abroad to find a manager. Nothing personal against Sven-Goran Eriksson, but I really would have preferred the FA to find somebody on our little island to take charge of our team. It's a question of pride in your country and the belief that we ought to be able to find one of our own capable of producing a decent side from the best group of players in the land.

I don't care if Eriksson eventually goes on to win the World Cup and a European Championship to go with it. I hope he does but I would still prefer one of ours to be in charge. It's a scandal when England cannot find somebody good enough for the top job. Mind you, when they did have the chance to appoint the best, they shoved him to one side. Me! But it's not resentment that has me wishing we didn't need someone from outside England to teach the players how to perform together. I wouldn't have minded so much if the chance had been offered to one of two Irishmen – David O'Leary from the south or Martin O'Neill from the north of the Emerald Isle. At least they played and earned their living in the English game. They were household names in most homes, certainly in more homes than Eriksson was. The wider public would have felt some kind of affinity towards them and felt reasonably comfortable that we had one of our own, or near enough, in charge.

As I've already made clear, when Keegan walked out, I would have opted for the reappointment of Terry Venables. After all, he had been there and done it and done pretty well at it, but I gather his name was barely considered, if at all. He was discounted for reasons that had nowt to do with the ability to pick and motivate a successful football team. How daft can they get, those who are supposed to have the best interests of English football at heart!

Ah well, the world can't be perfect for all of us, I suppose, but for a long time mine was, as near as damn it. It keeps me warm in winter, saving money on the central heating, when I mull over the lovely memories that football brought me – and the perks that come from success and so-called stardom as a manager who won two league titles with relatively small clubs. Controversy helped although when I said things that others considered outrageous, I was only expressing an honest opinion. I suppose that came from my conceit. I am just a conceited man, that's all. Barbara describes me as somebody who seemed to have been born in a cocoon, a shell. I suppose she meant I was unaware of what went on outside my own little sphere and how I sometimes affected or offended others. 'Where angels fear to tread,' she is forever telling me. 'You didn't have enough intelligence to walk round delicate areas – you just walked straight through them.'

But I gathered friends along the way and the last couple of years have not been good in that sense. I've already mentioned the death of Brian Moore and the passing of my dear pal Colin Lawrence. We lost Harry Secombe as well. Sir Harry was not a close friend or somebody I was in regular contact with but a friend from many years ago when I bought that apartment of ours in Cala Millor. Harry and his wife had a beautiful villa just round the coast. We first met in Majorca and often linked up at holiday times. One of the first occasions was when I had the Derby County team with me and Harry came round to the hotel and gave us a song. He was an overpowering man, he dominated the surroundings, took over a room the moment he walked in, and if you were fortunate enough to be in his company for more than half an hour, you left as his friend.

You couldn't regard him as anything less than a friend because apart from his immense talent and versatility, he was such a nice, nice man. How could anybody fail to laugh when he was present? Harry could laugh at owt or at nowt and I can see that jolly round face of his whenever I look for it, those sparkling, laughing eyes.

I close mine sometimes when I think of Harry Secombe, and I remember that song of his, one of so many associated with the man, the one that includes the line that summed him up. And it makes an old, former football manager who was not too bad at his job, either, give a contented little smile of his own. It makes me think that if things had been a wee bit different, if I had been Muhammad Ali, for instance, I'd still have enjoyed the sight of those crocuses popping up in March in time for my birthday on the twenty-first. I agree with Harry Secombe – 'If I ruled the world, every day would be the first day of spring.'

I N D E X

Note: The abbreviation BC is used to stand for Brian Clough.